I0845232

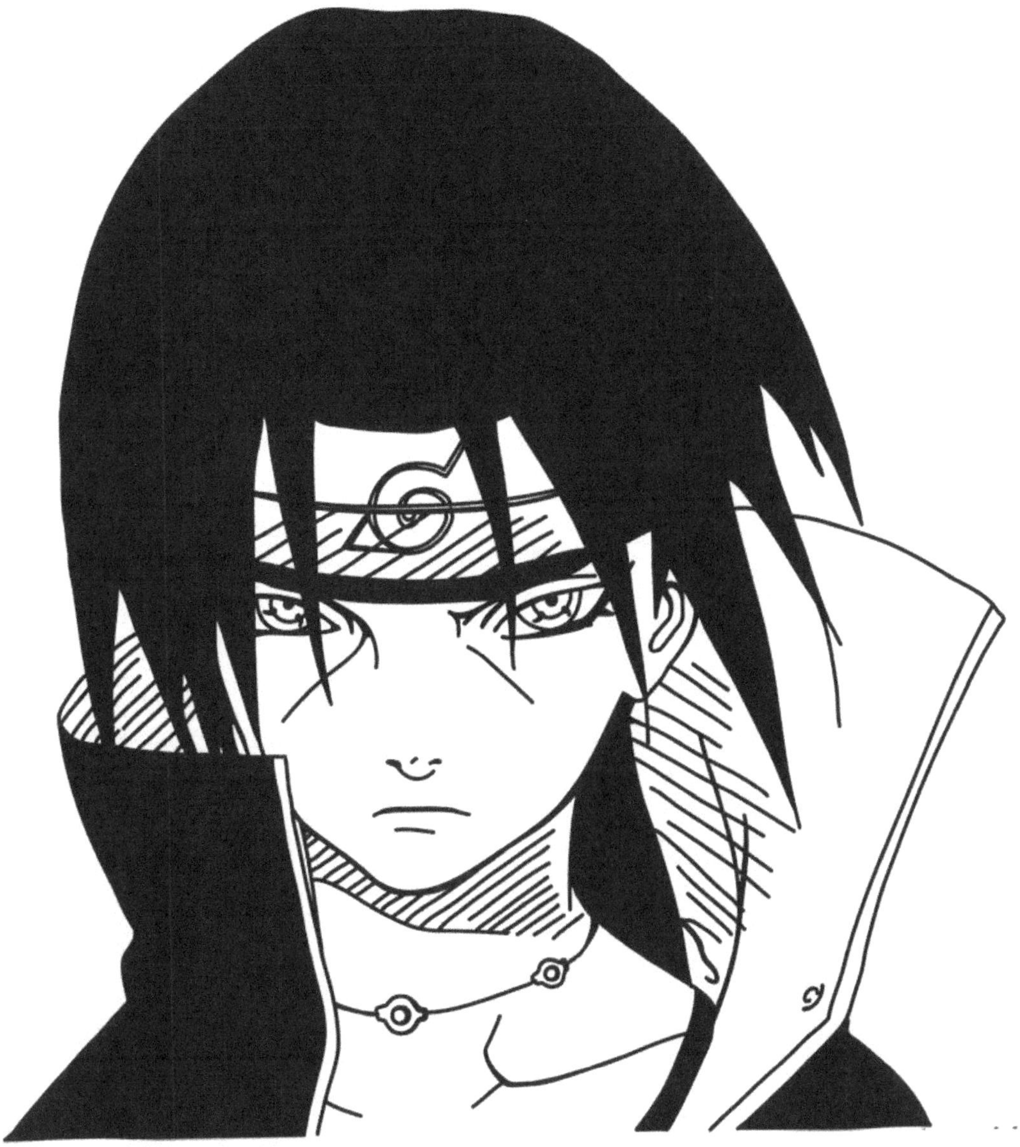

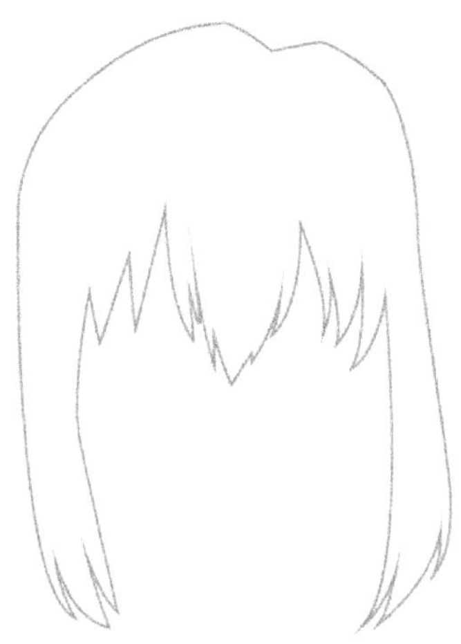

1

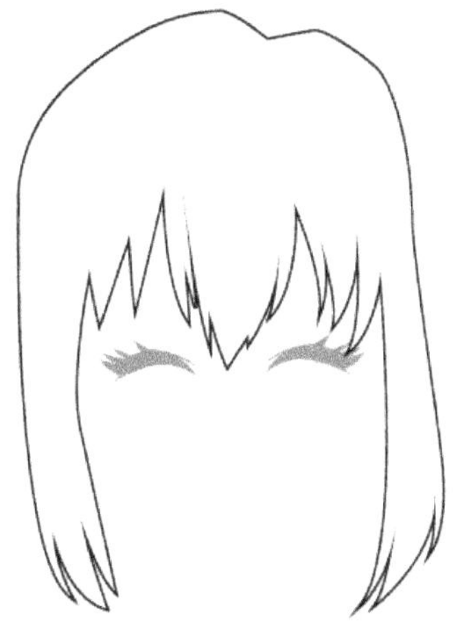

2

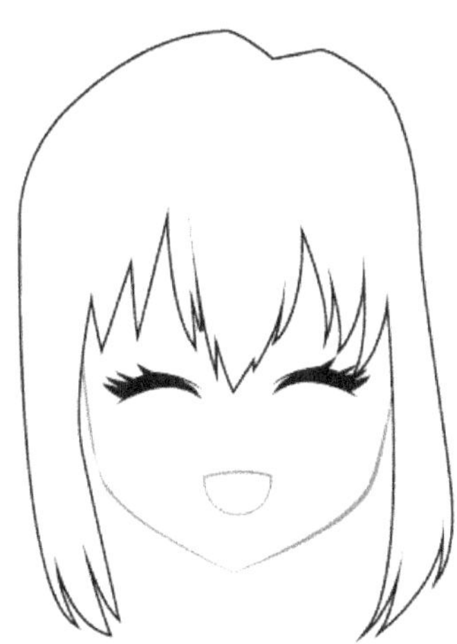

3

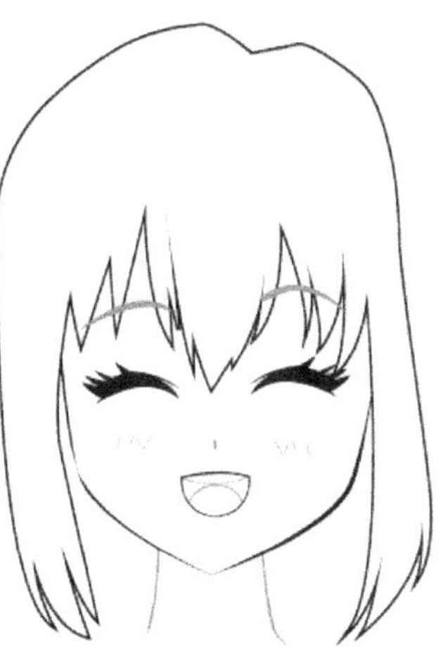

4

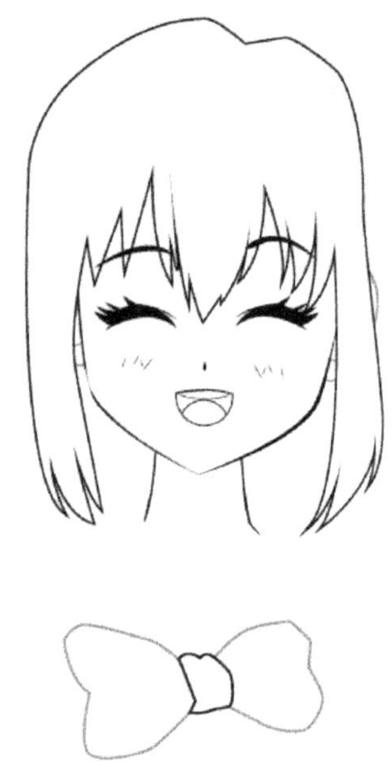
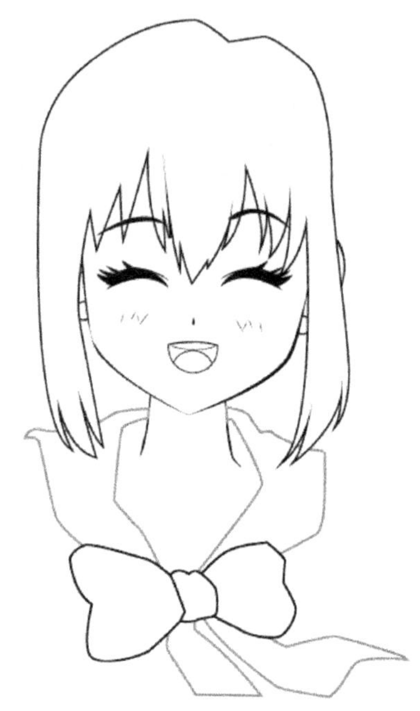
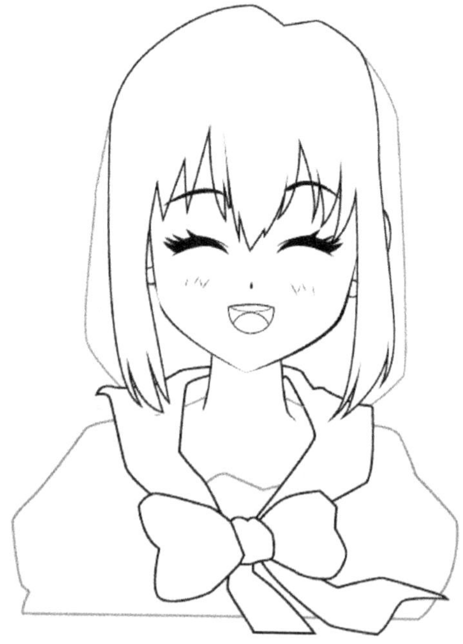
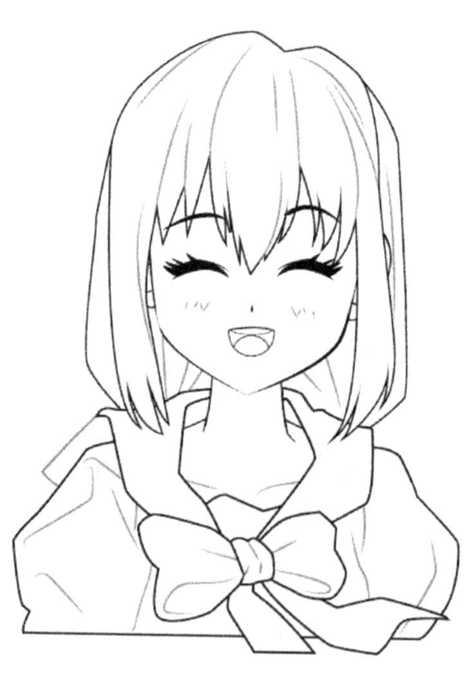

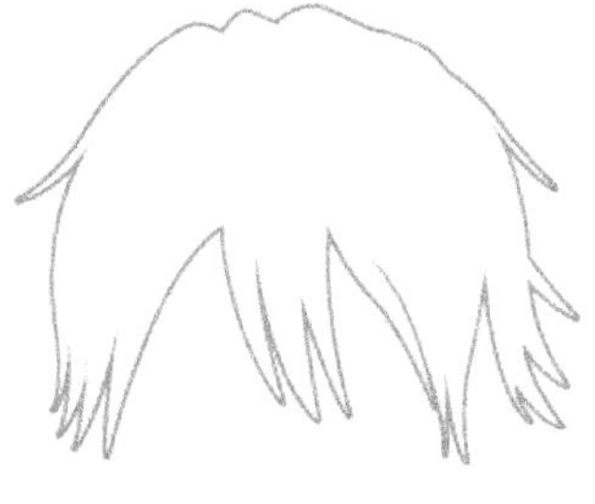
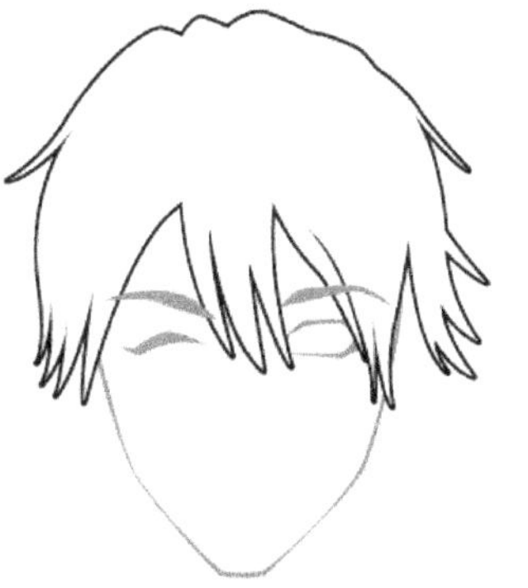
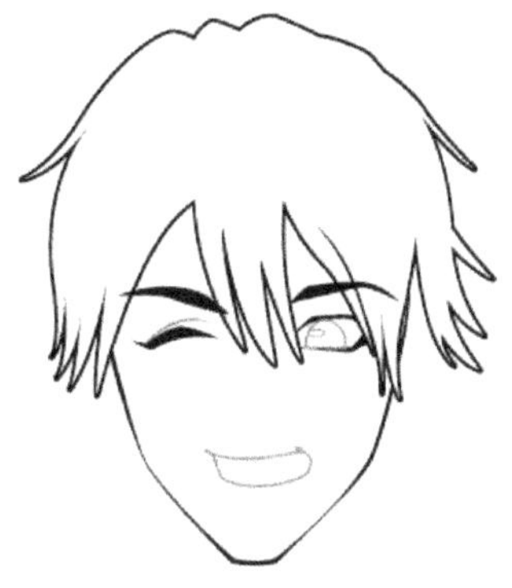
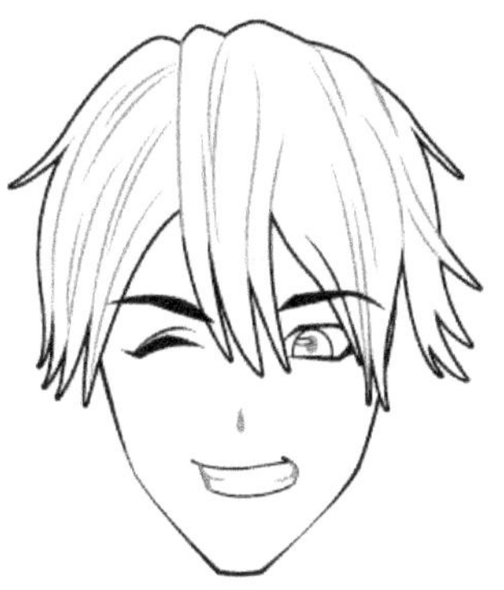

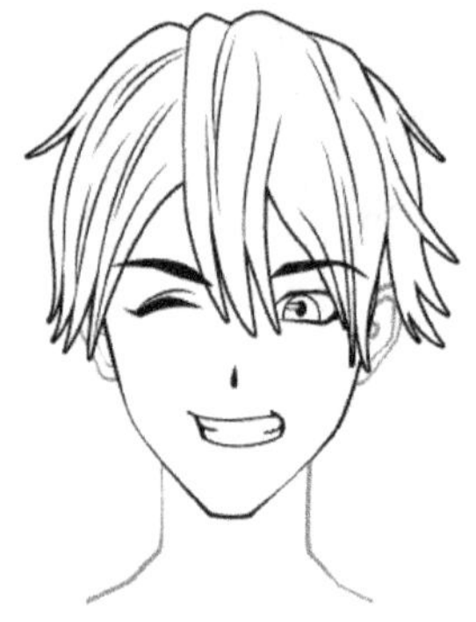

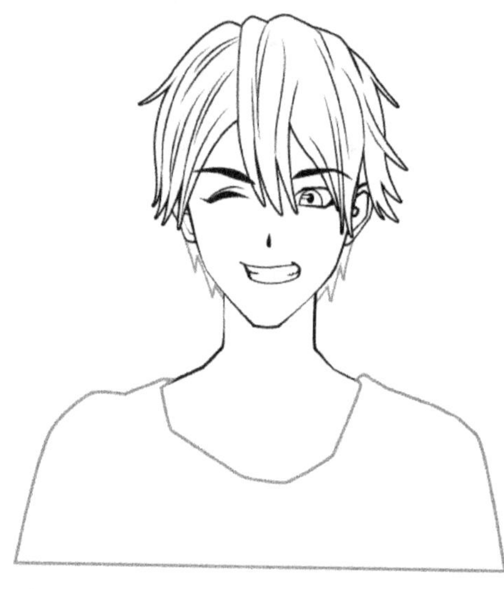

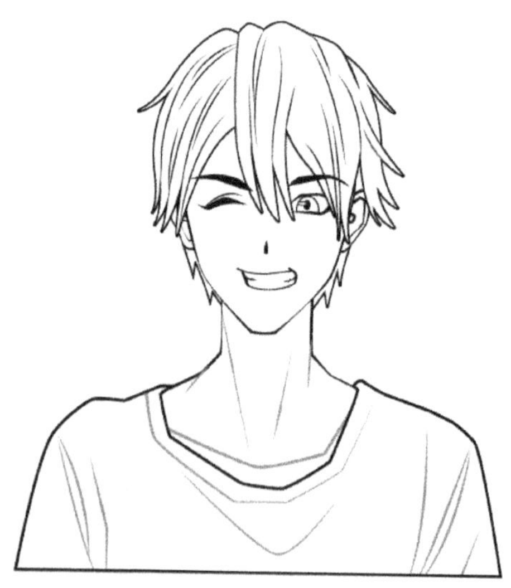

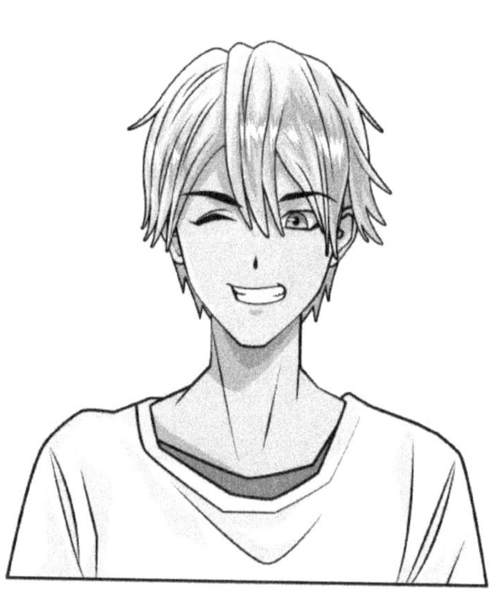

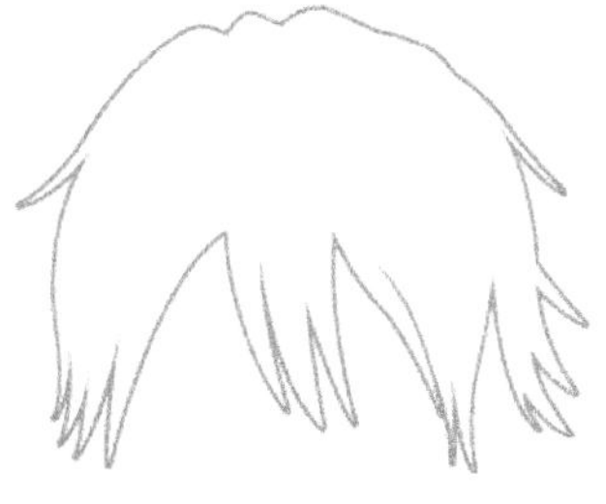

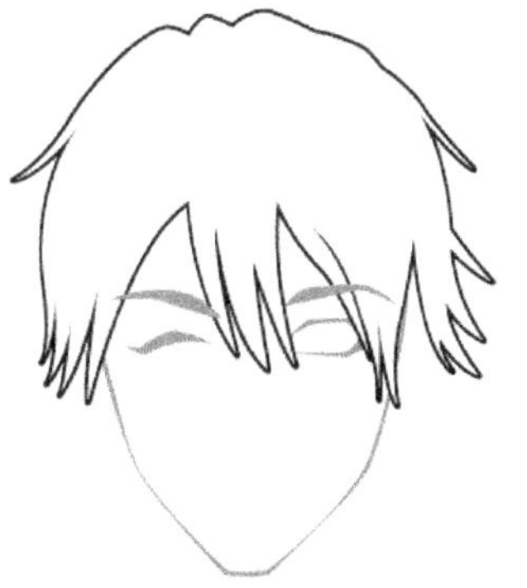

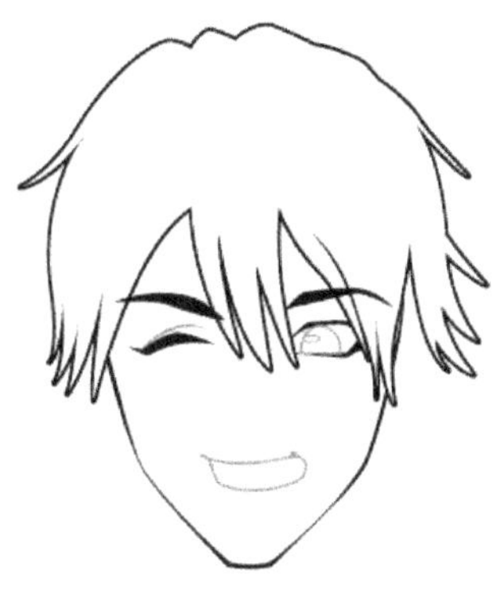

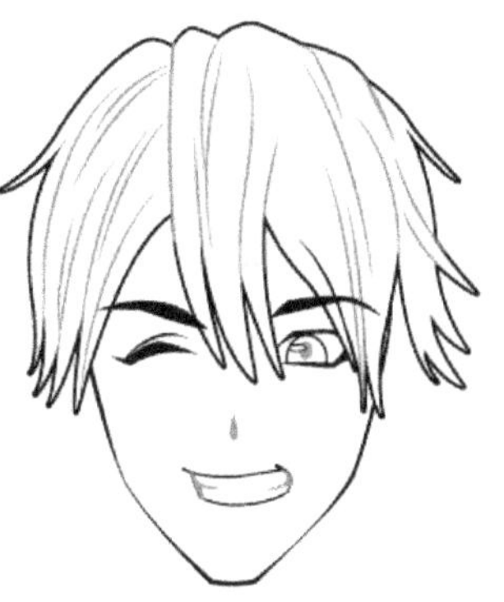

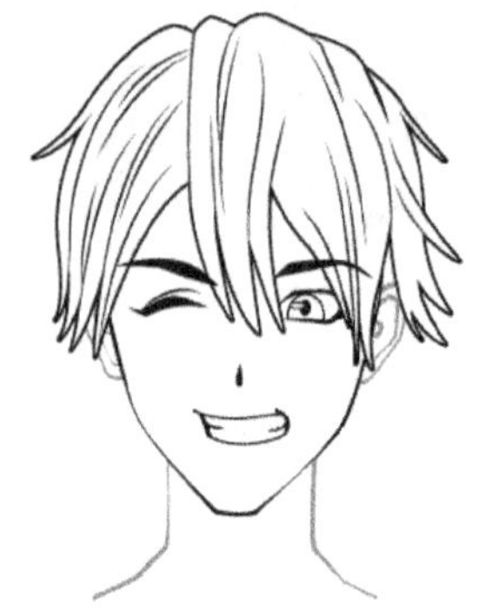
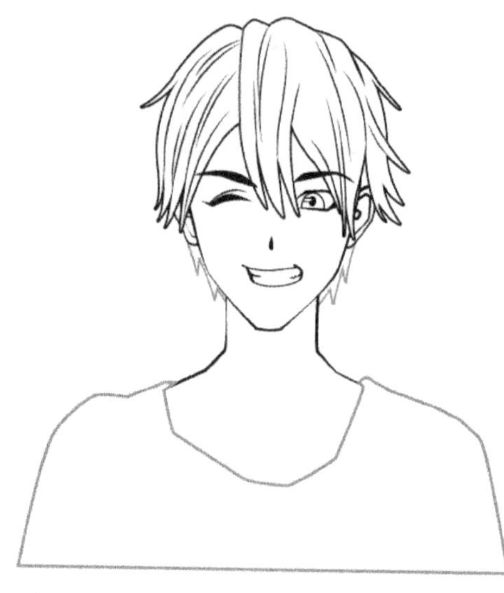
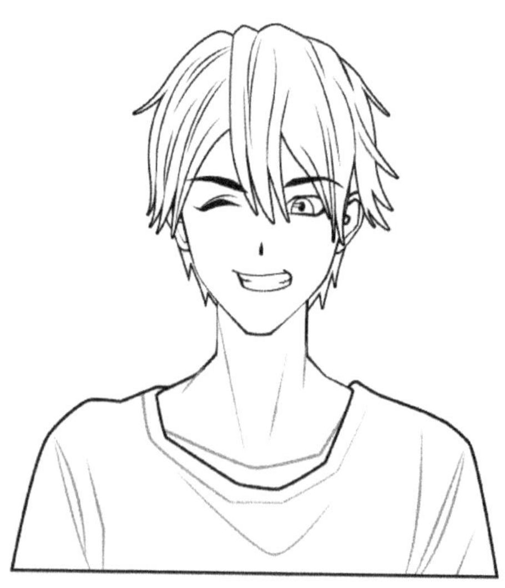
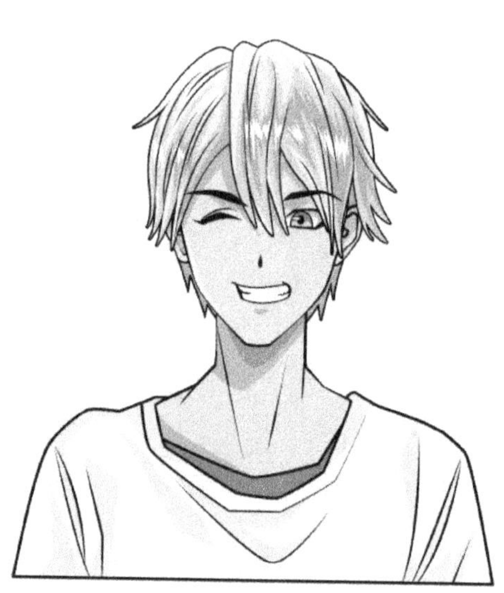

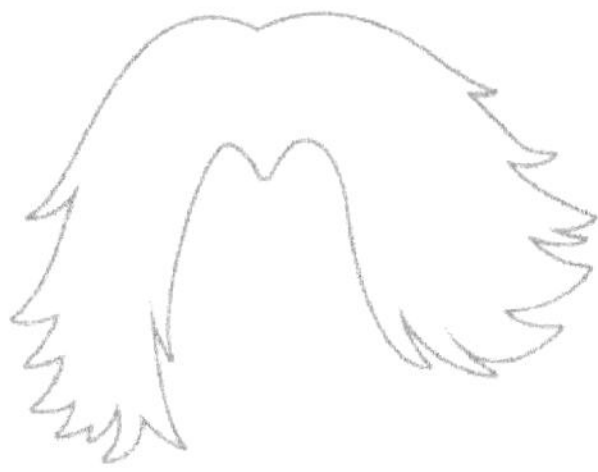

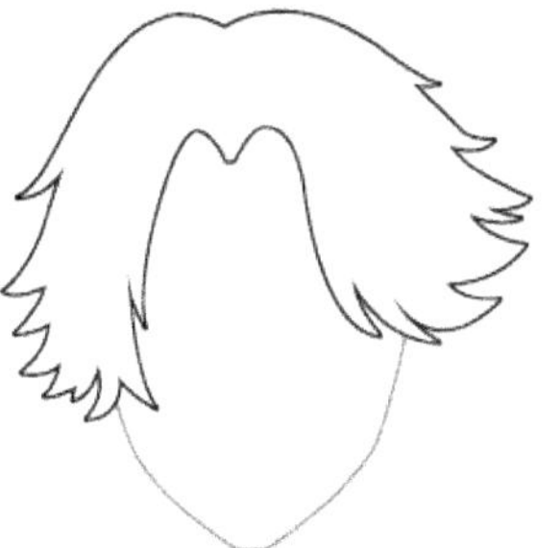

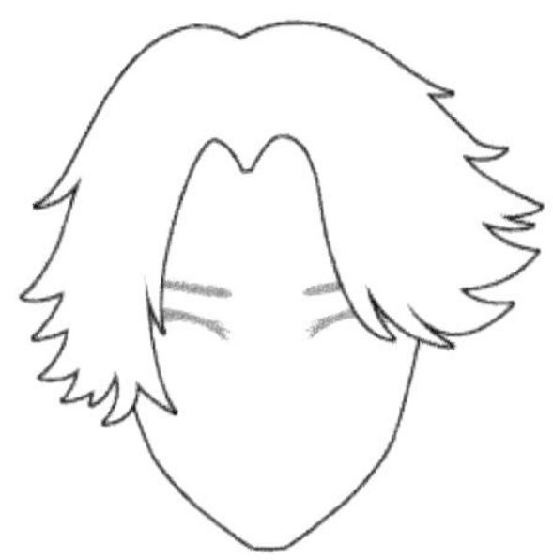

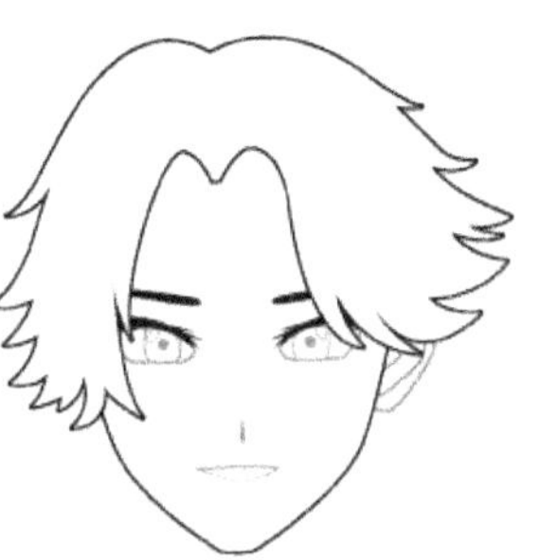

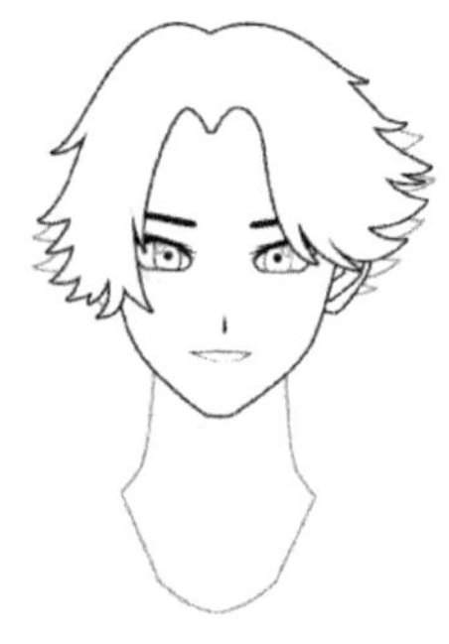

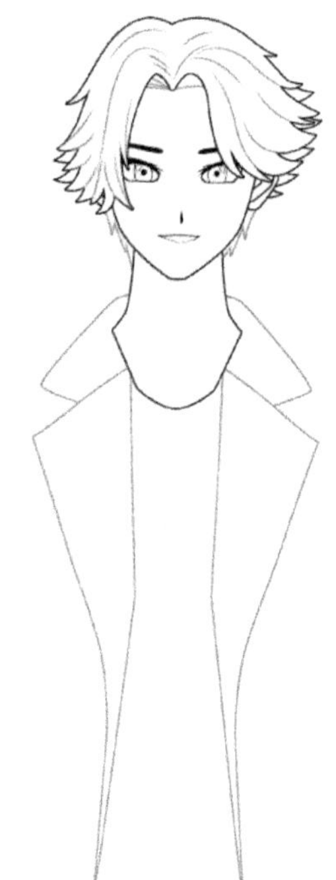

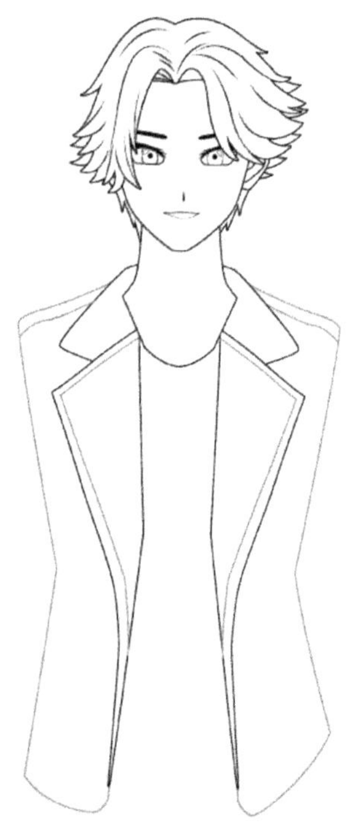

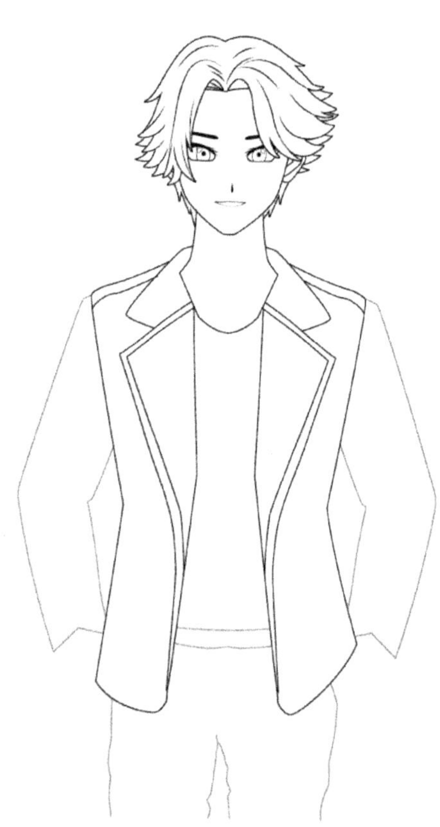

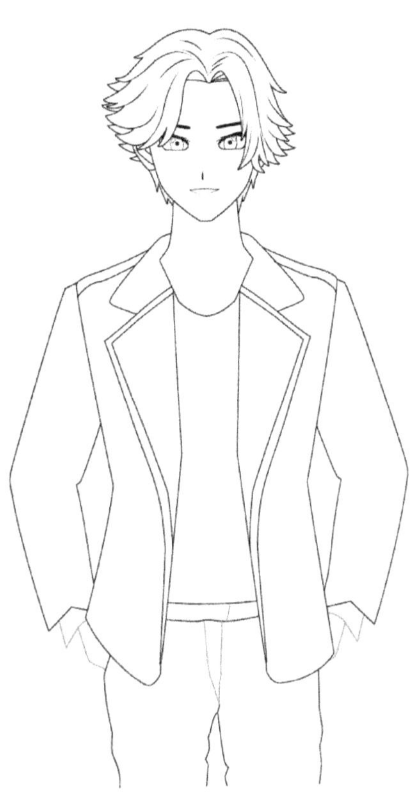
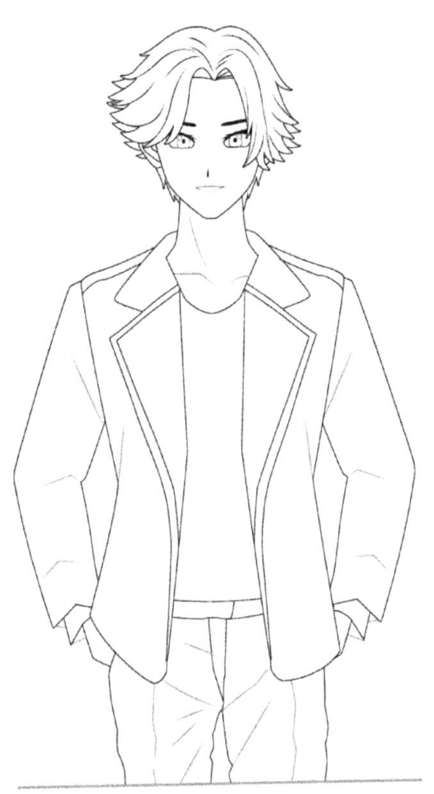
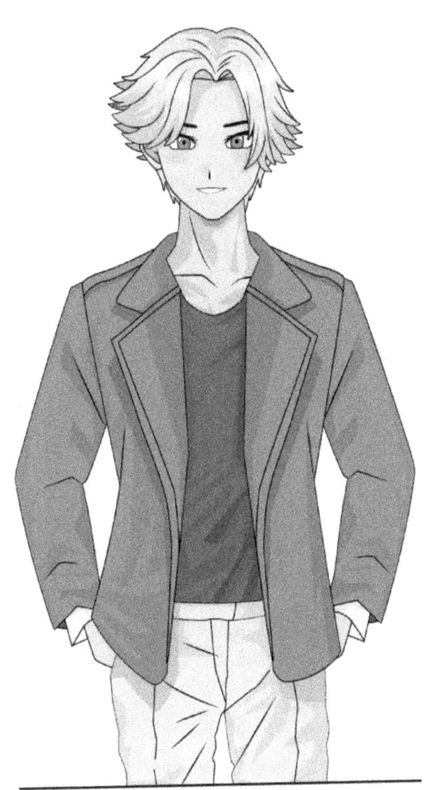

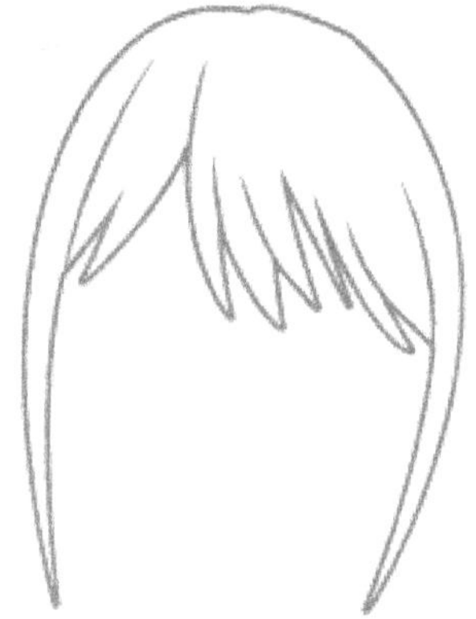

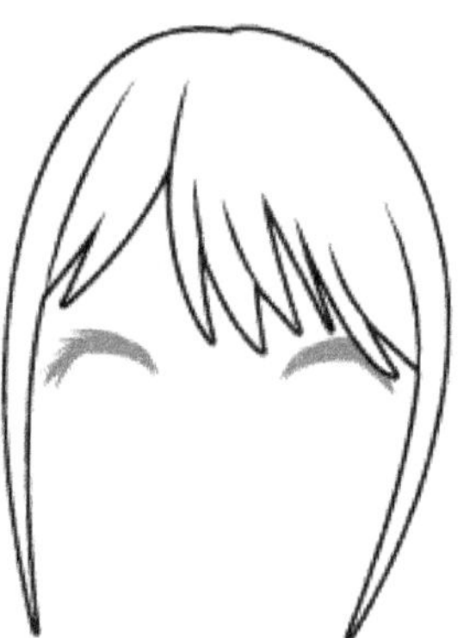

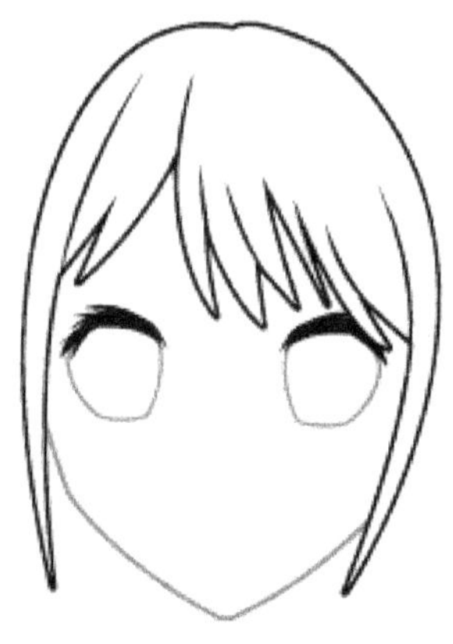

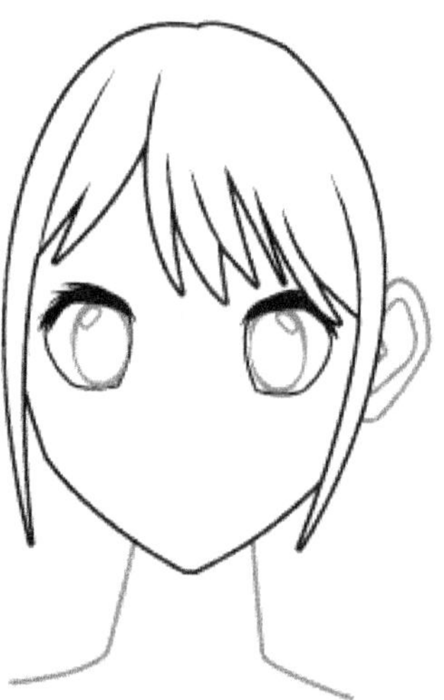

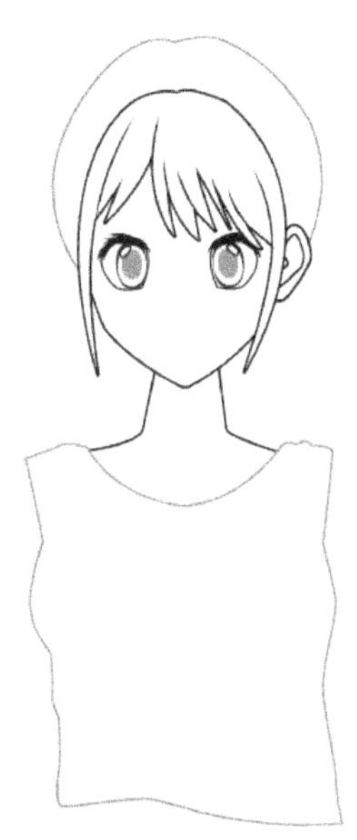

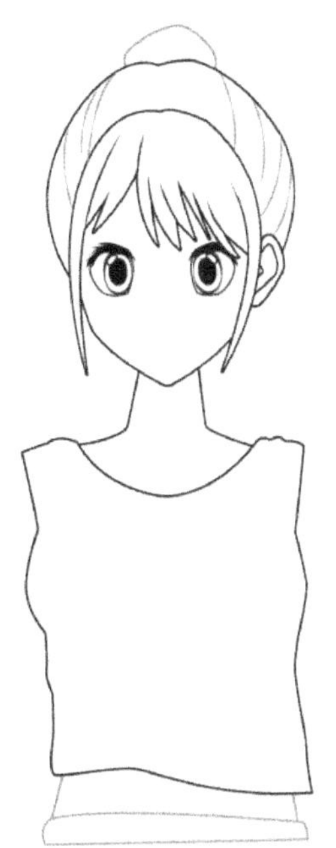

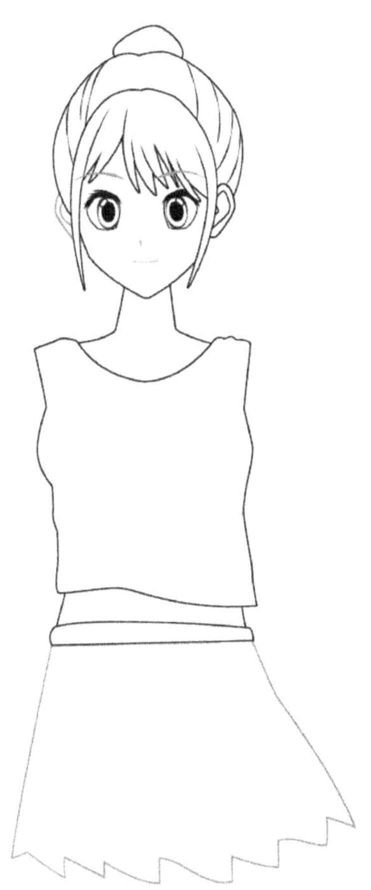

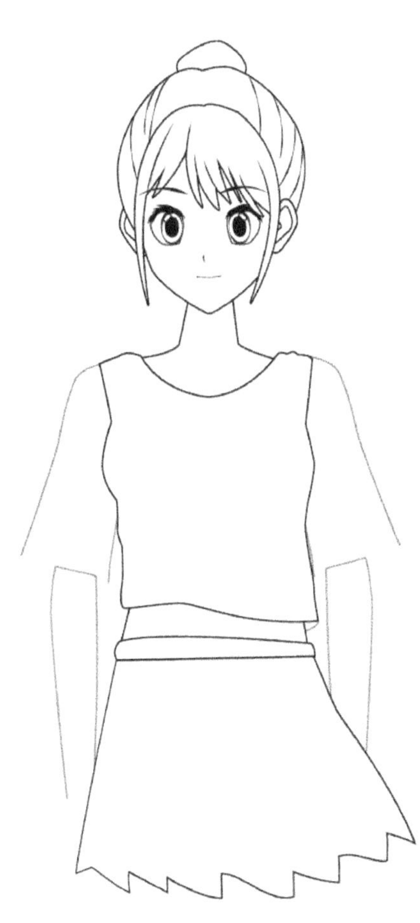

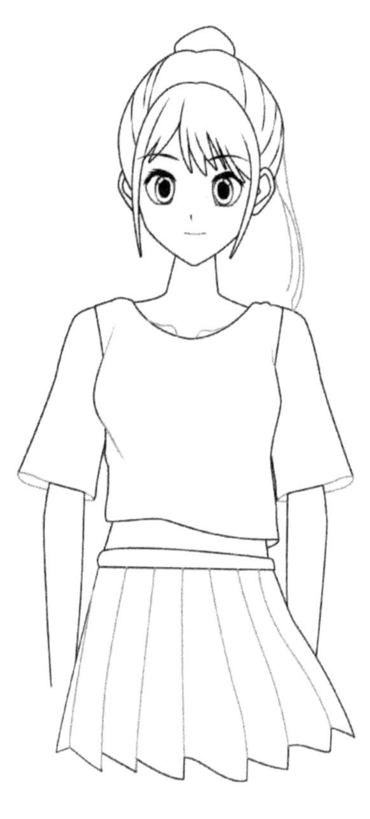

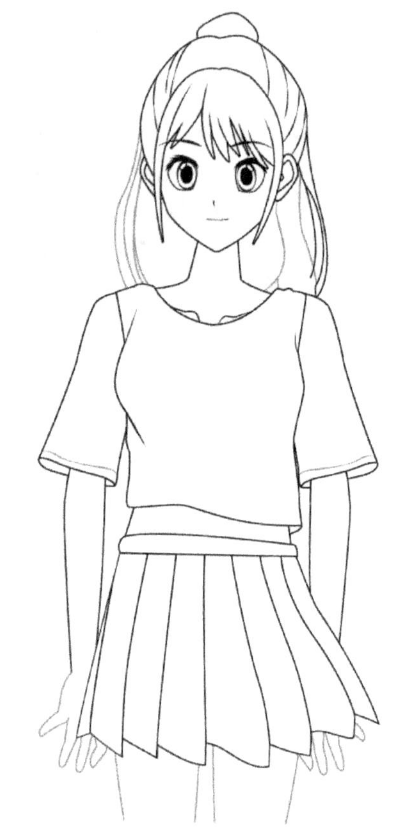

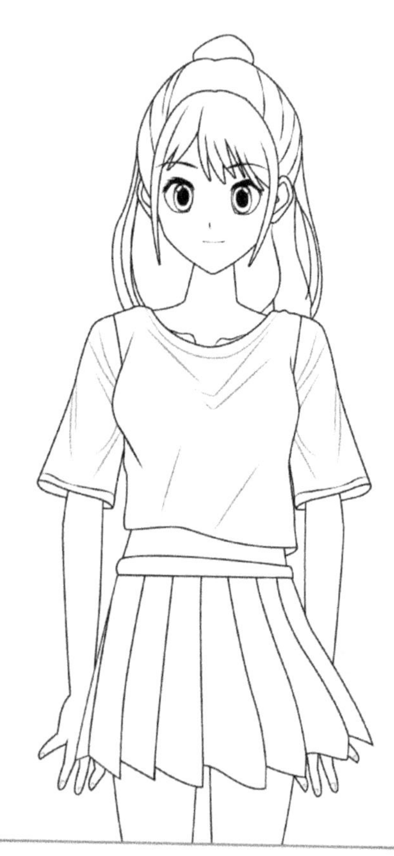

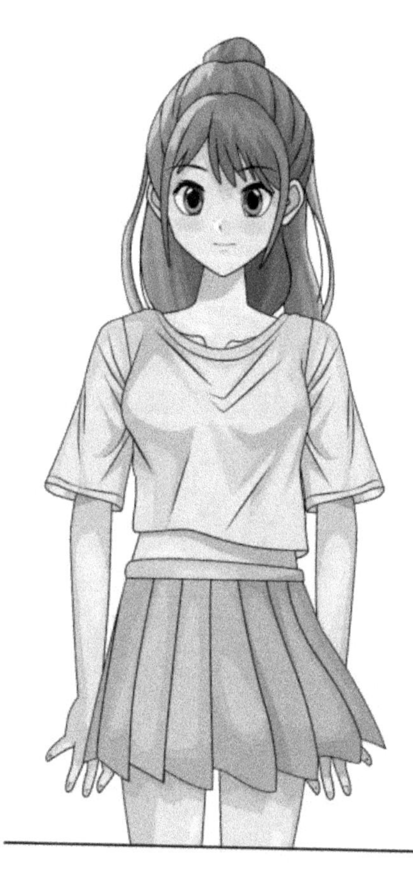

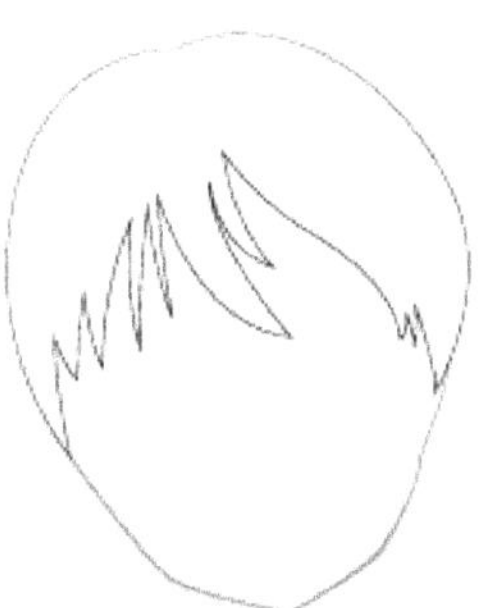

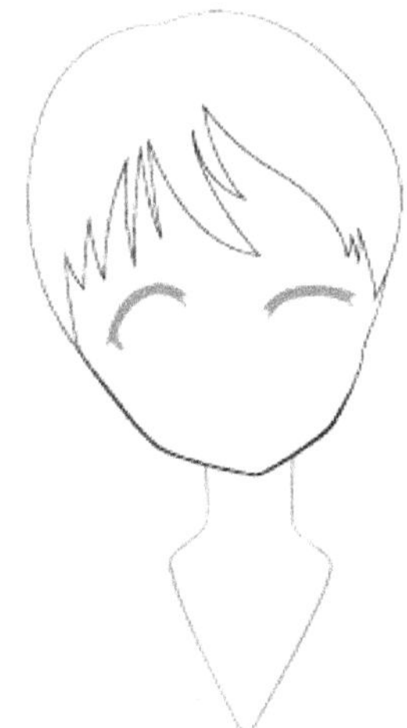

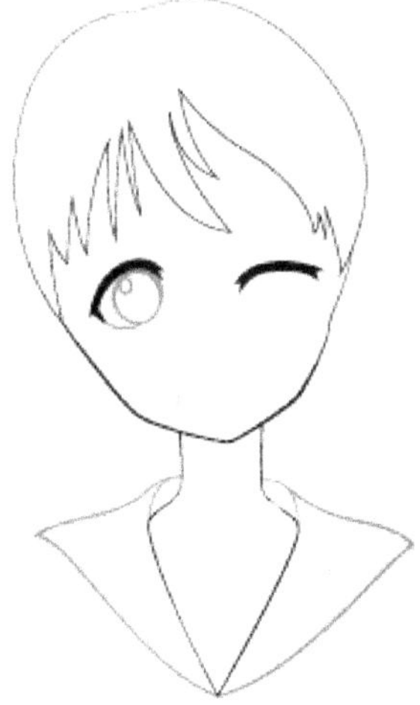

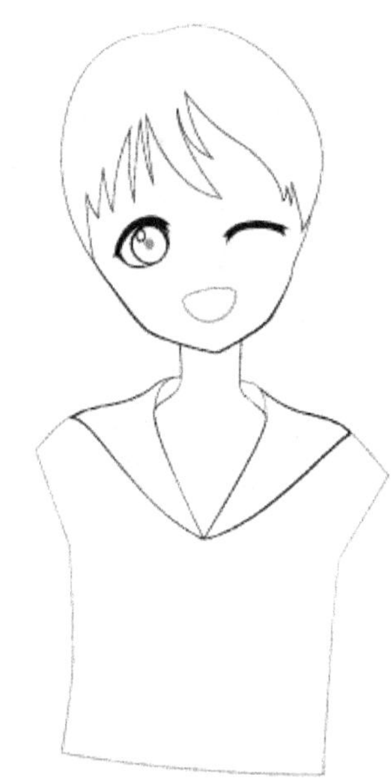

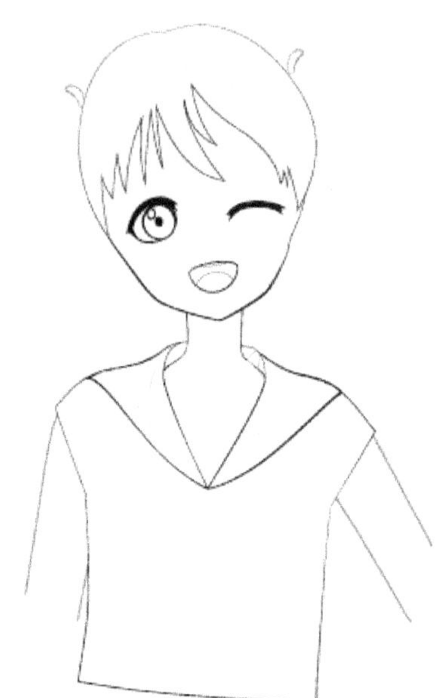

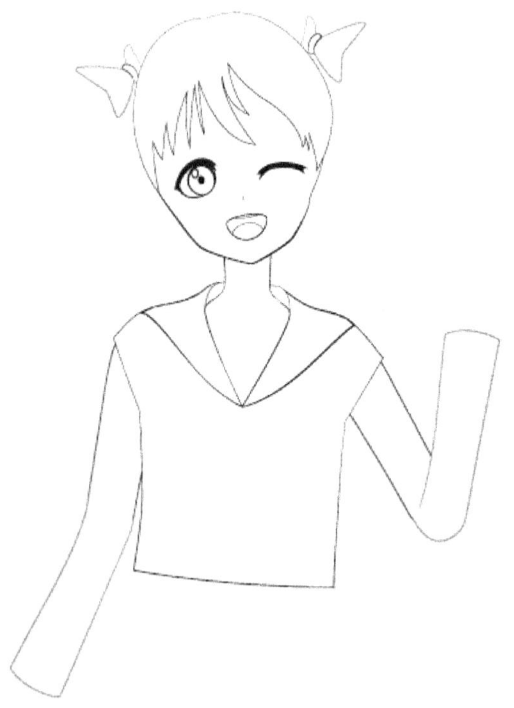

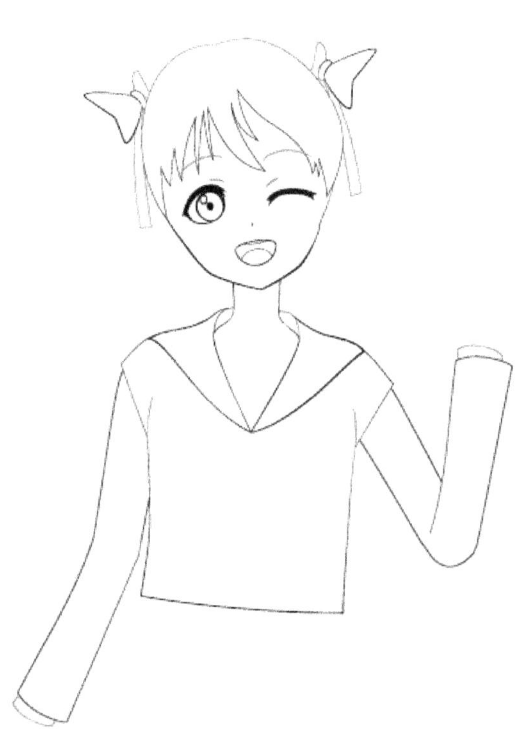

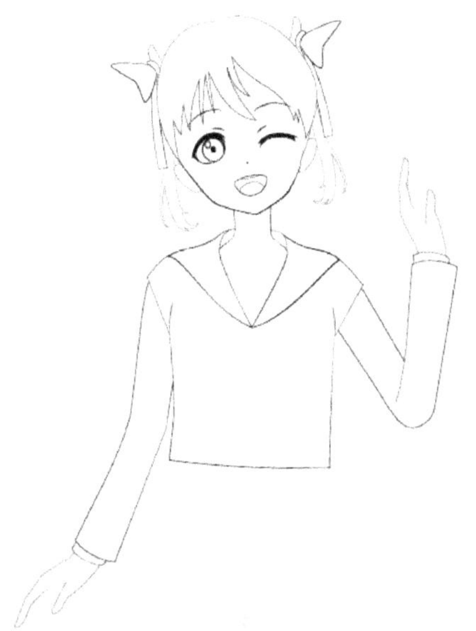
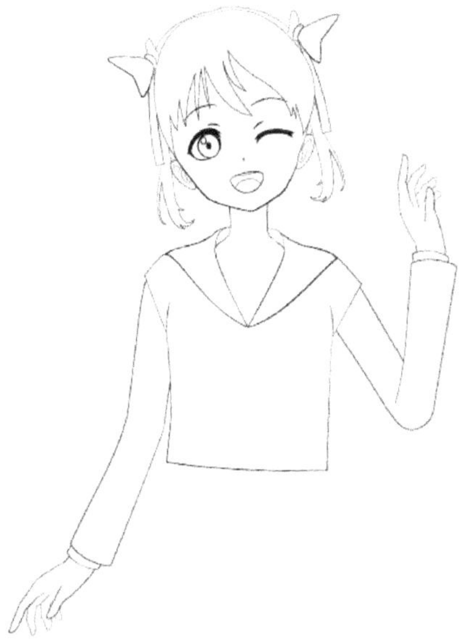
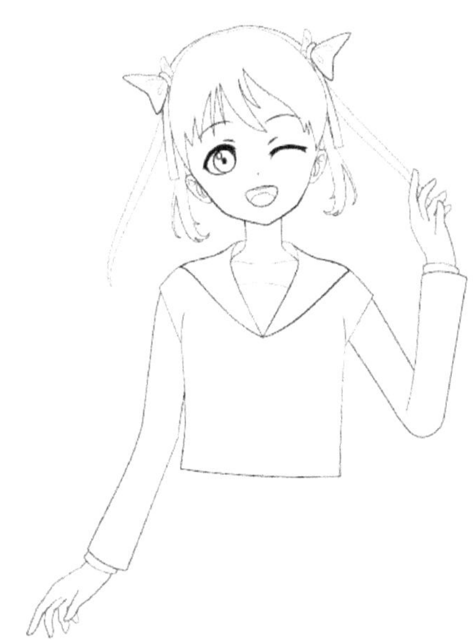
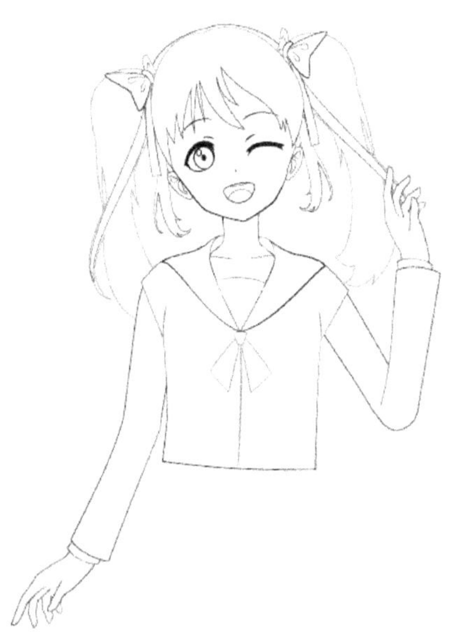

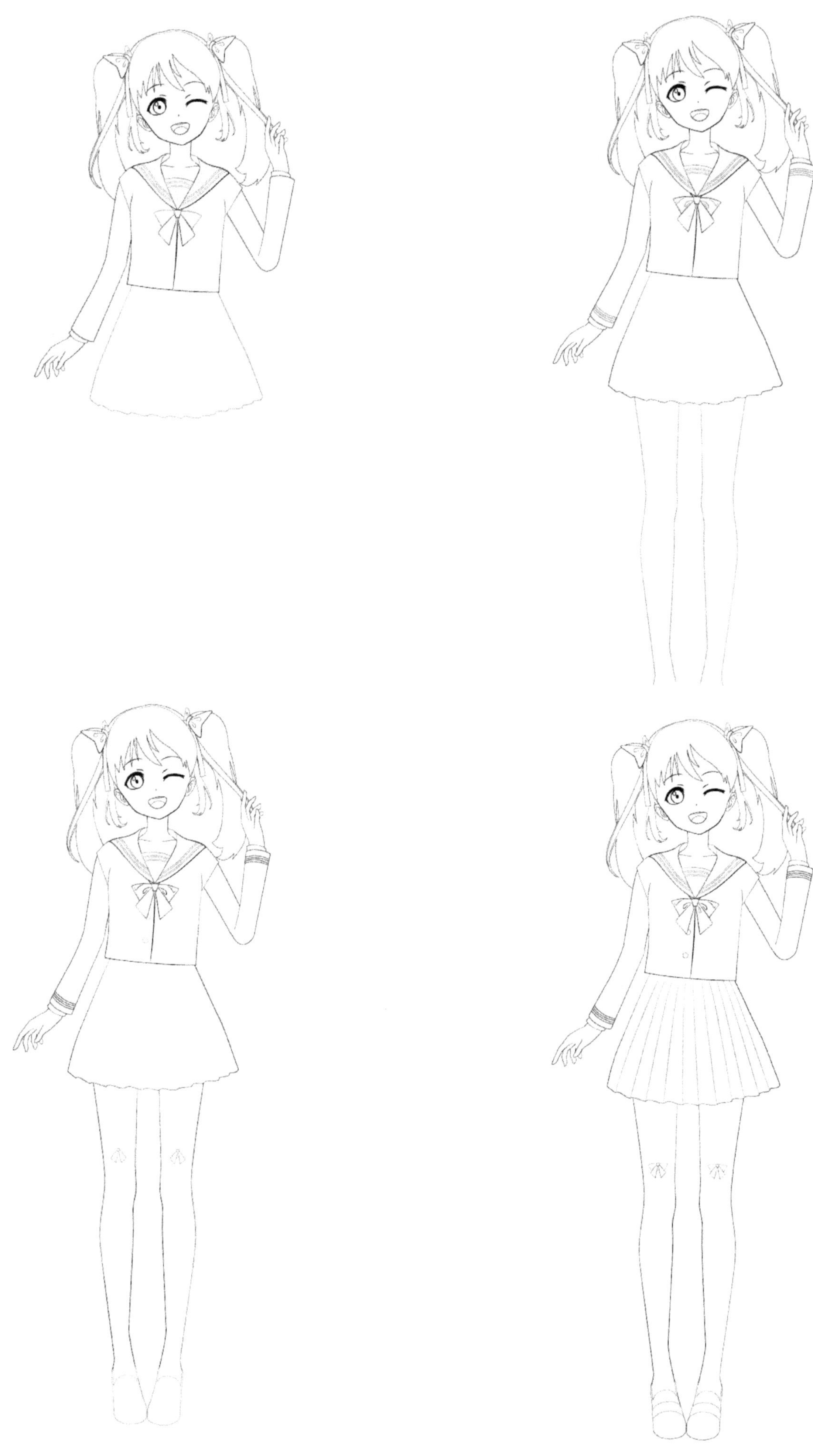

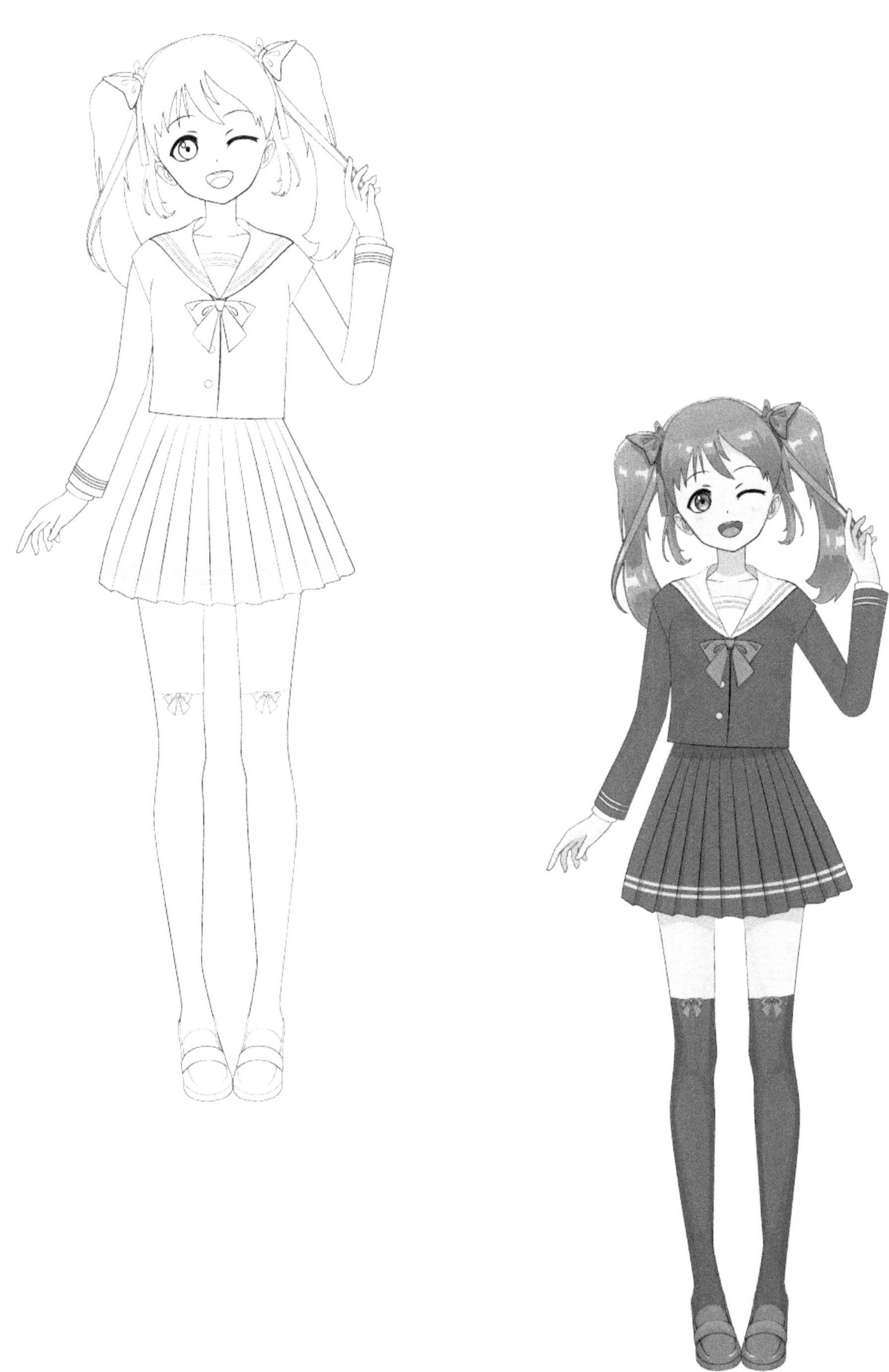

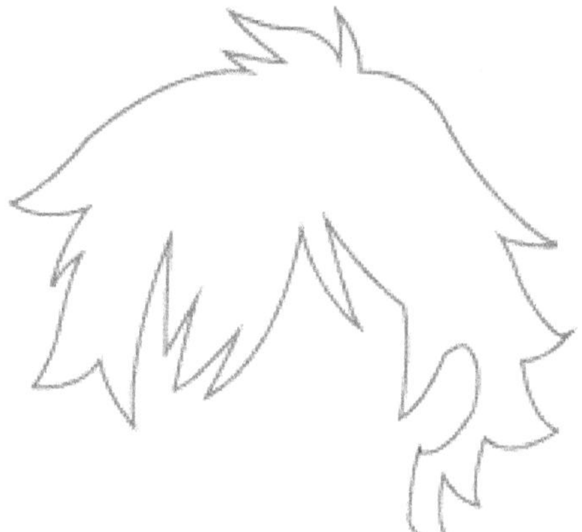

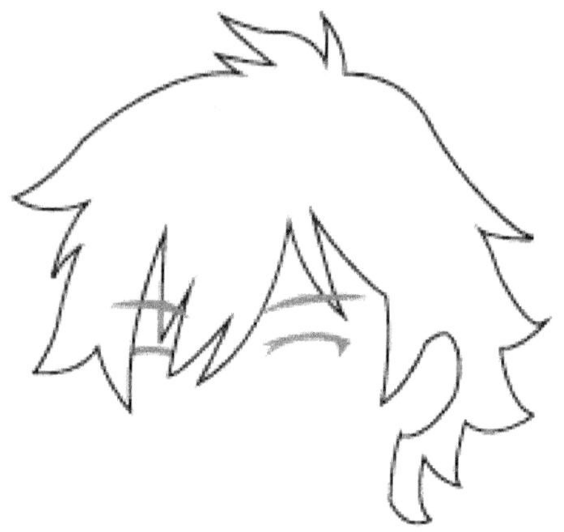

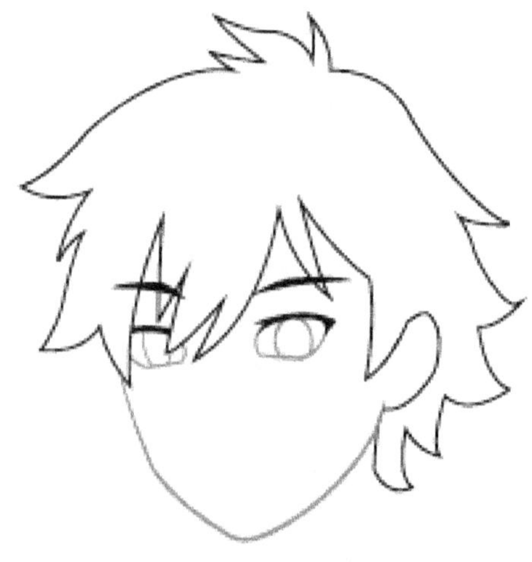

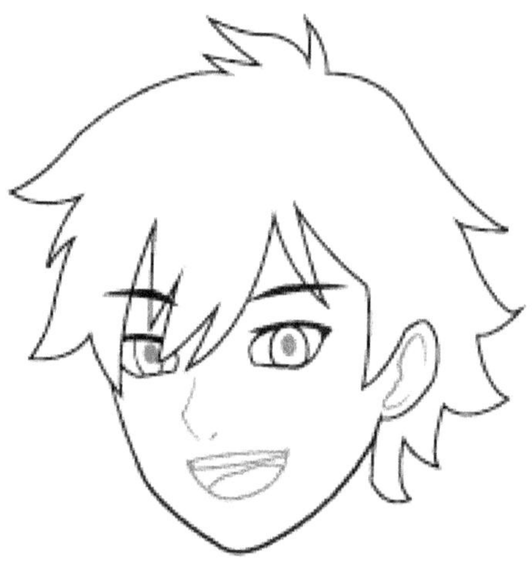

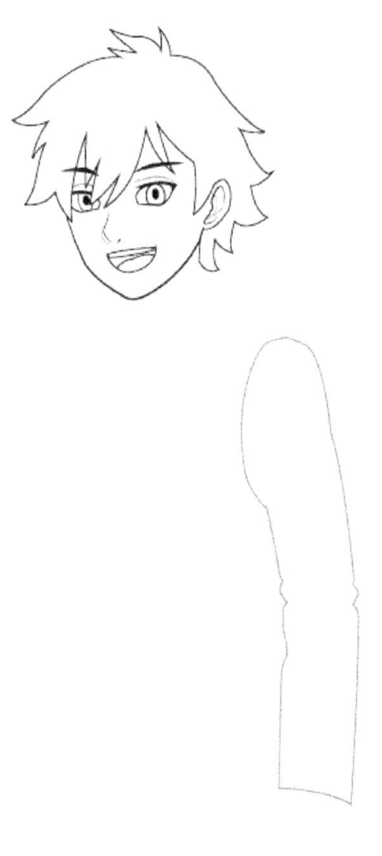

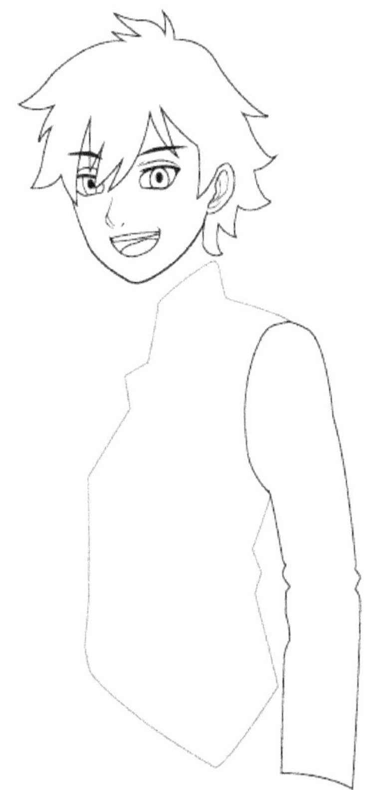

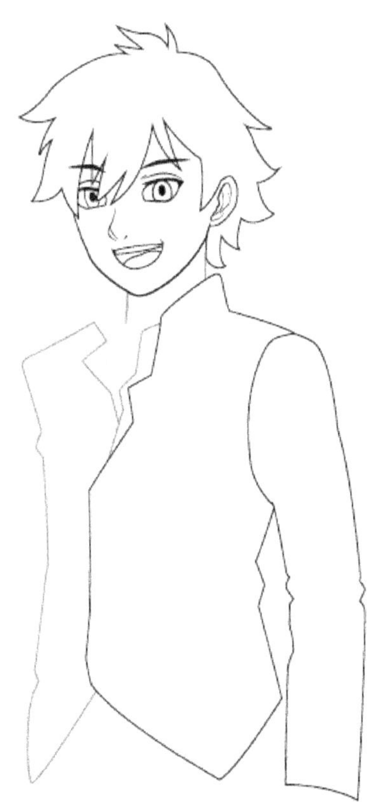

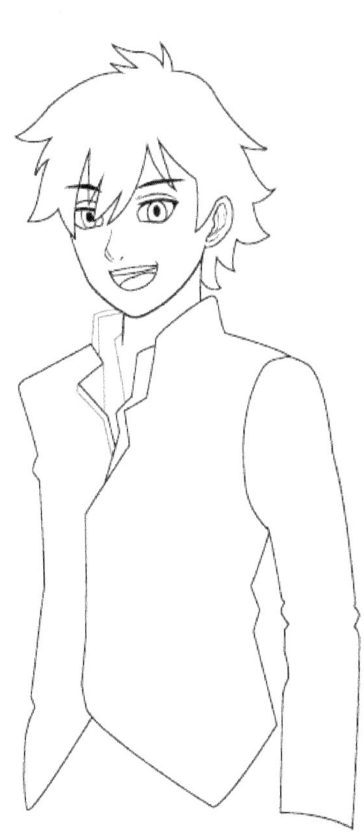

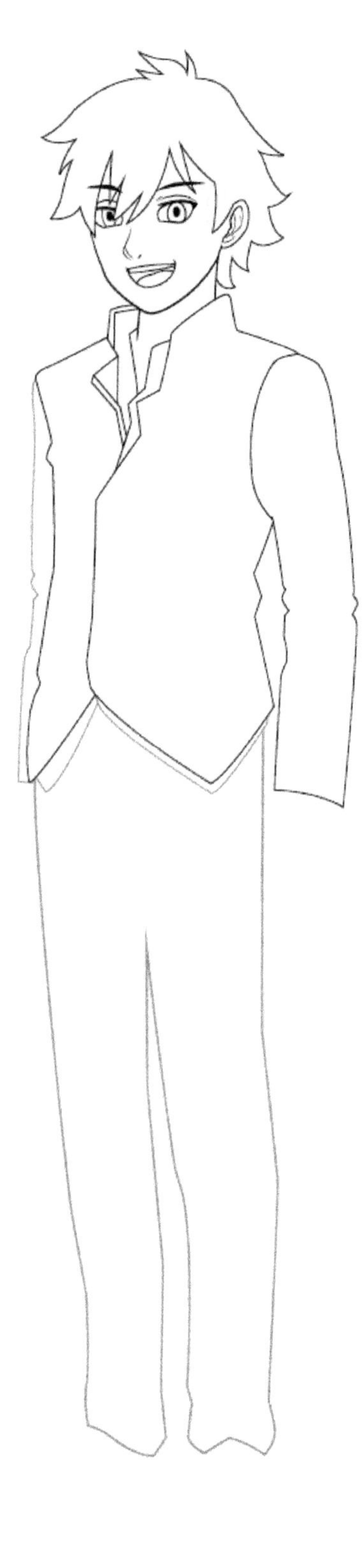
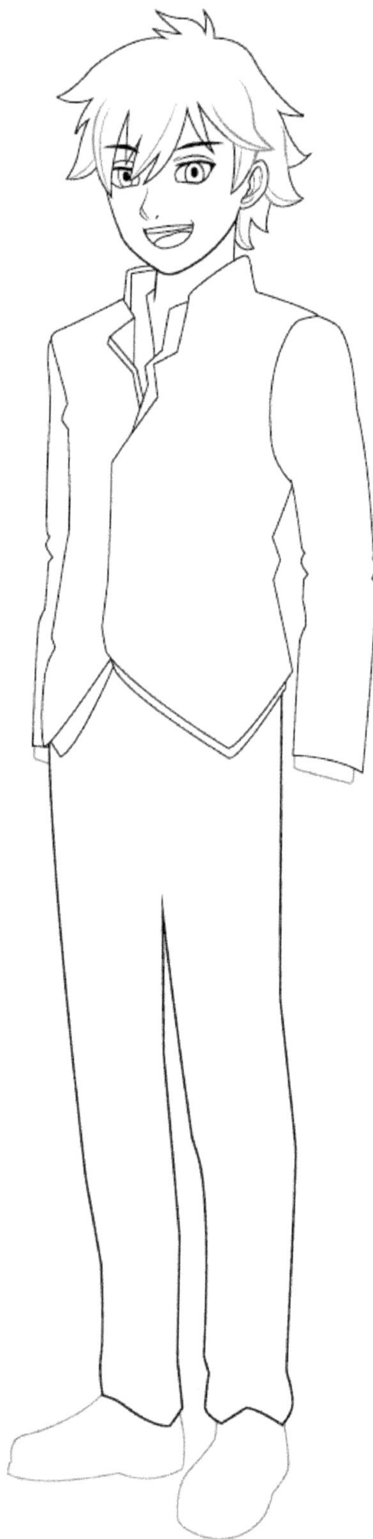

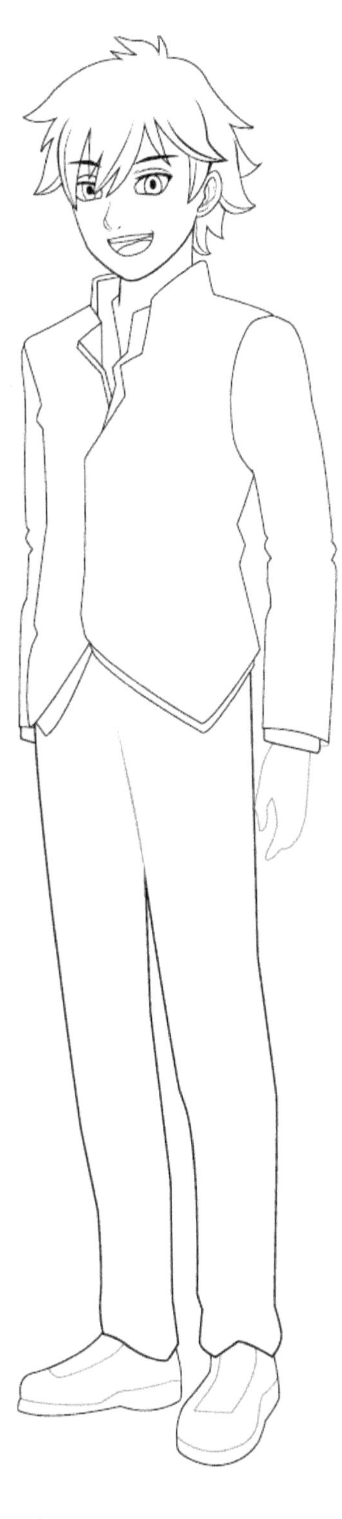

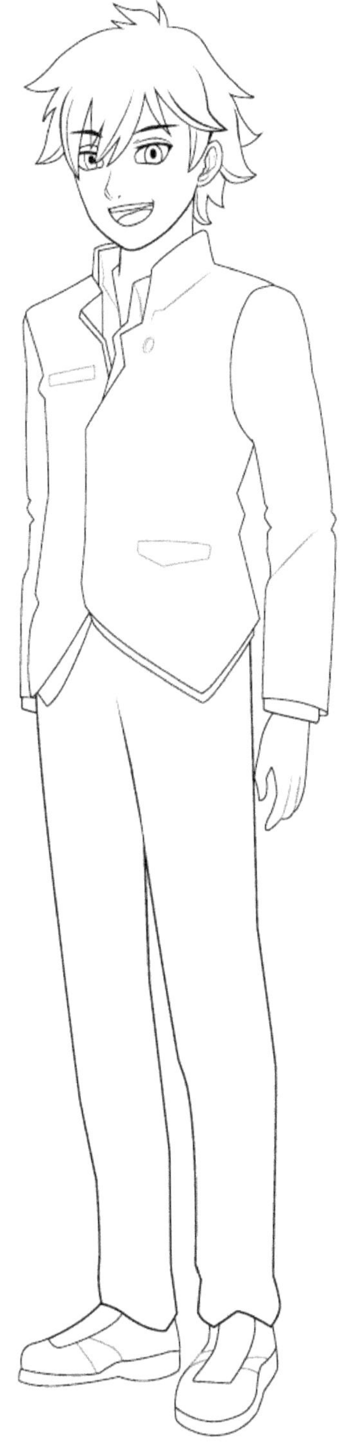

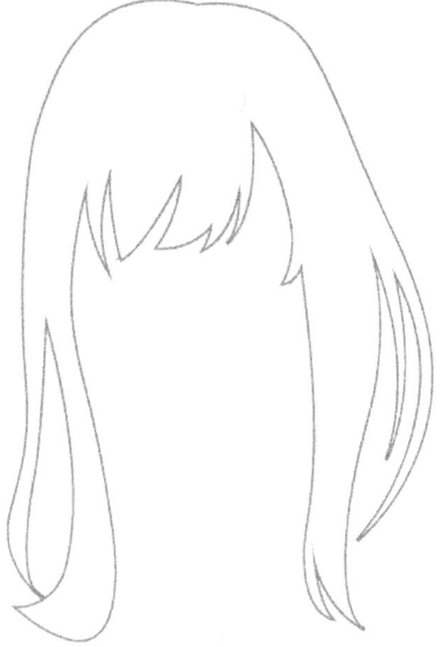
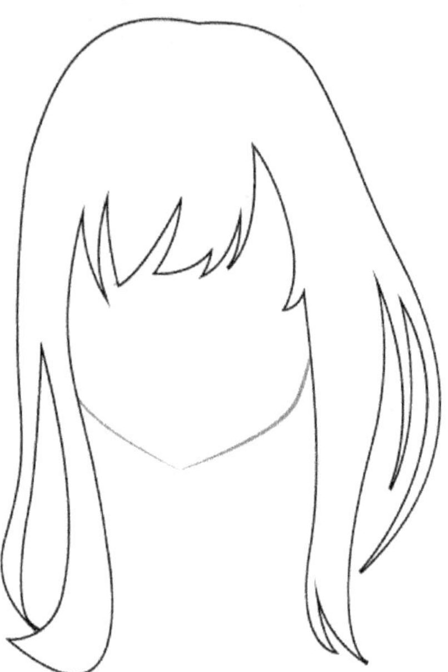
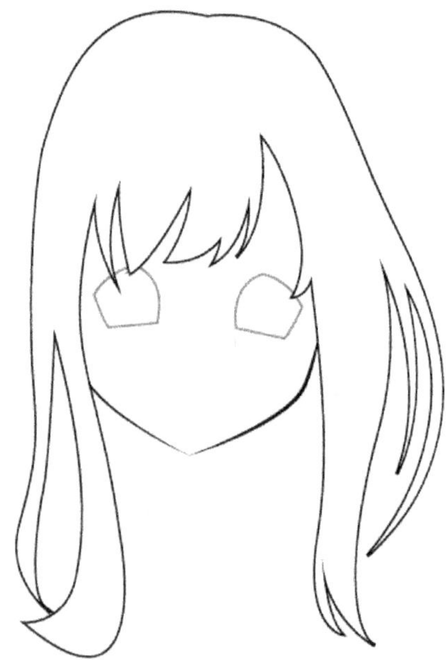
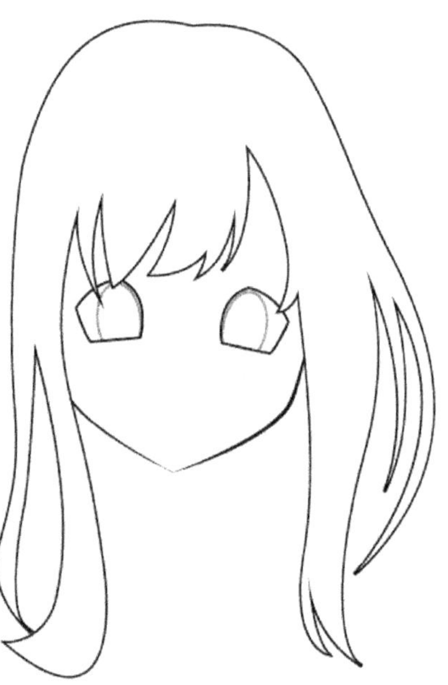

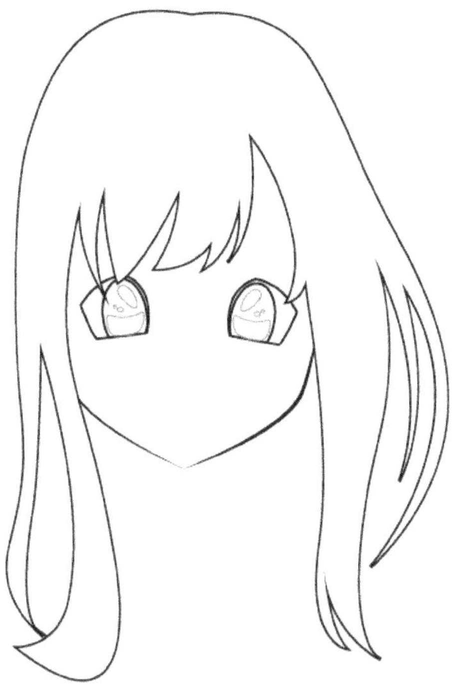
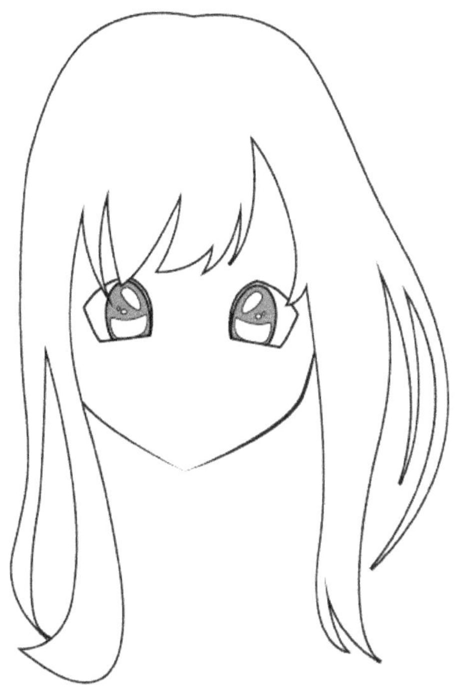
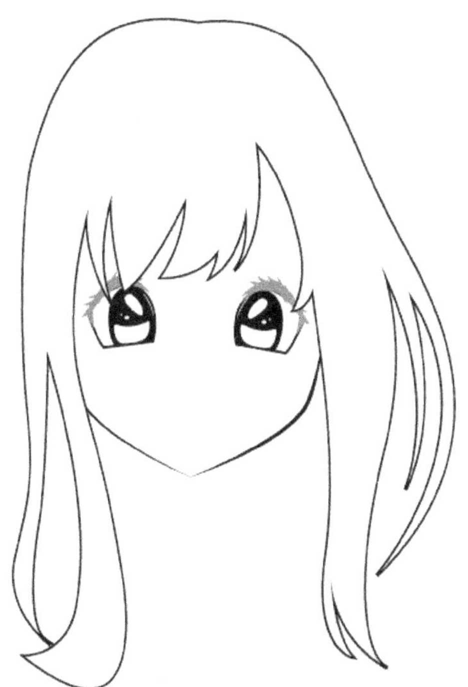
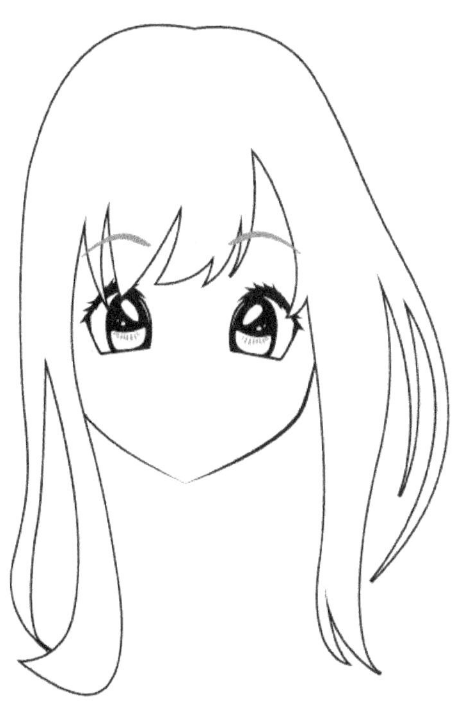

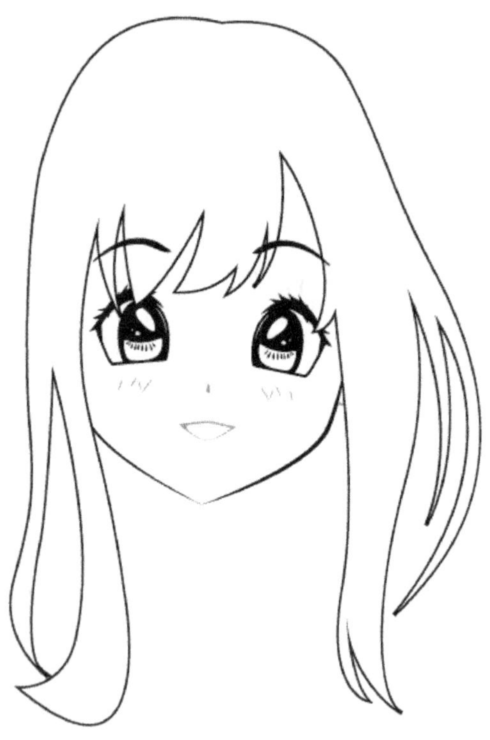
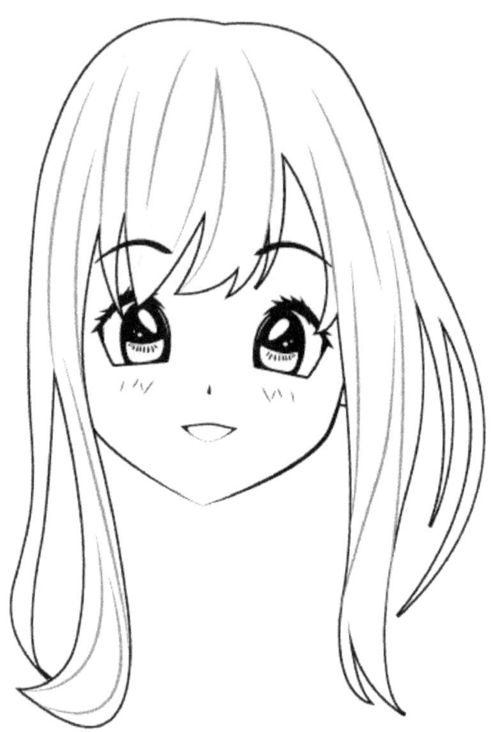
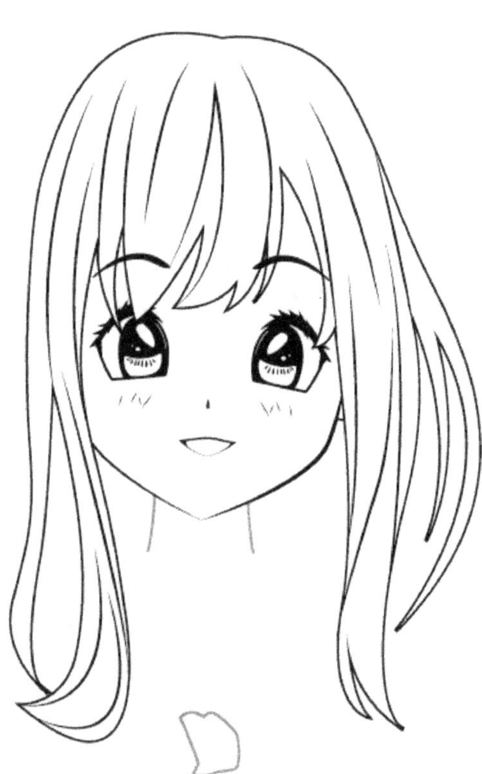
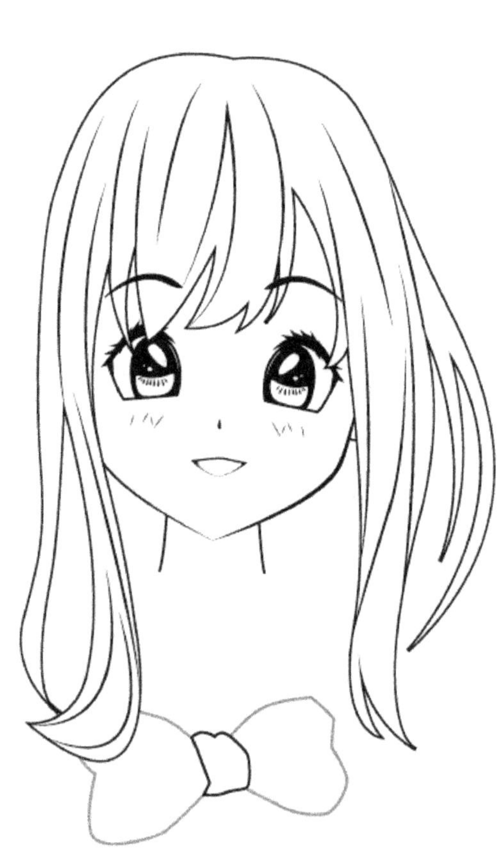

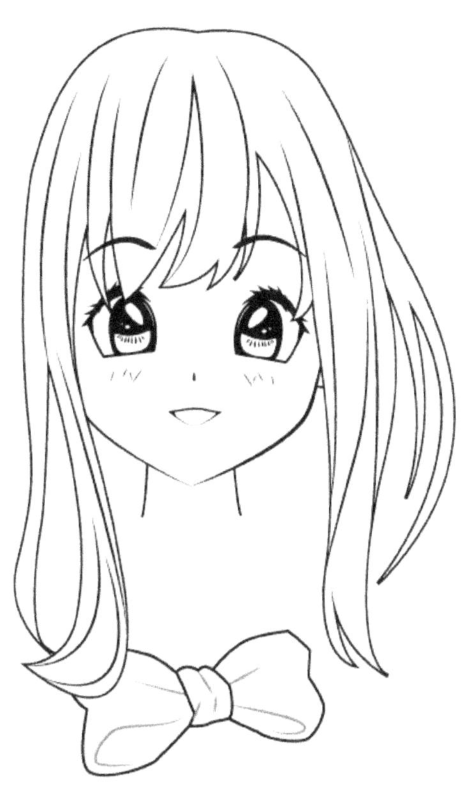
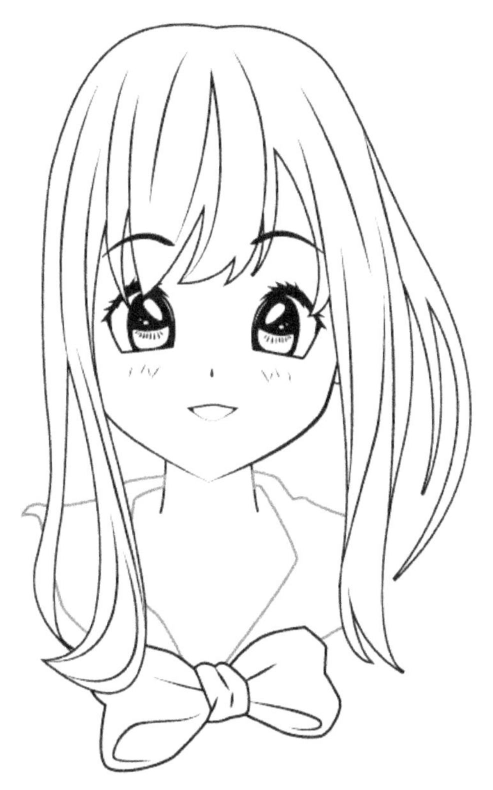
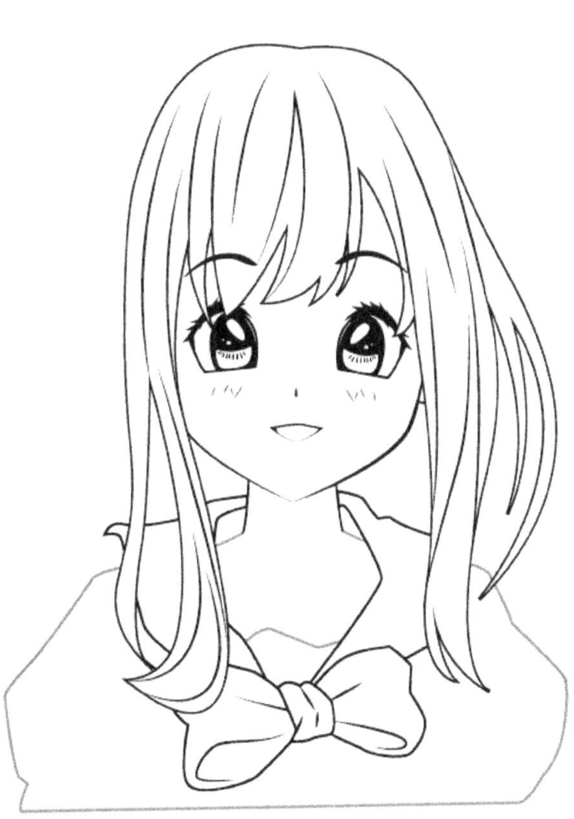
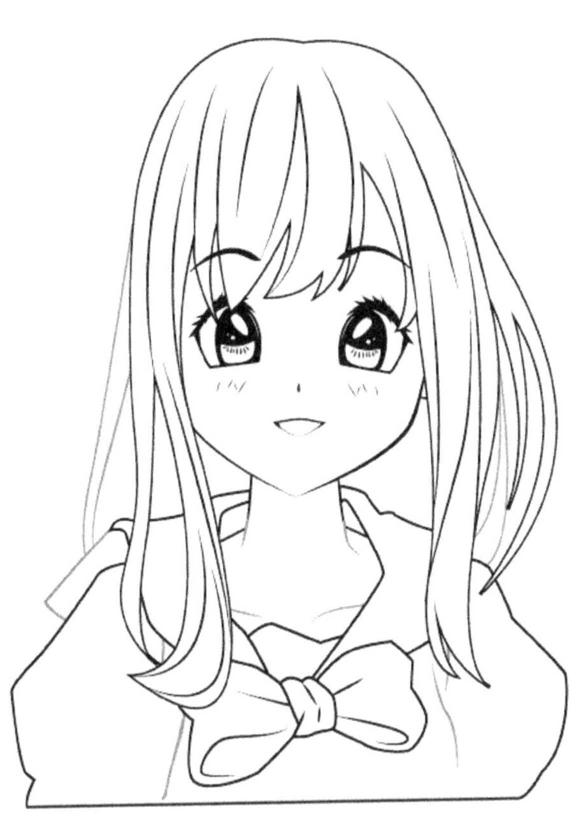

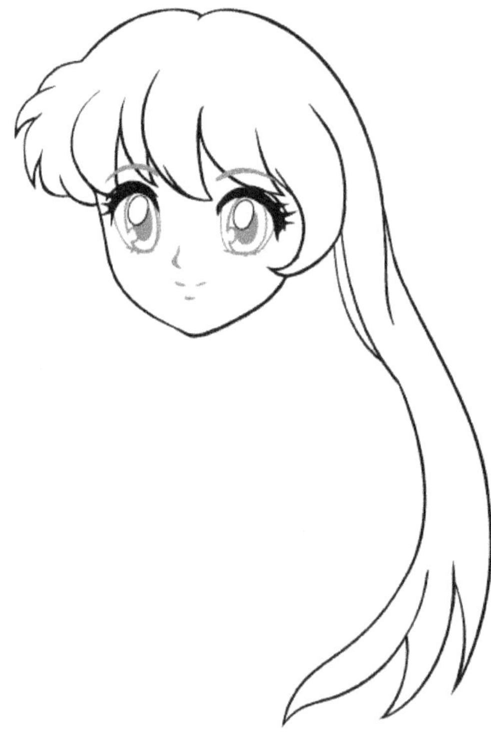

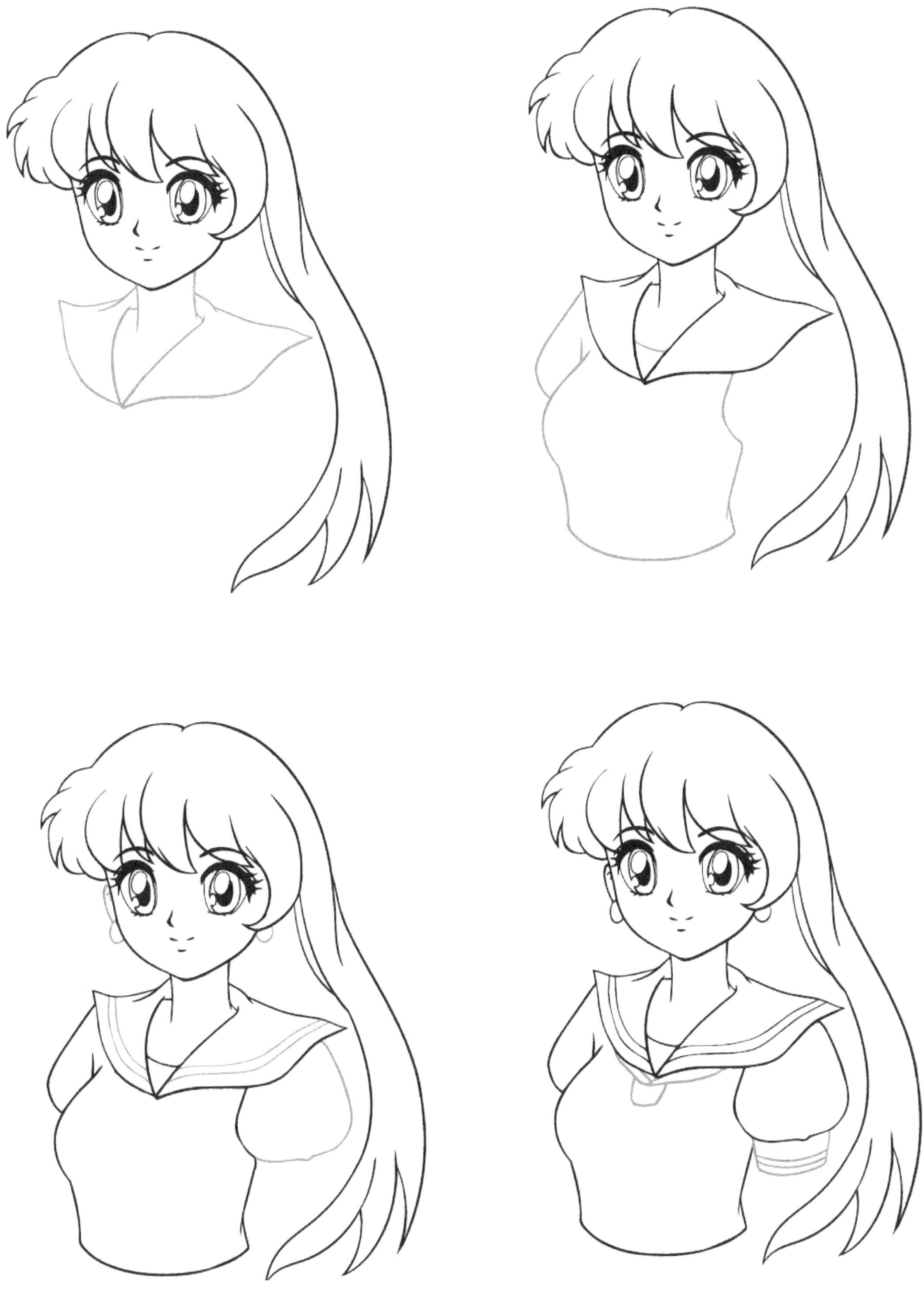

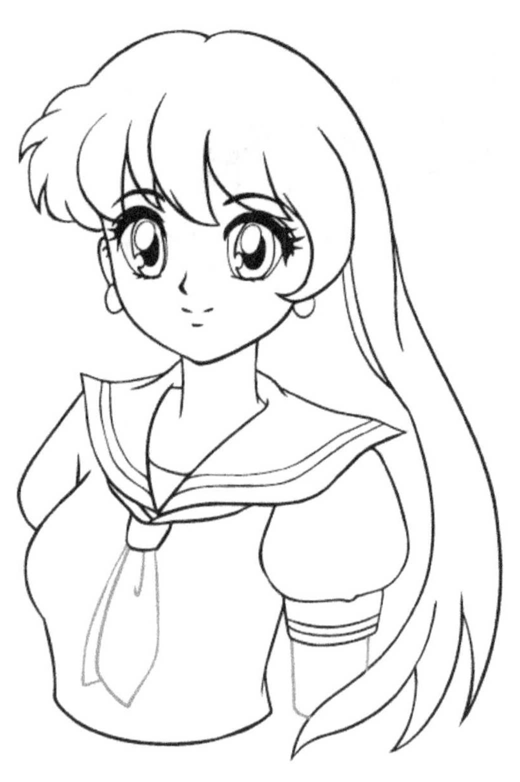
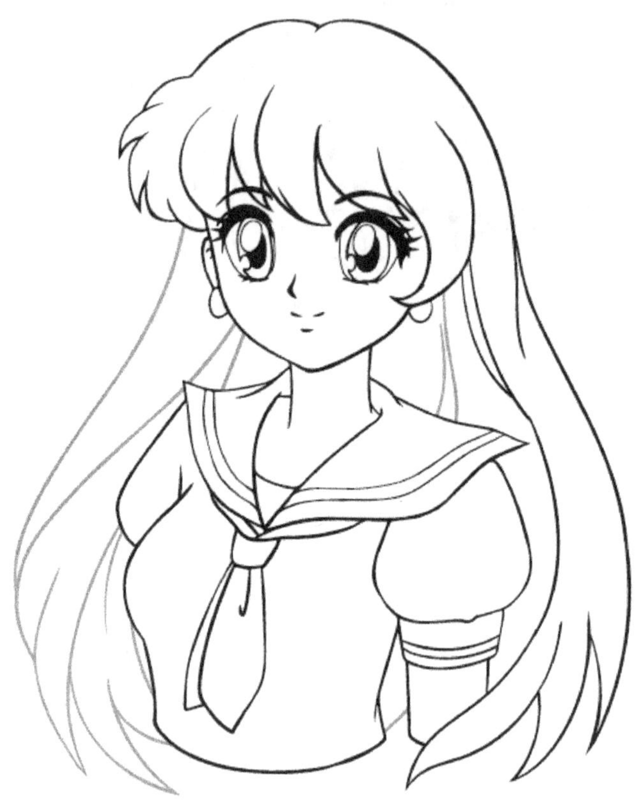
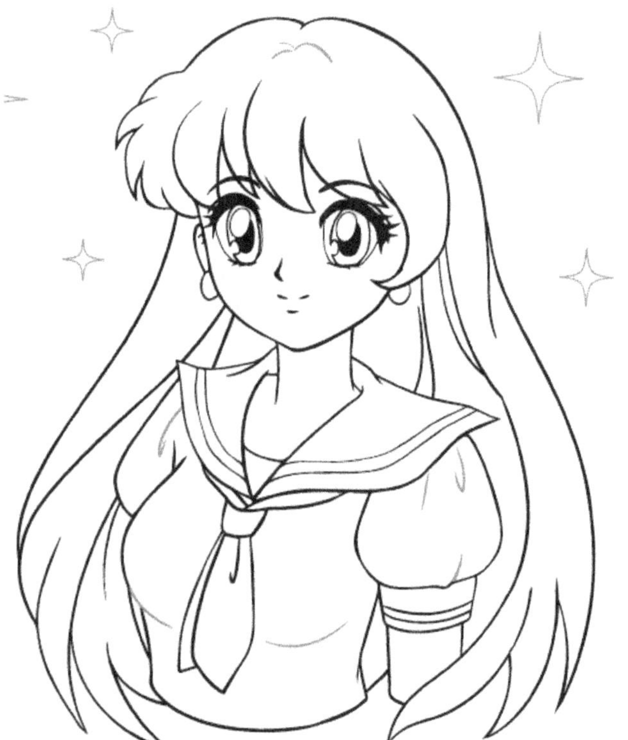
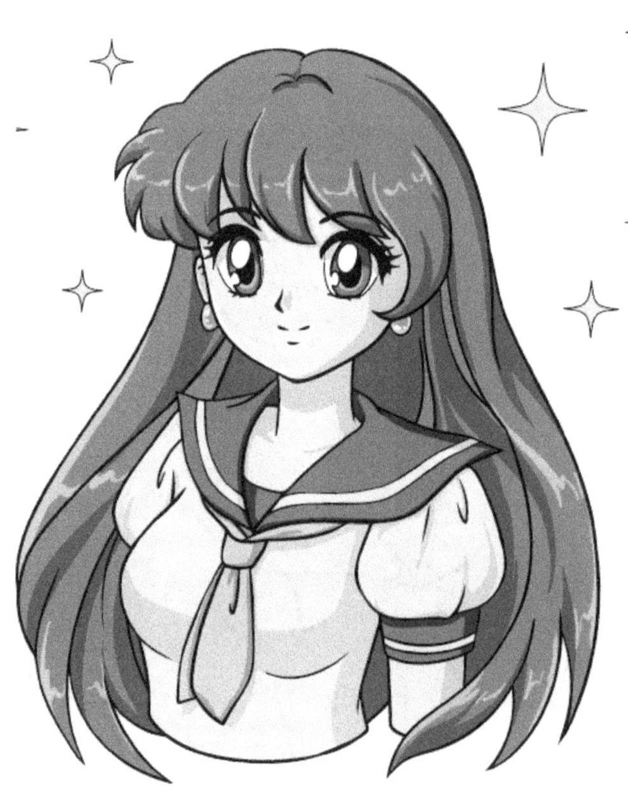

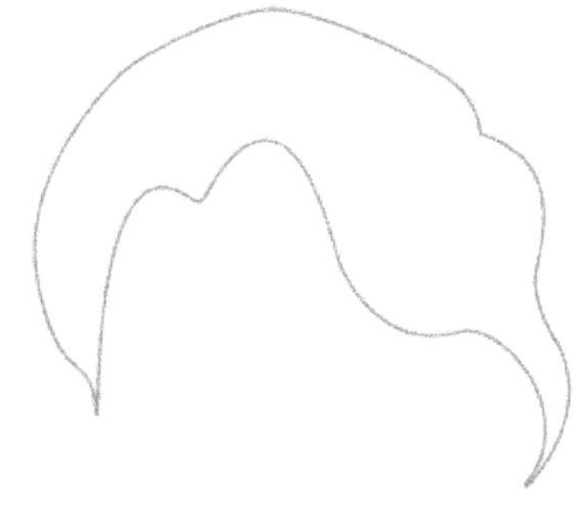

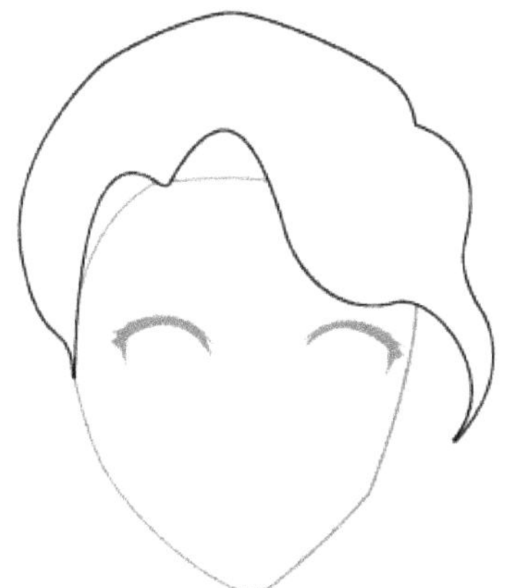

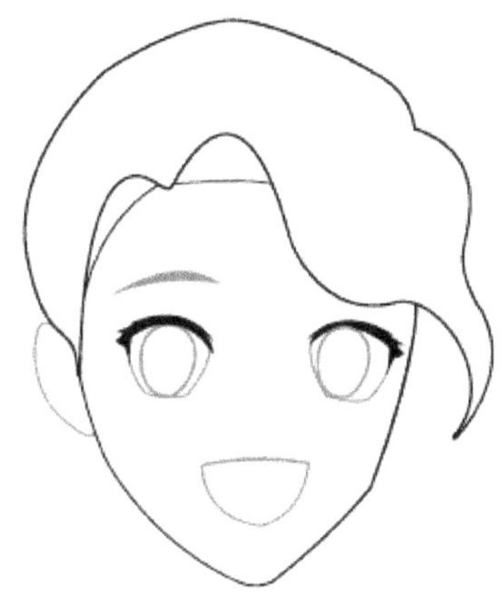

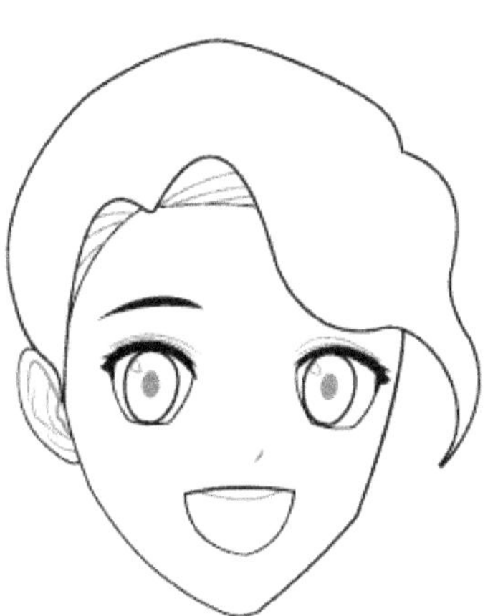

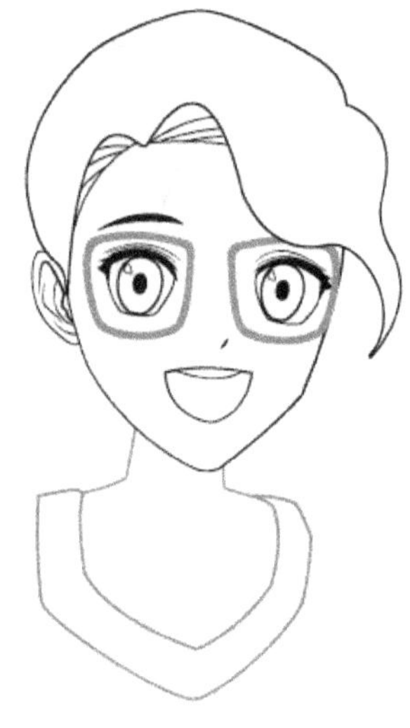

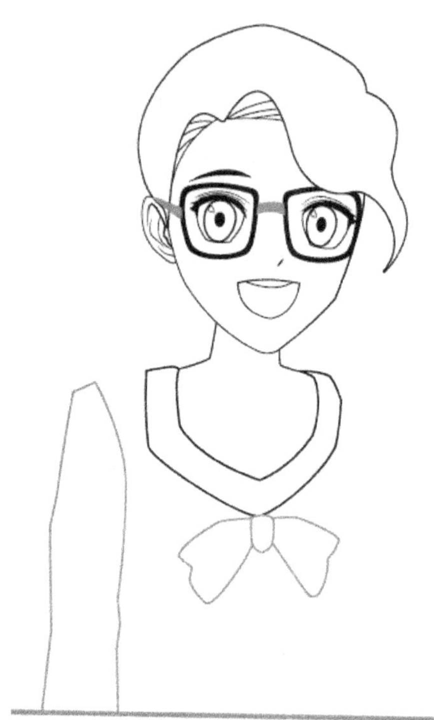

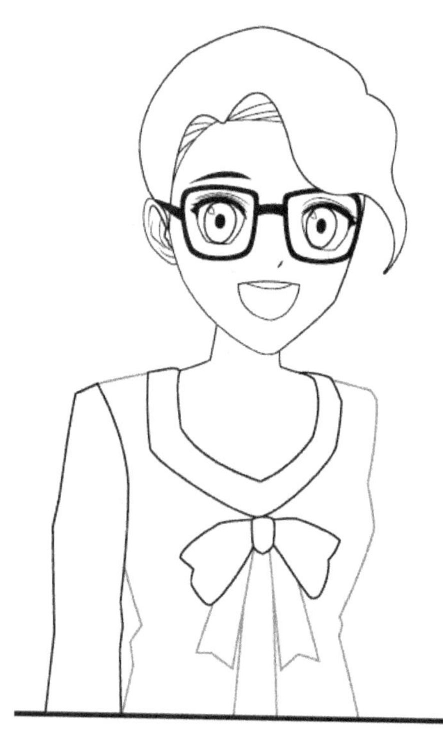

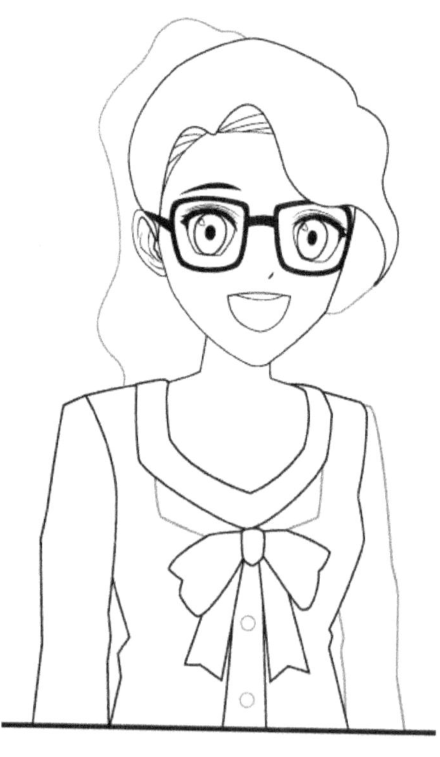

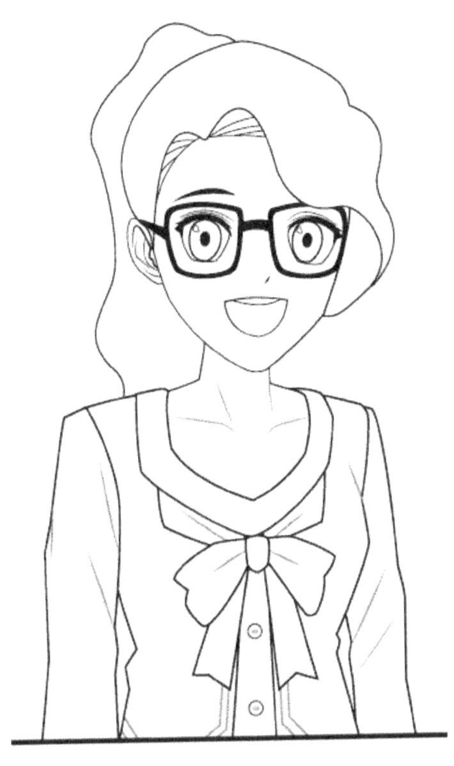

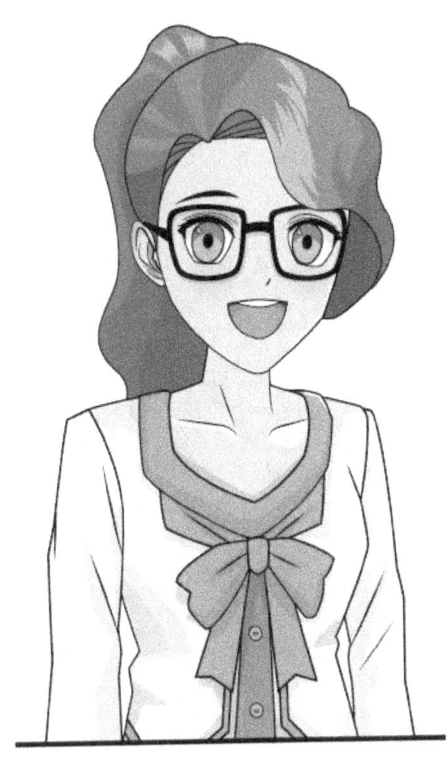

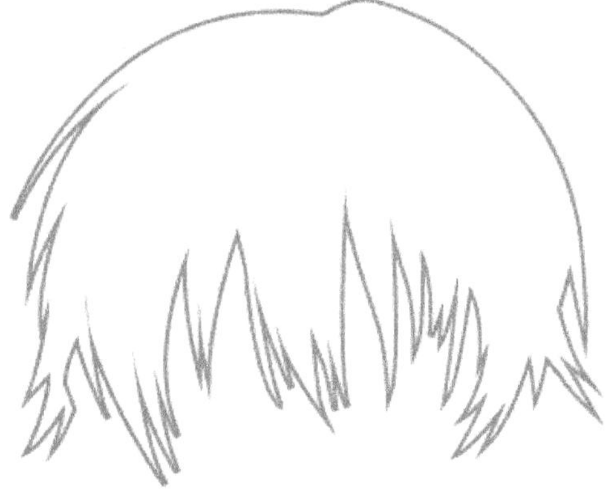

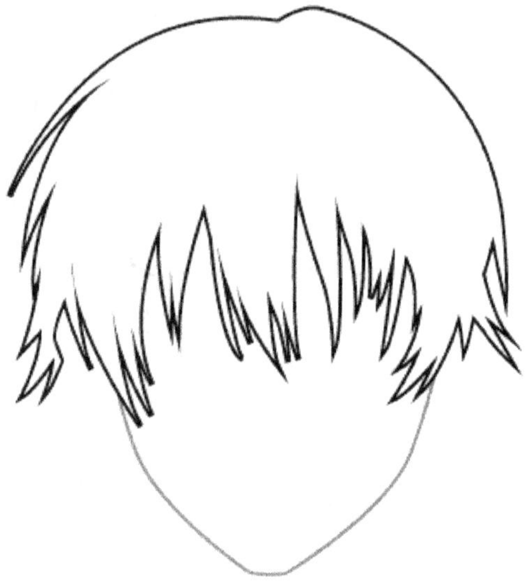

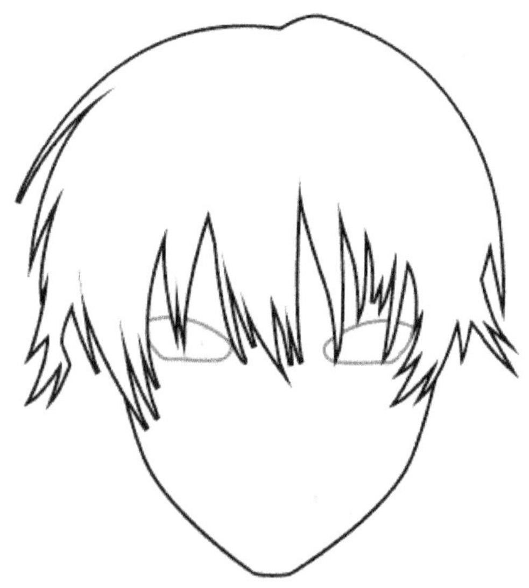

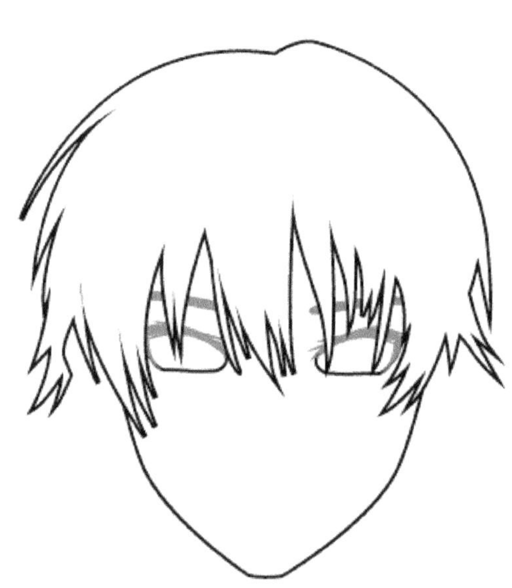

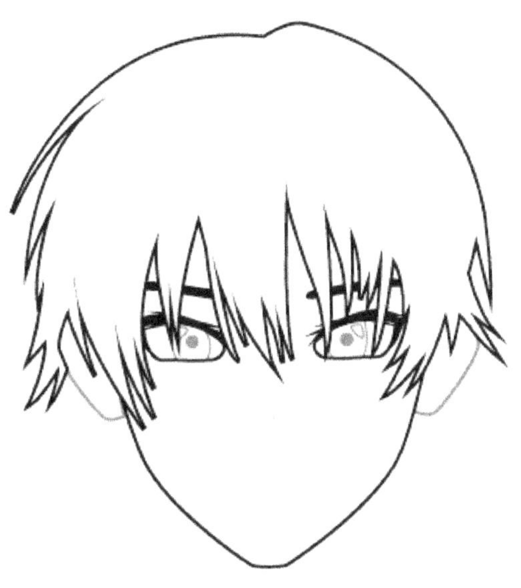
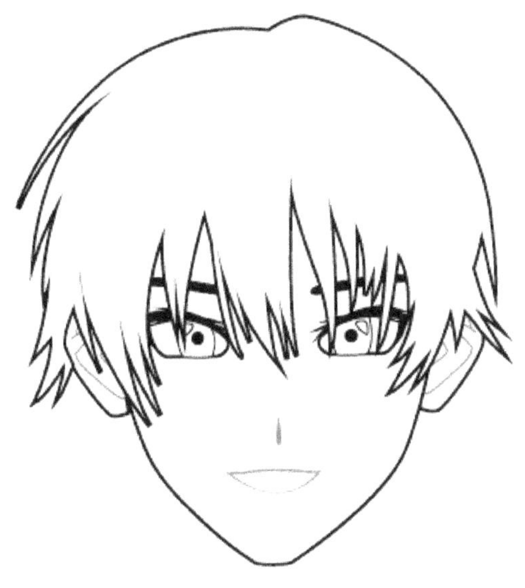
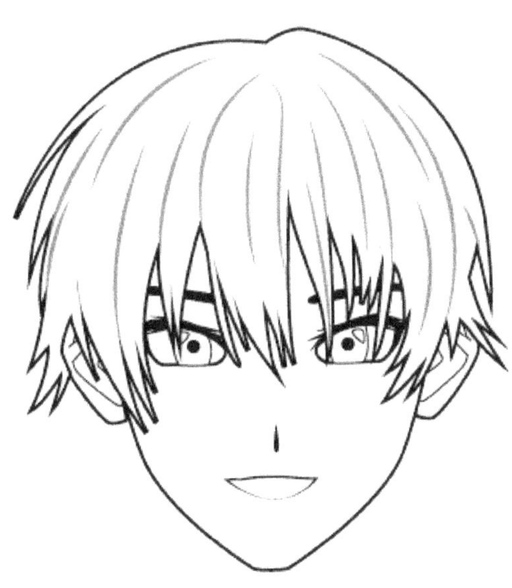
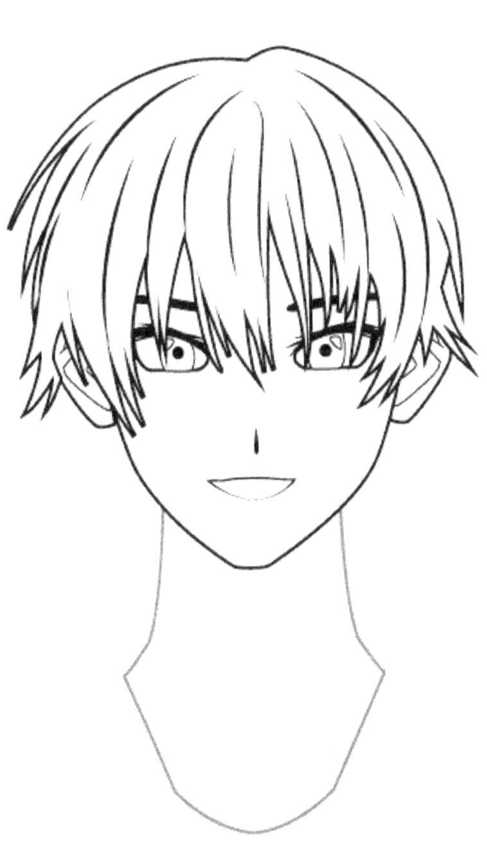

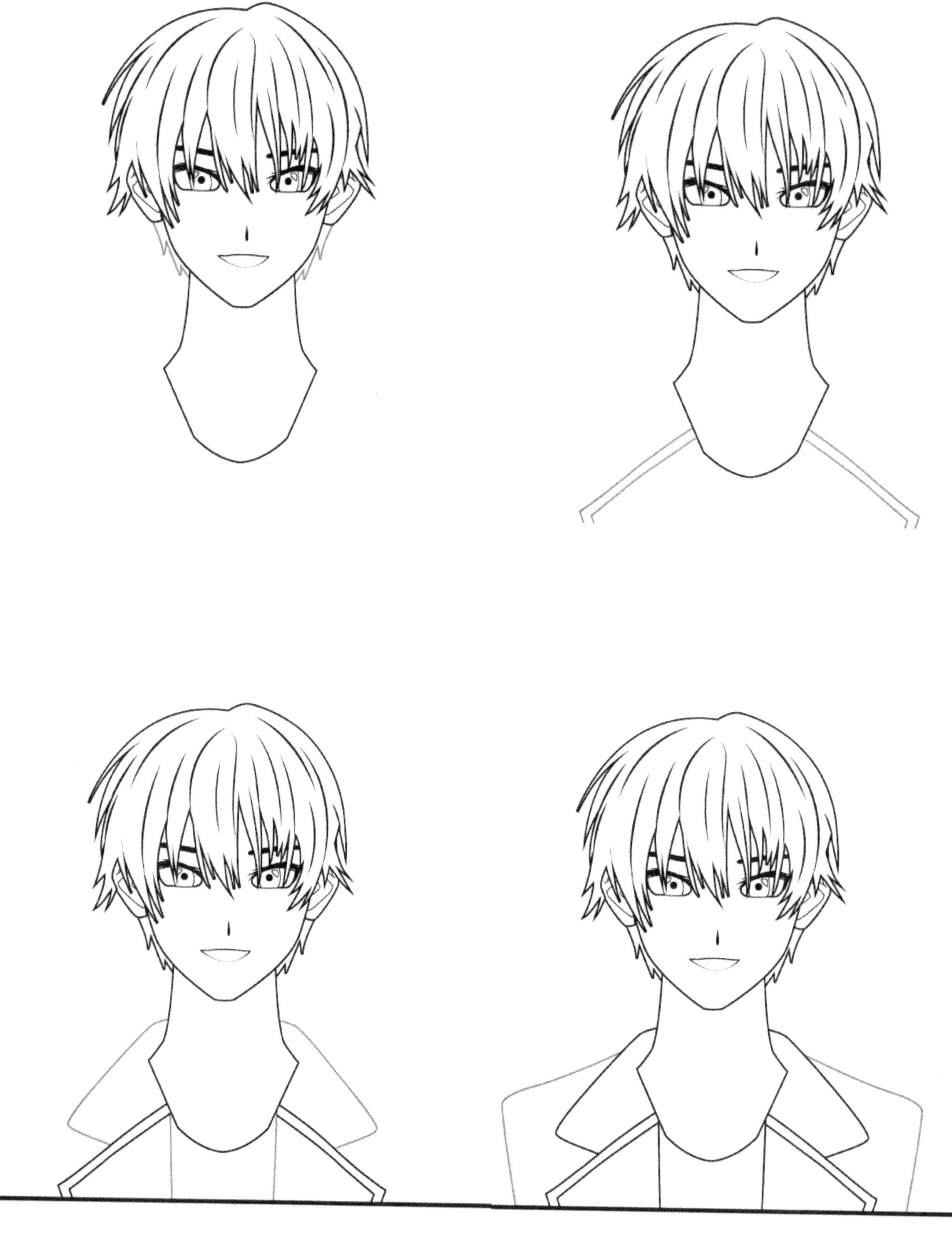

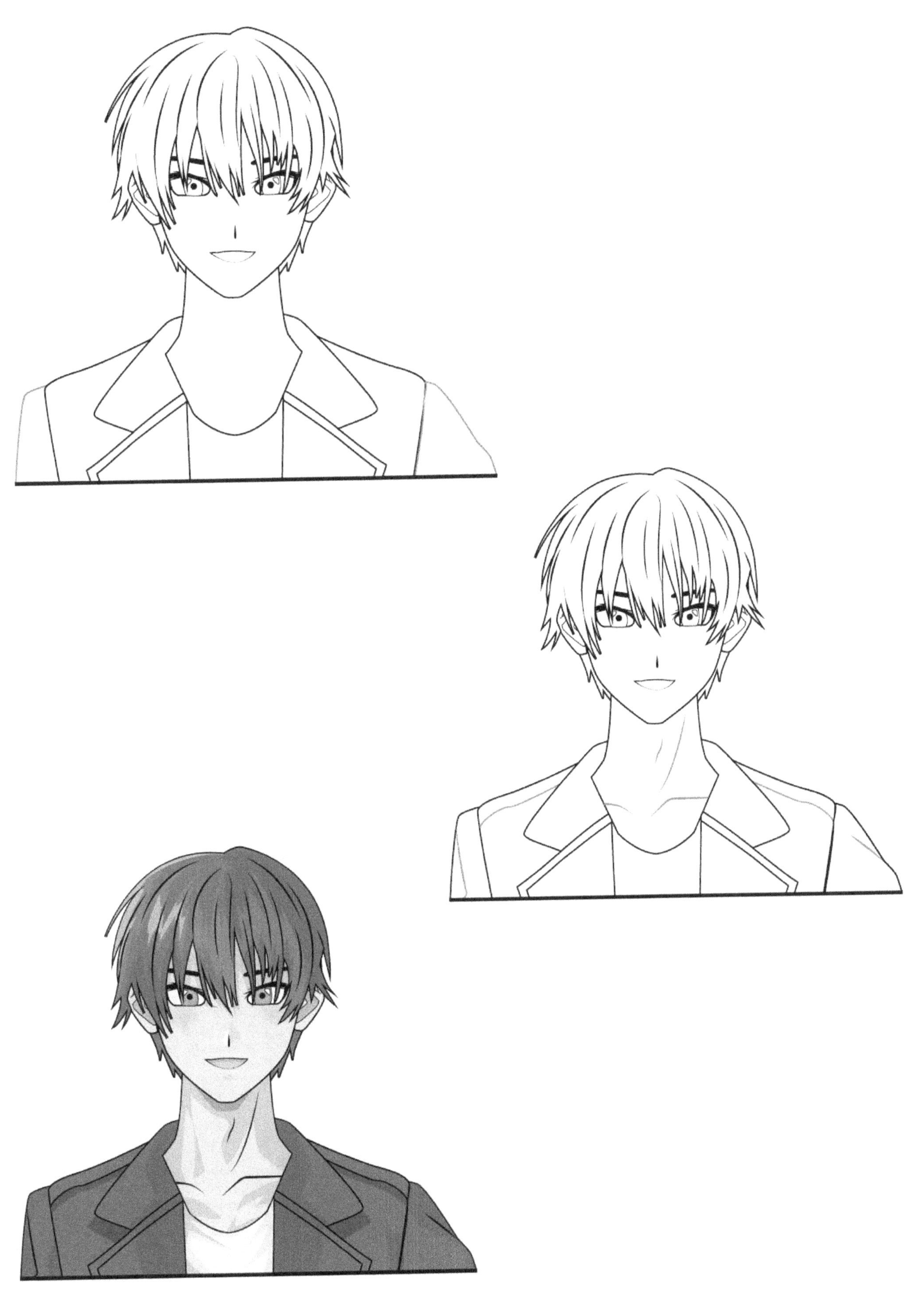

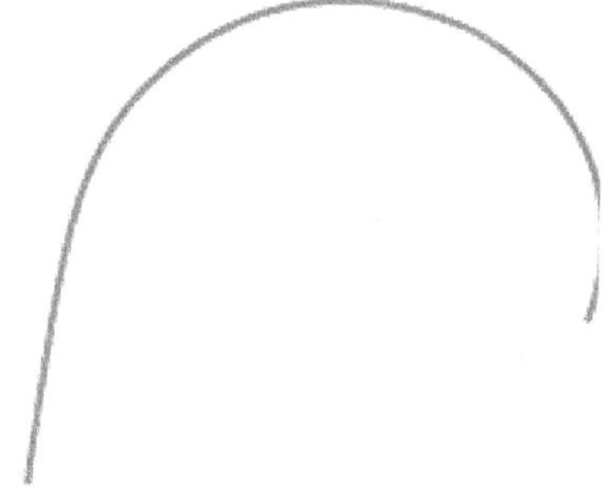

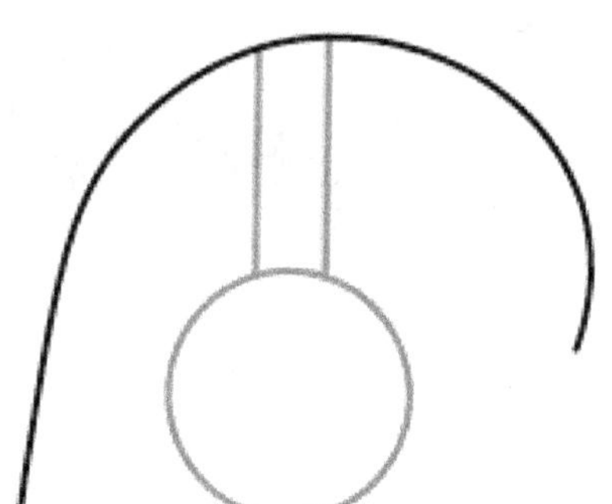

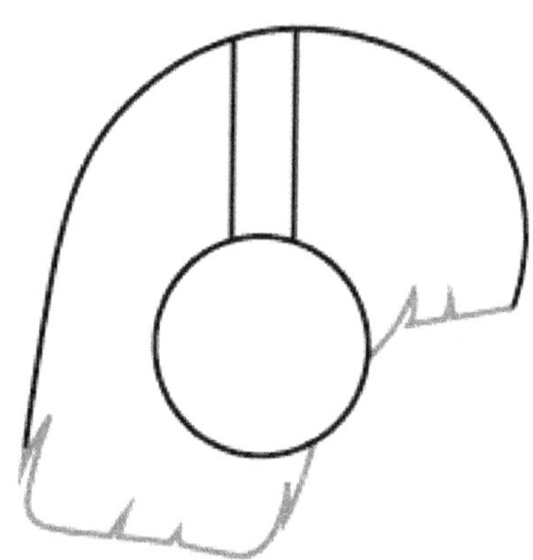

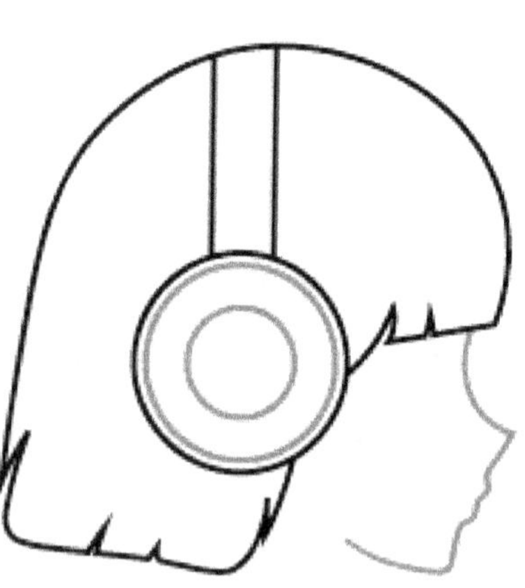

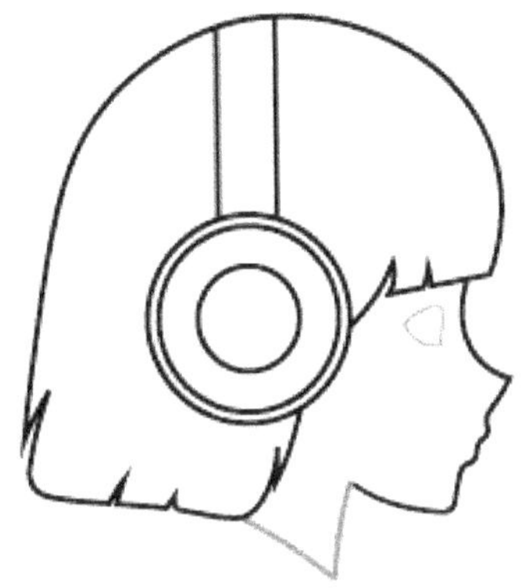
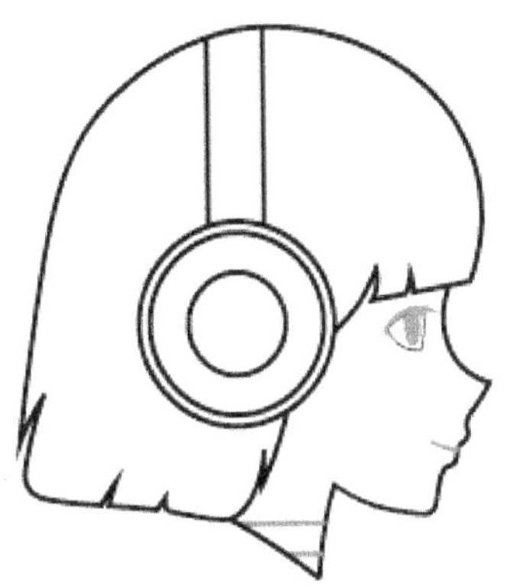
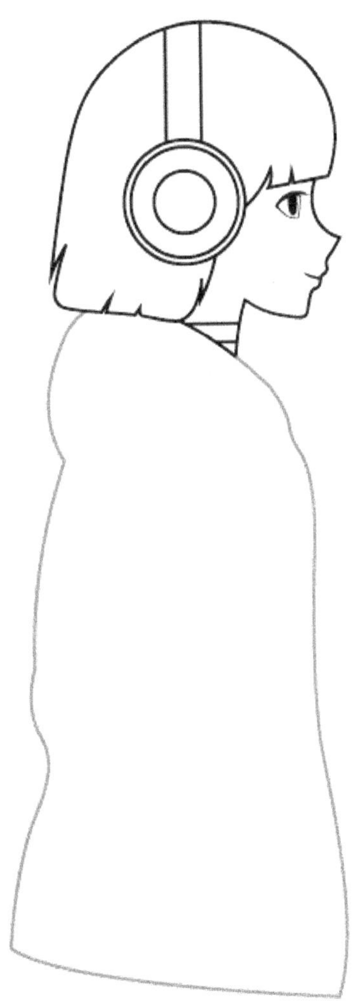
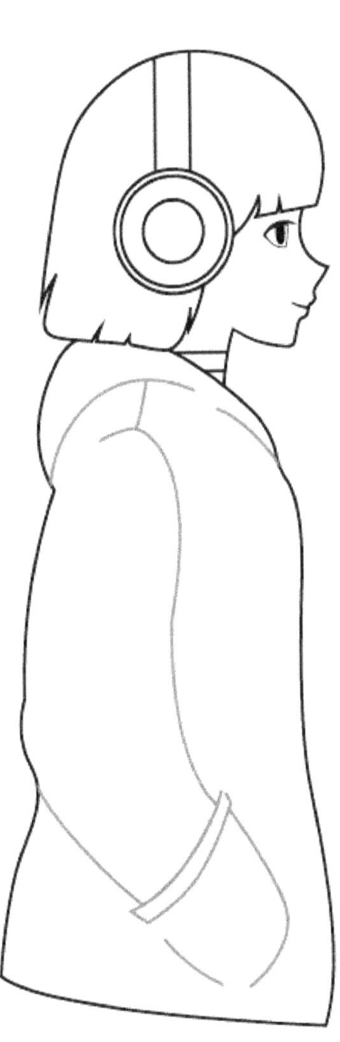

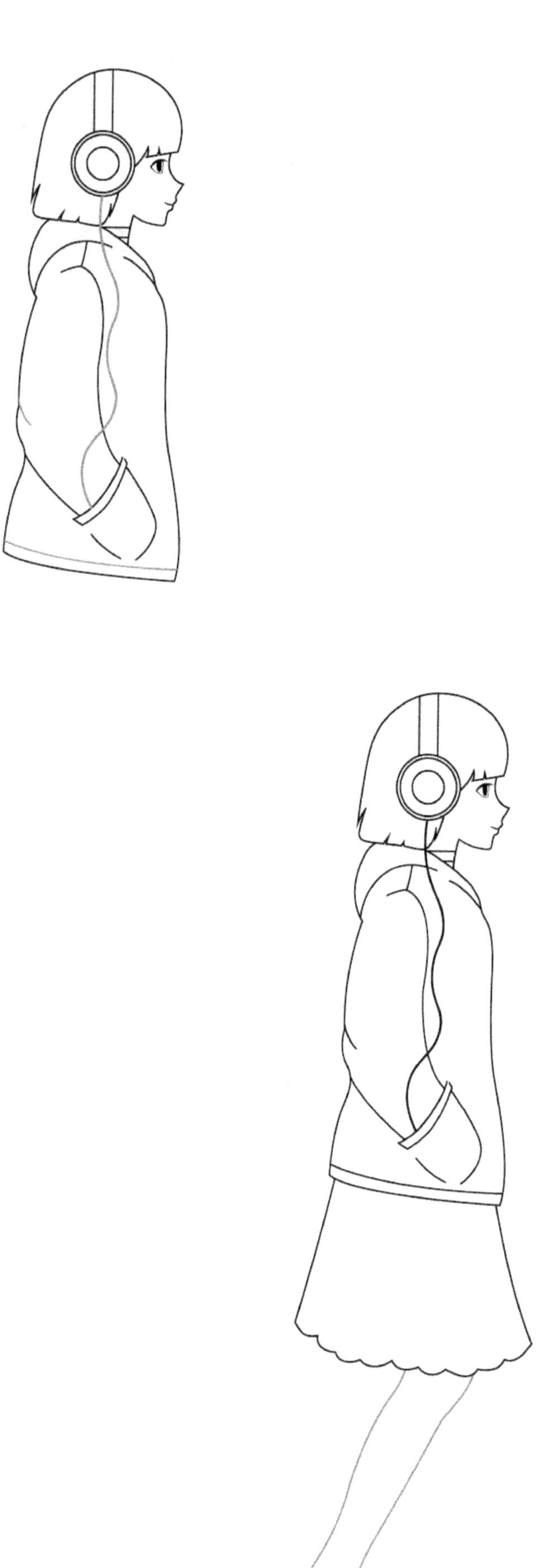
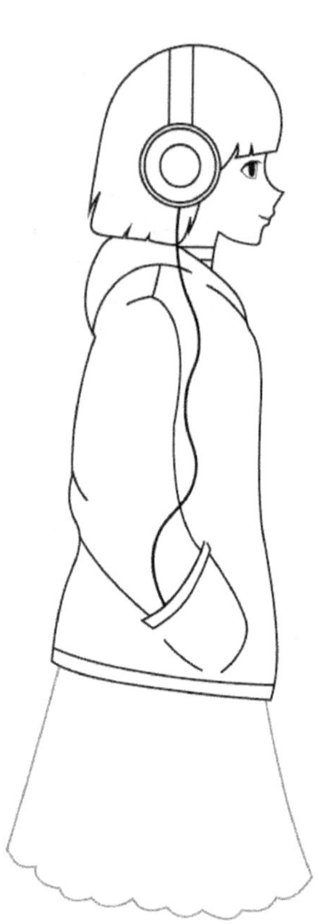

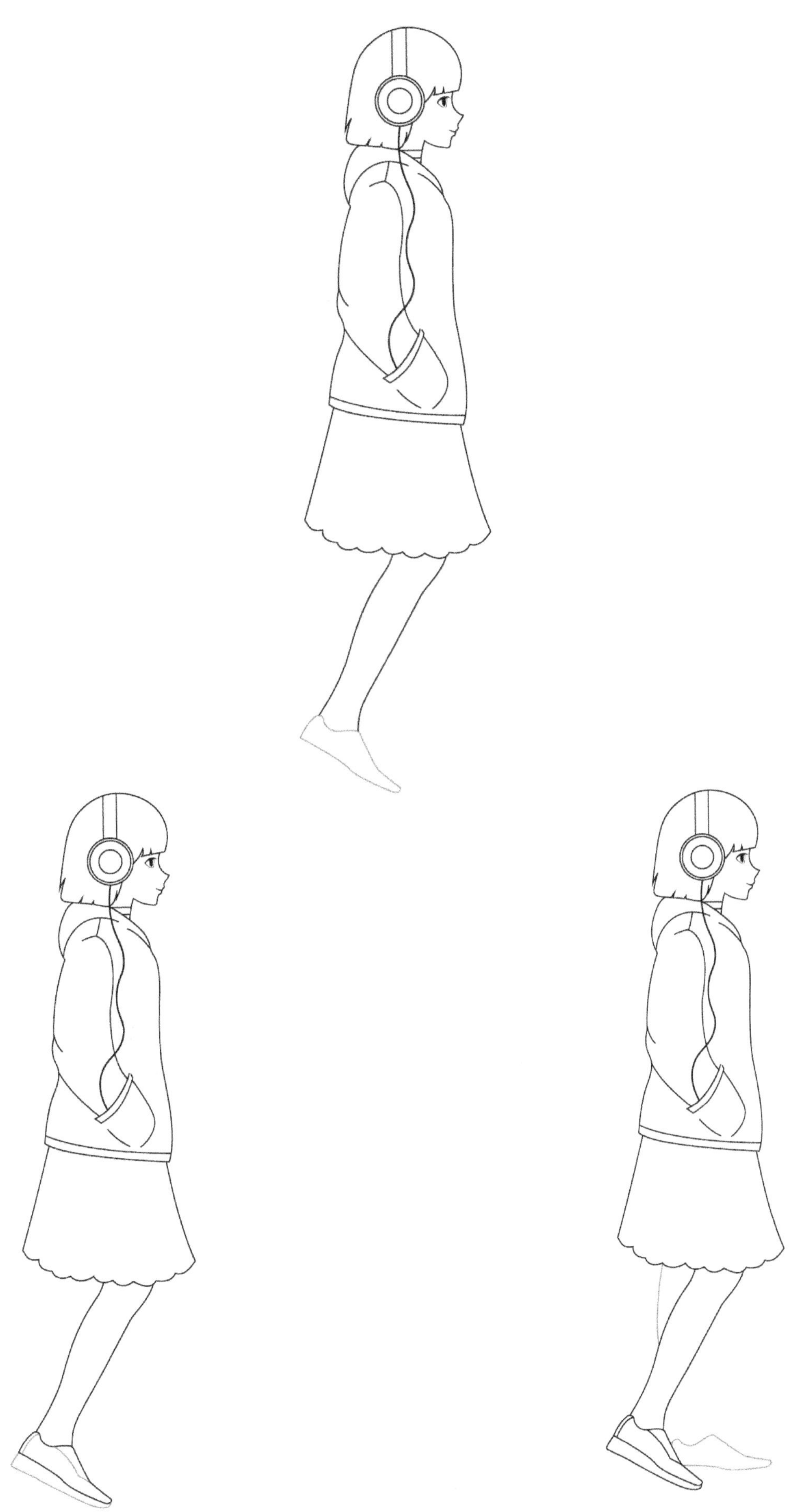

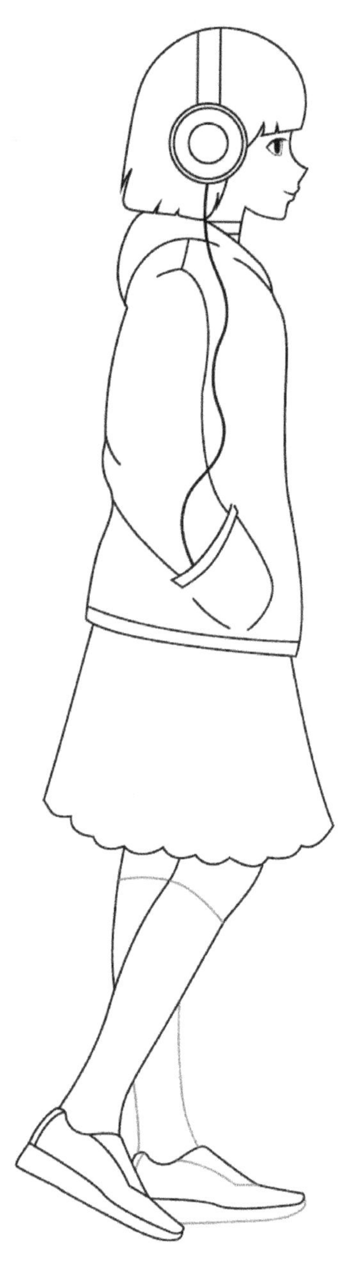
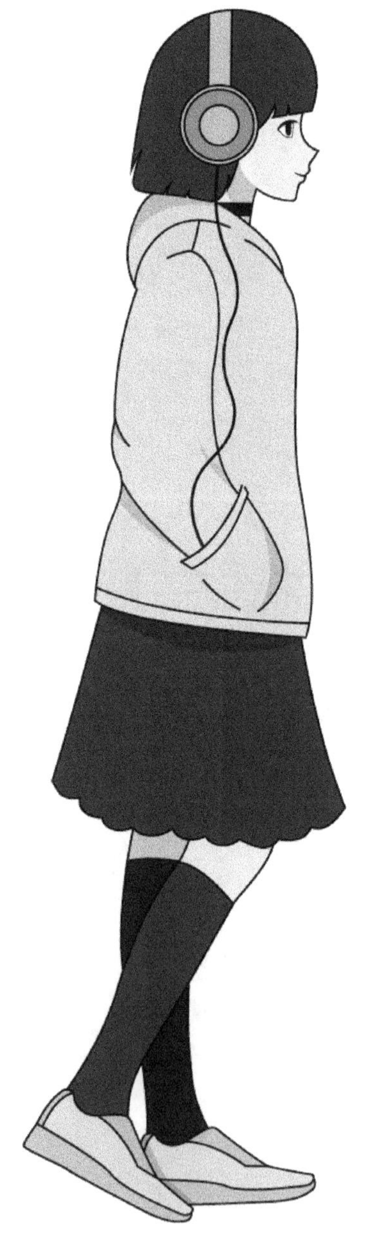

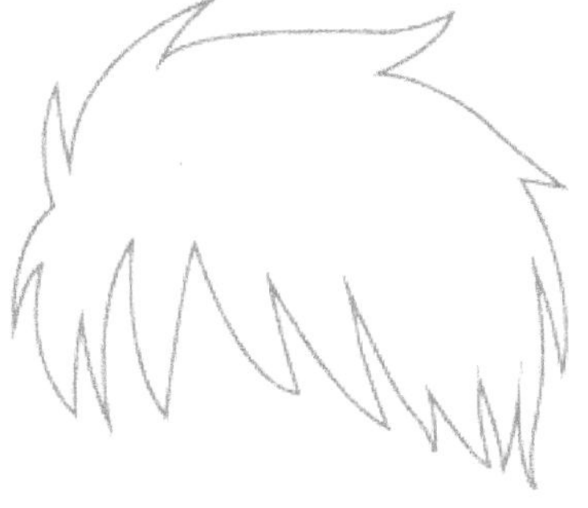

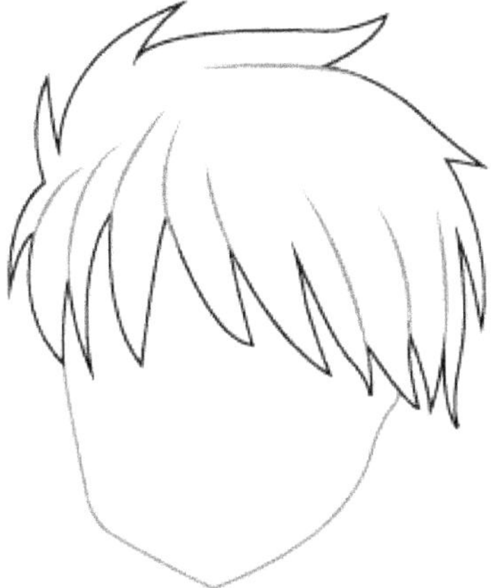

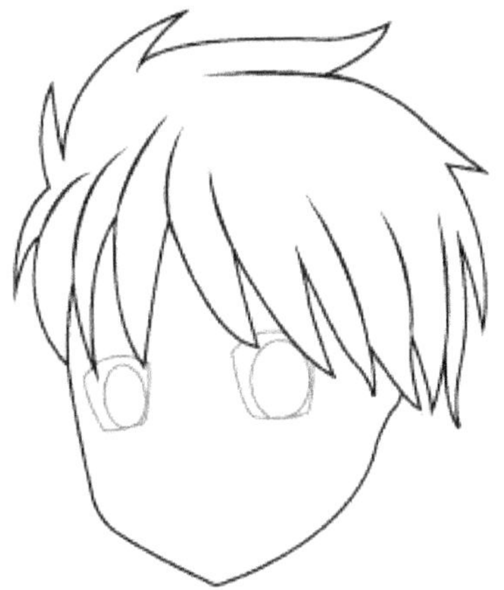

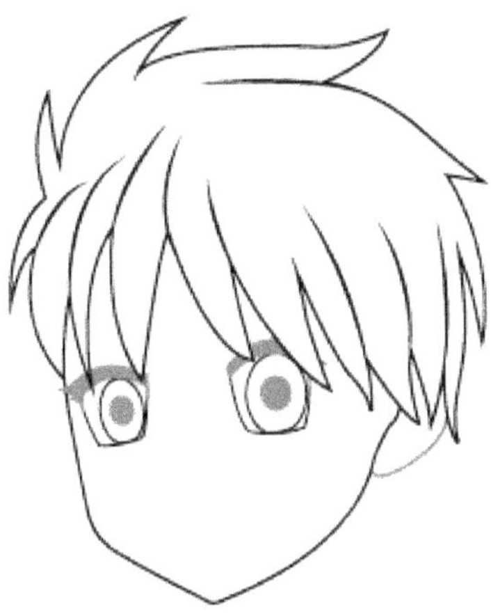

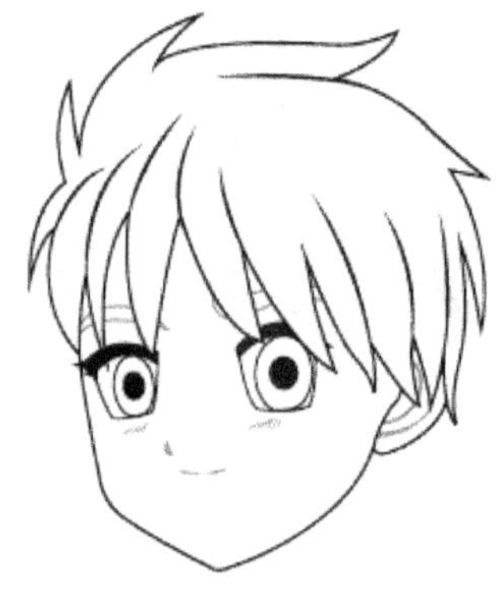

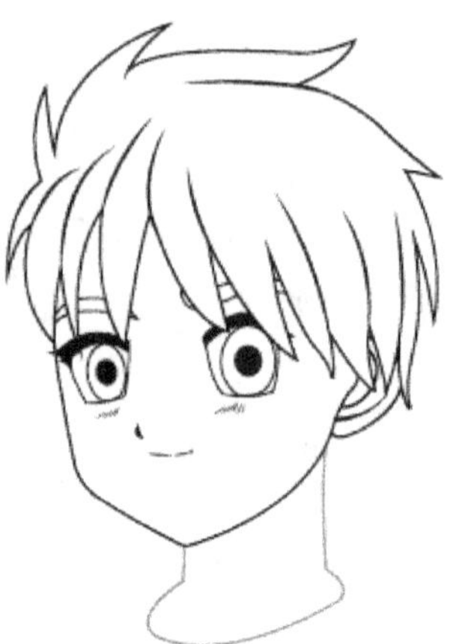

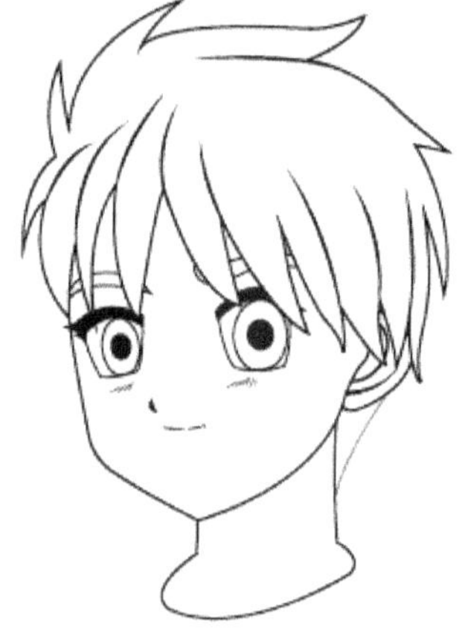

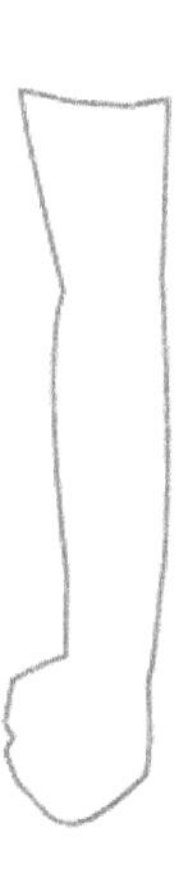

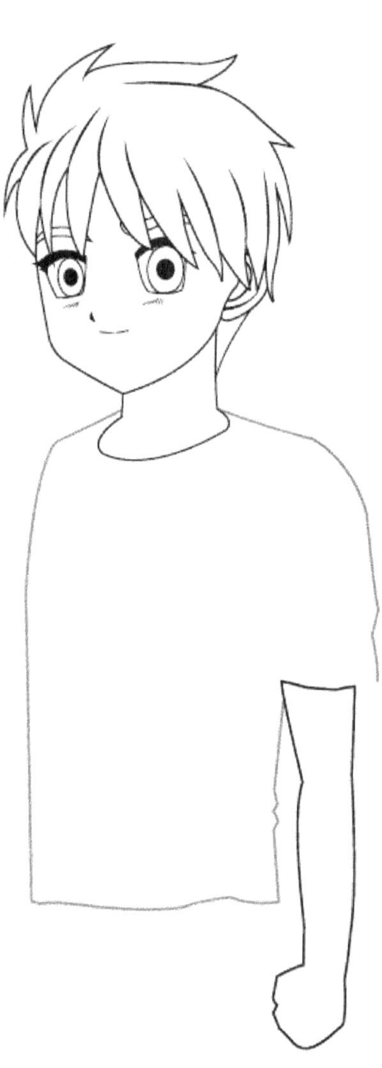

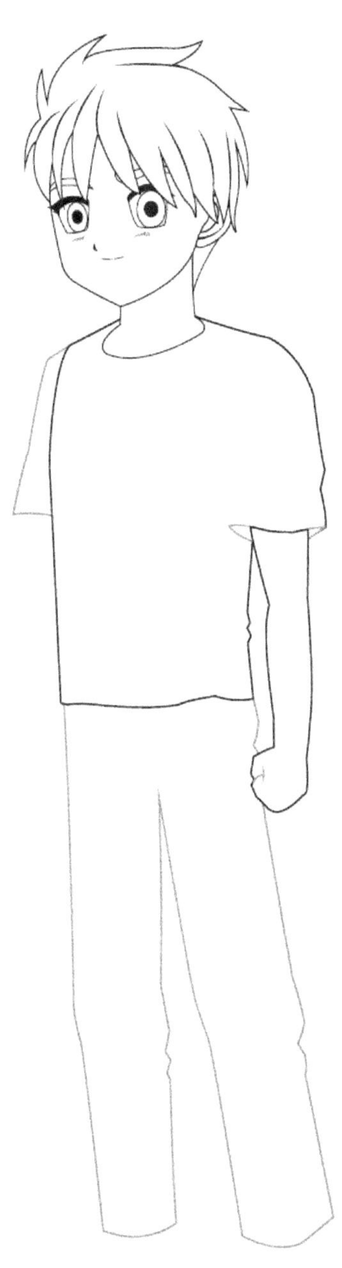
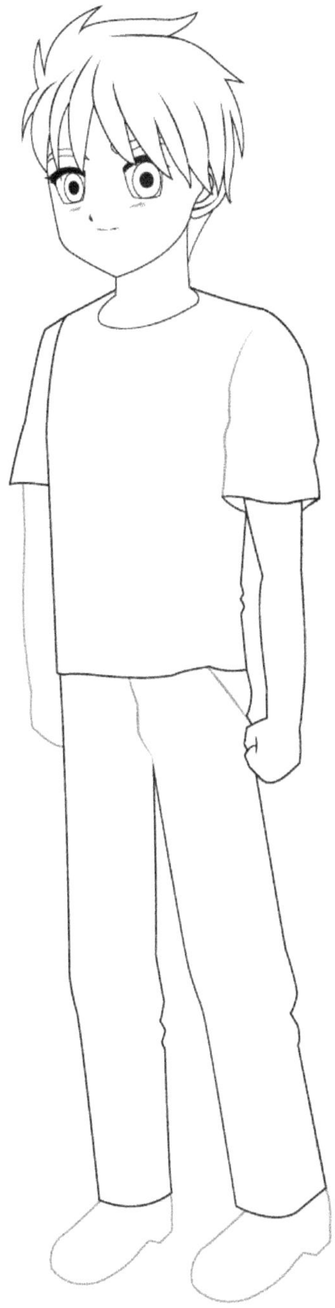

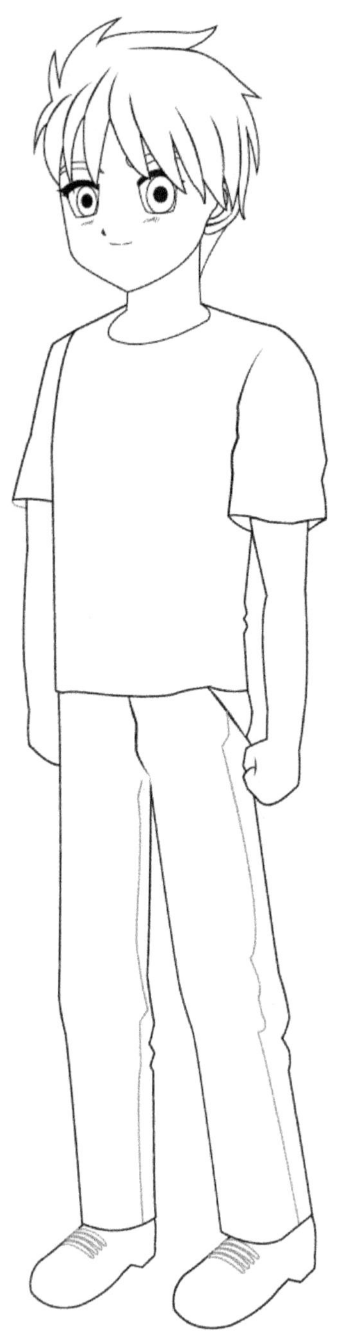
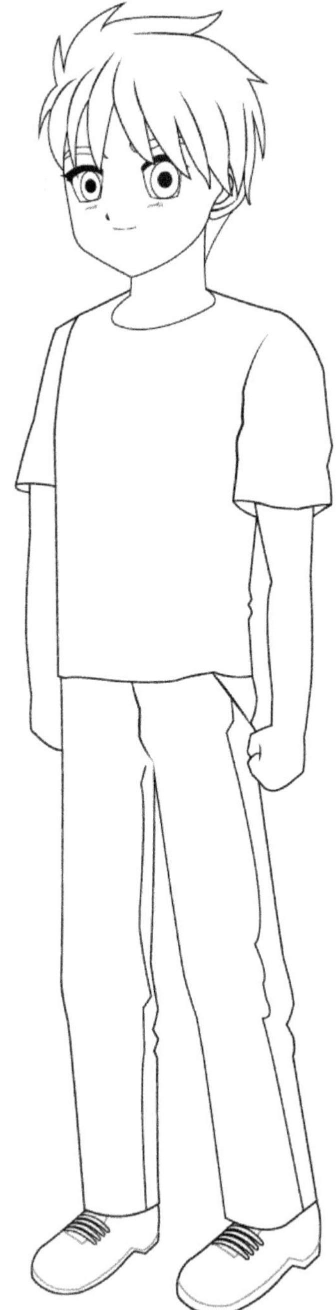

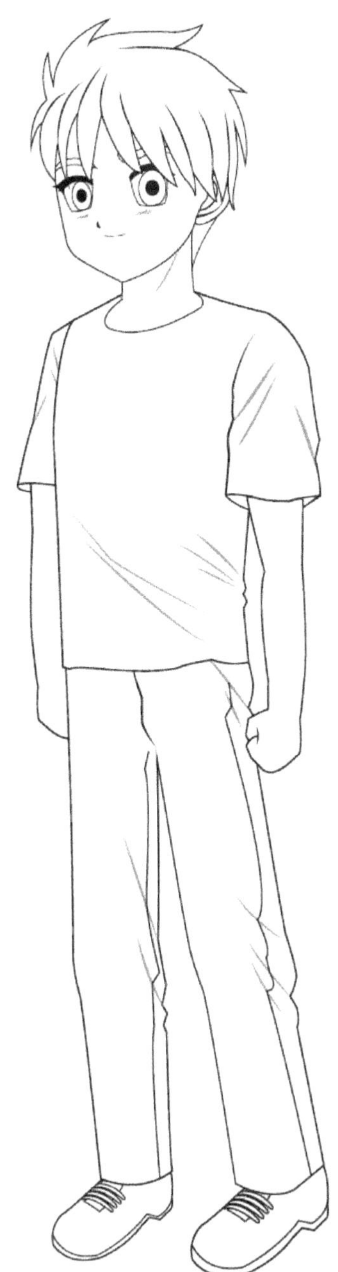
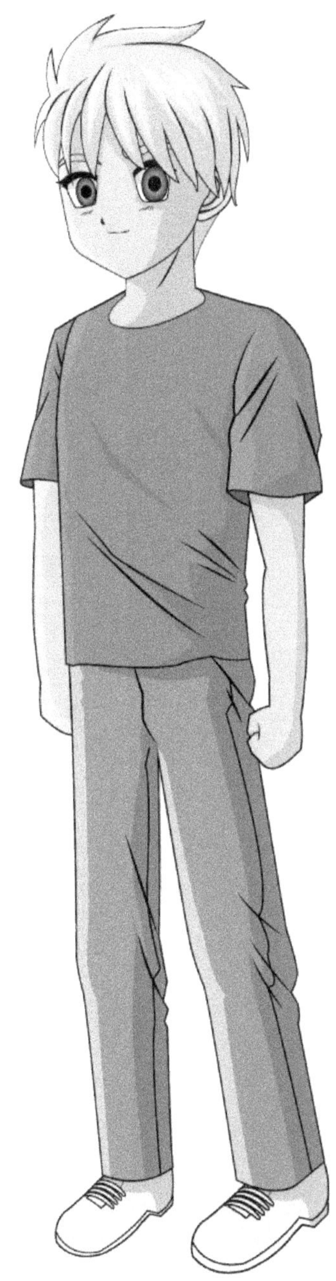

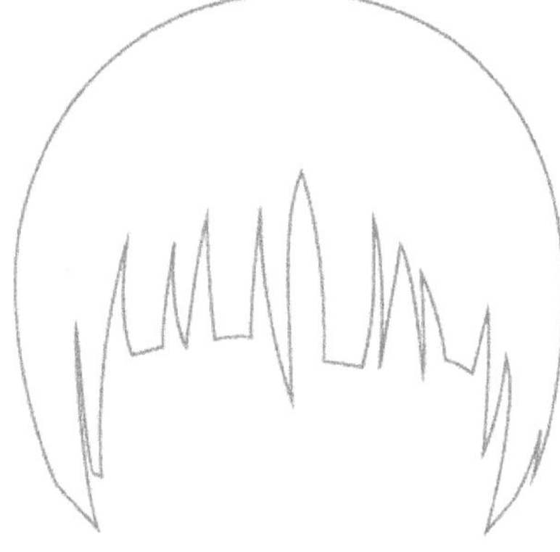

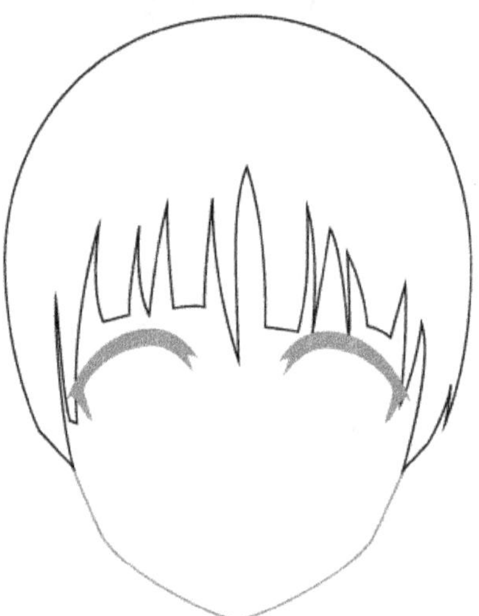

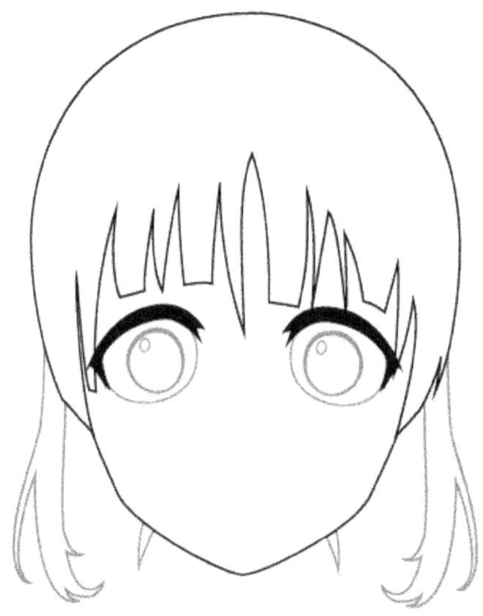

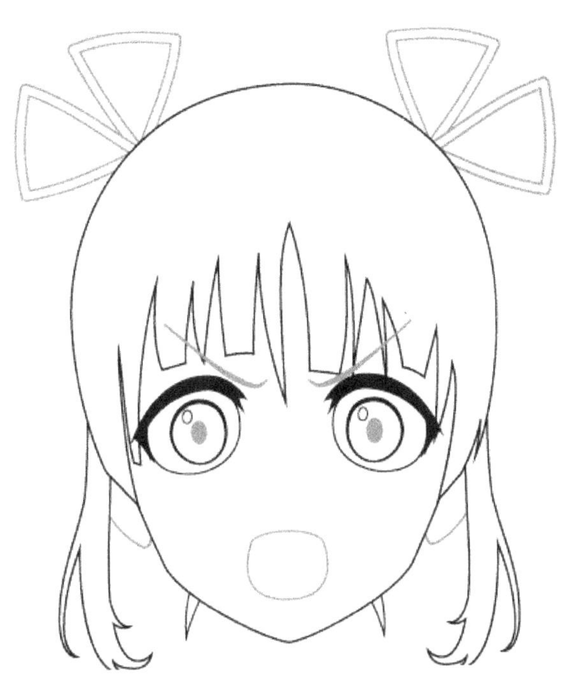
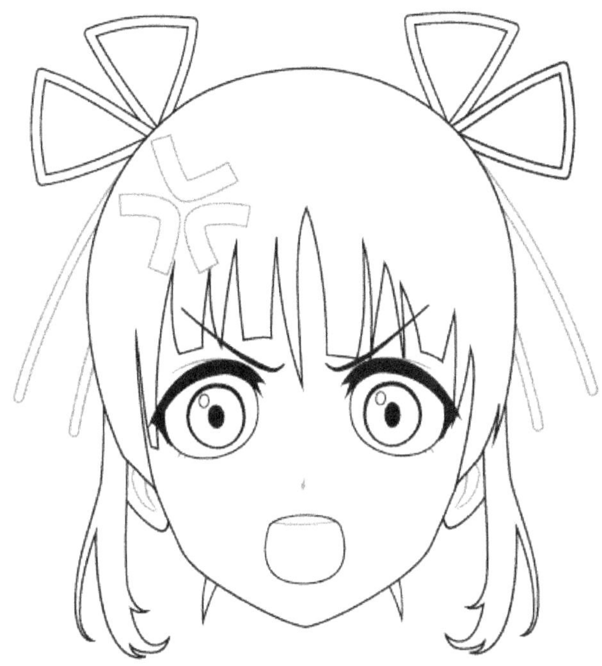
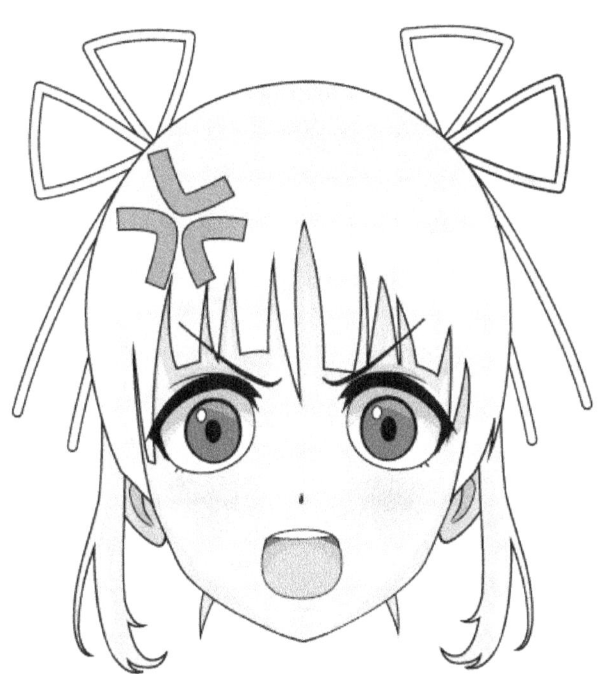

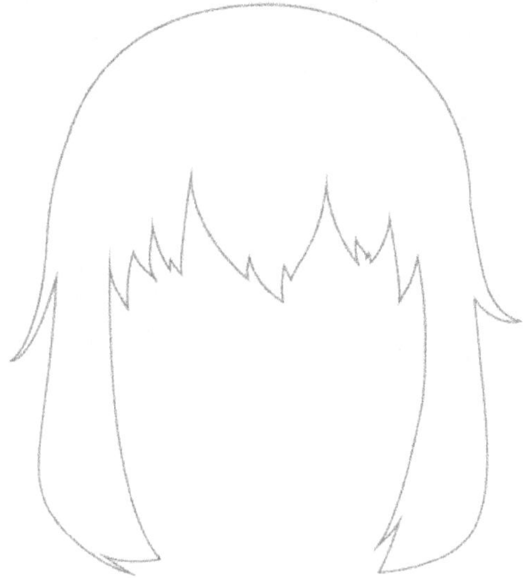

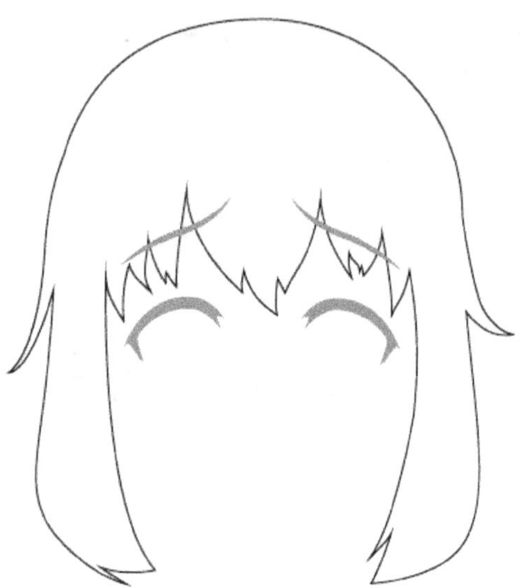

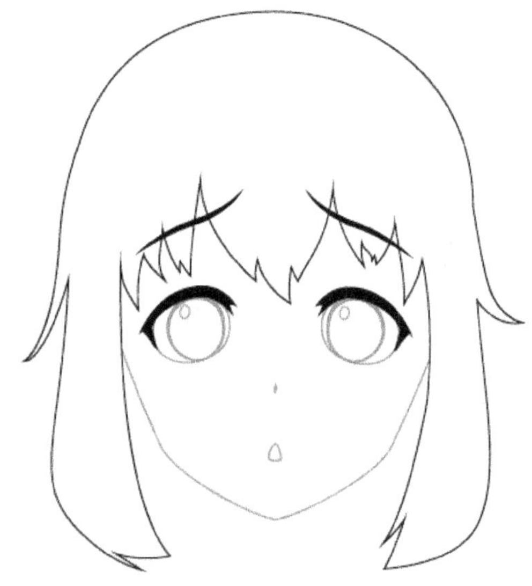

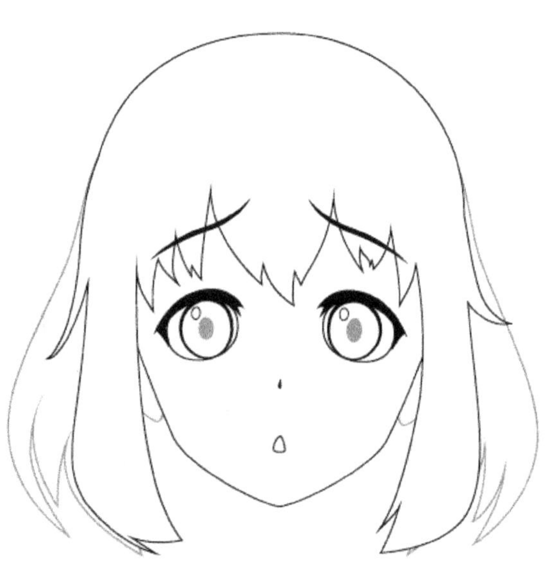

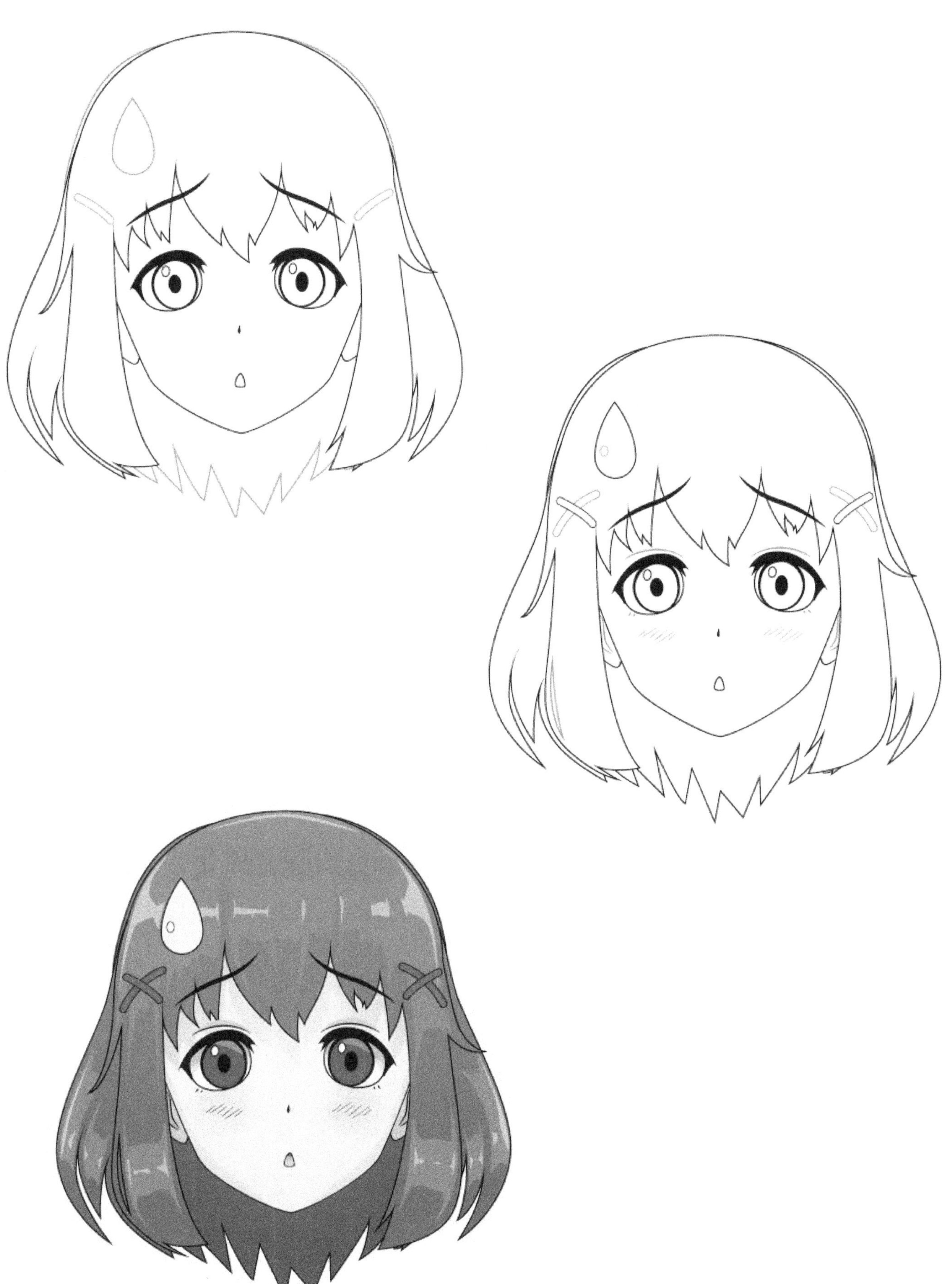

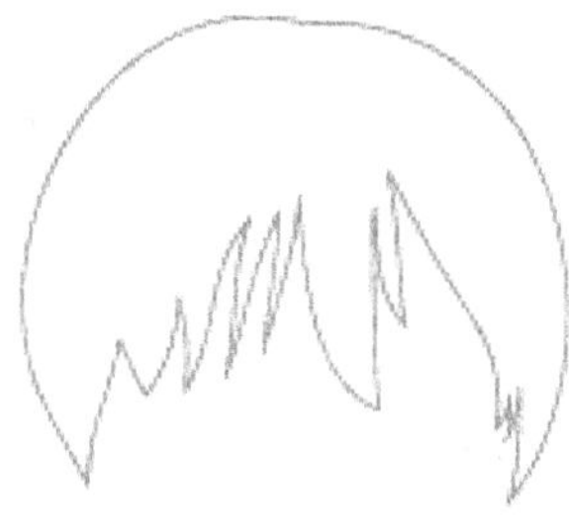

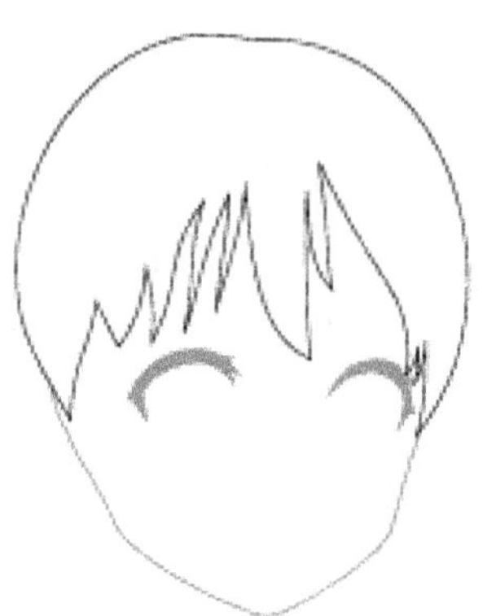

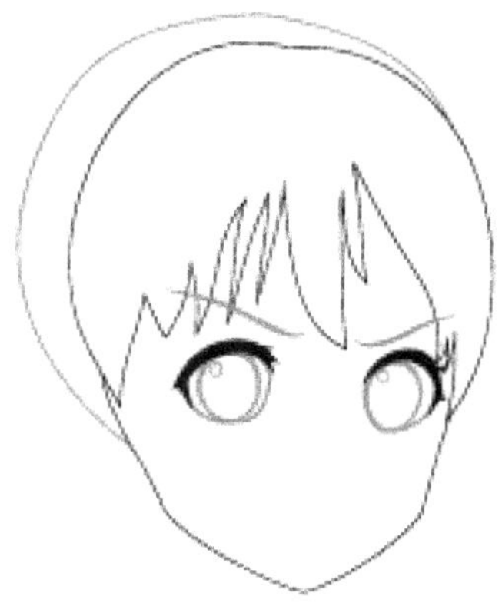

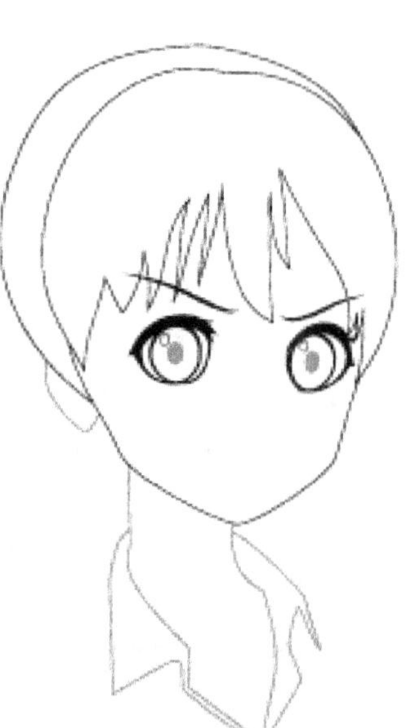

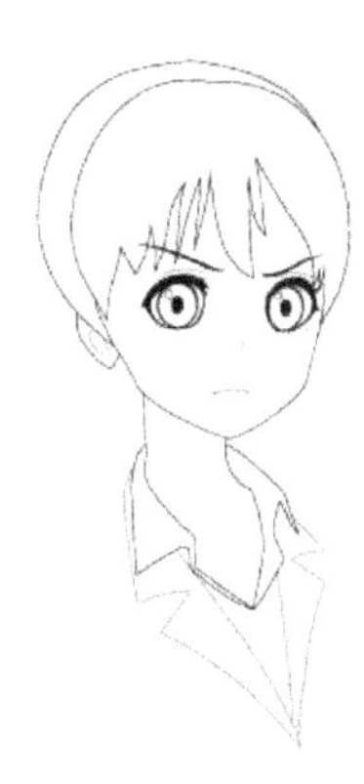
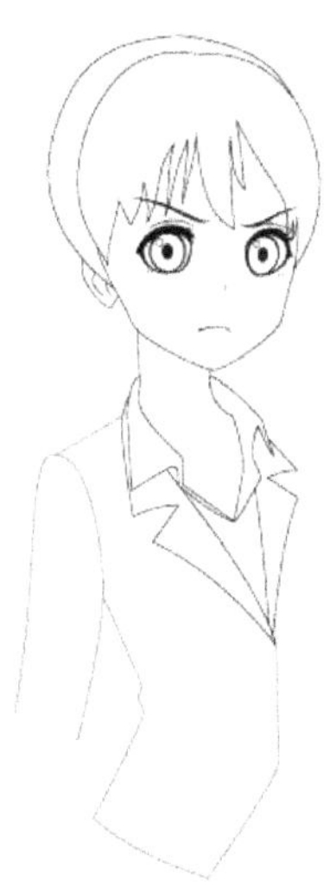
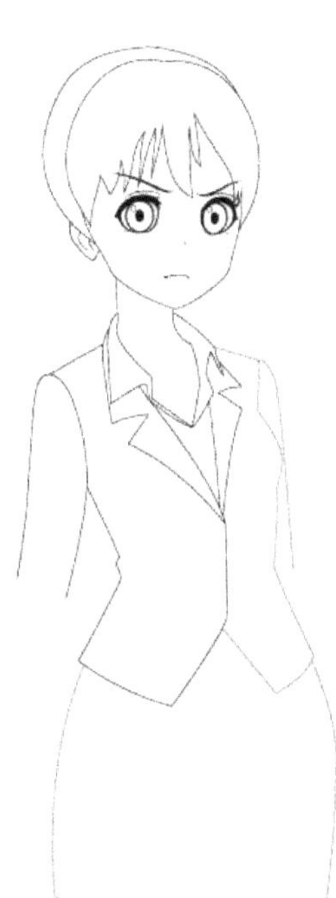
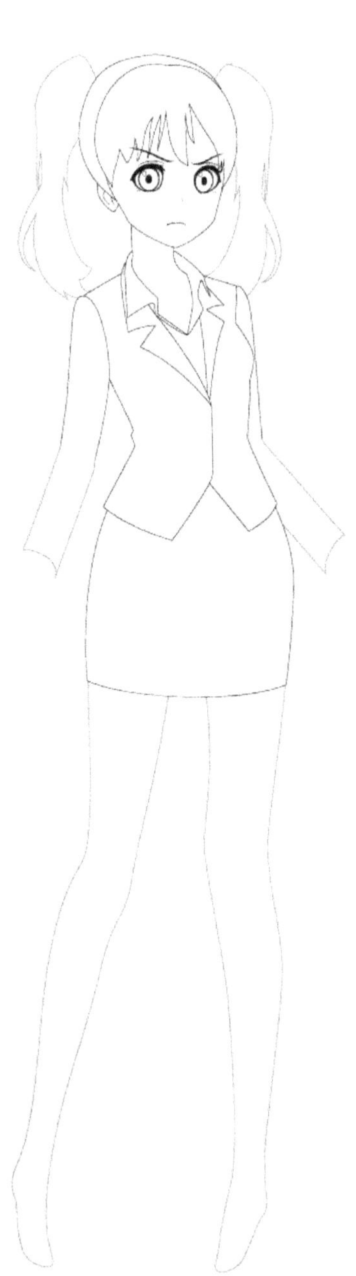

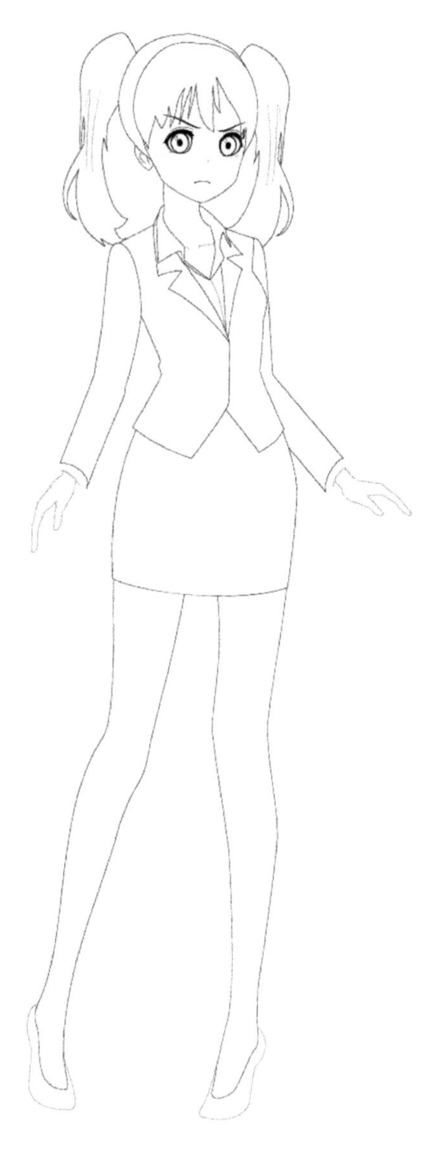

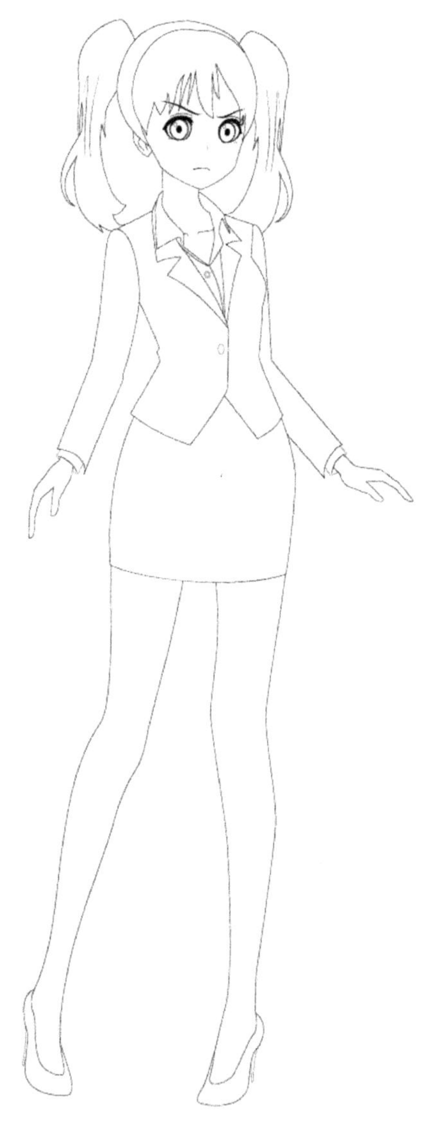

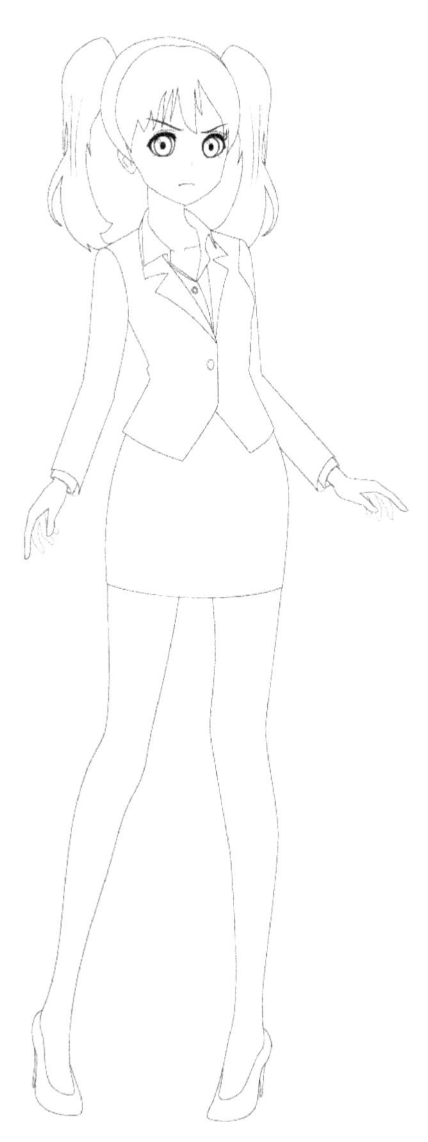
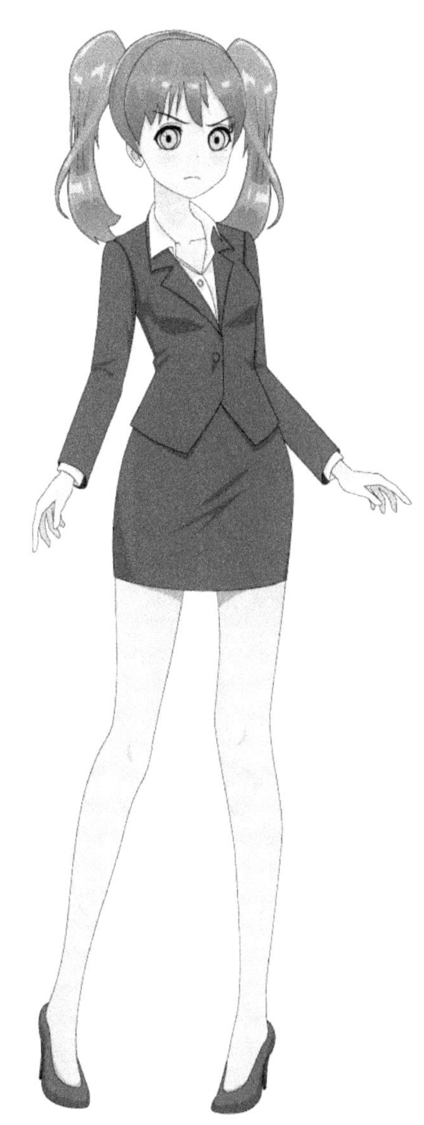

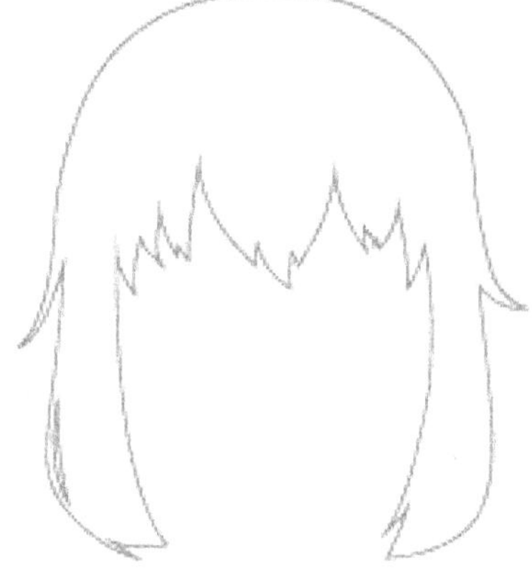

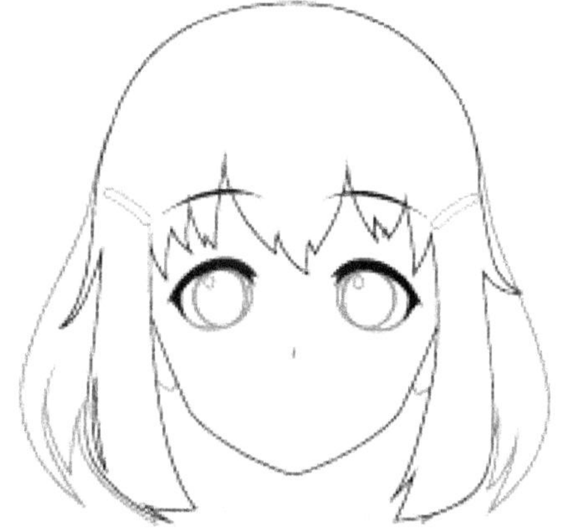
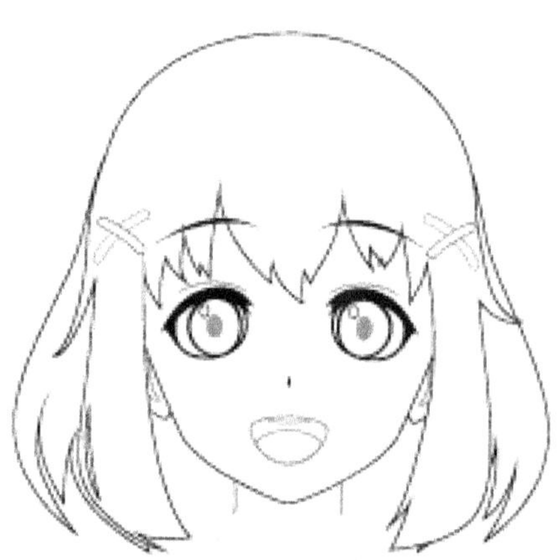

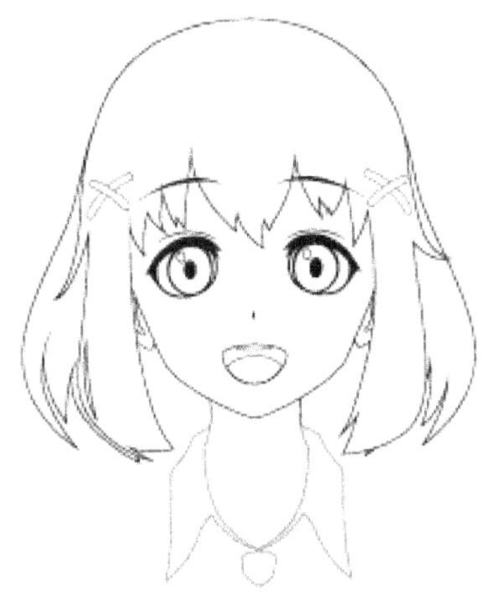
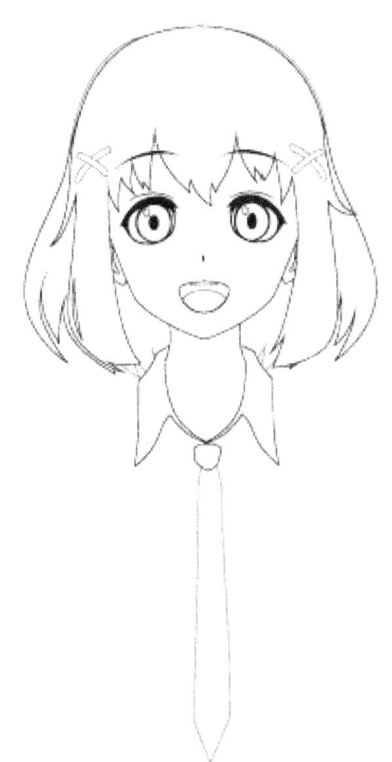
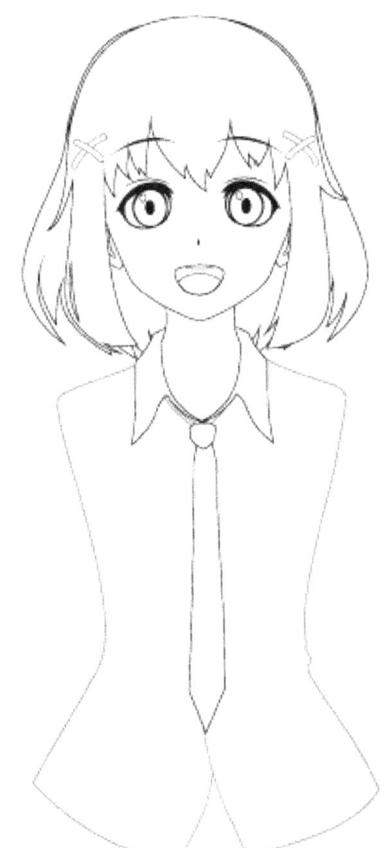
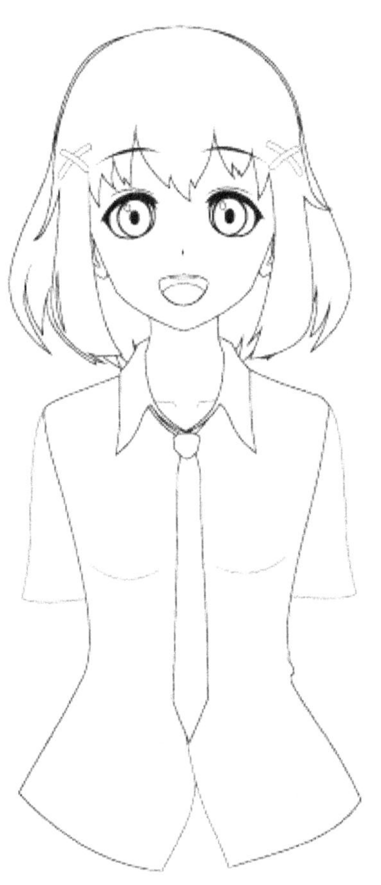

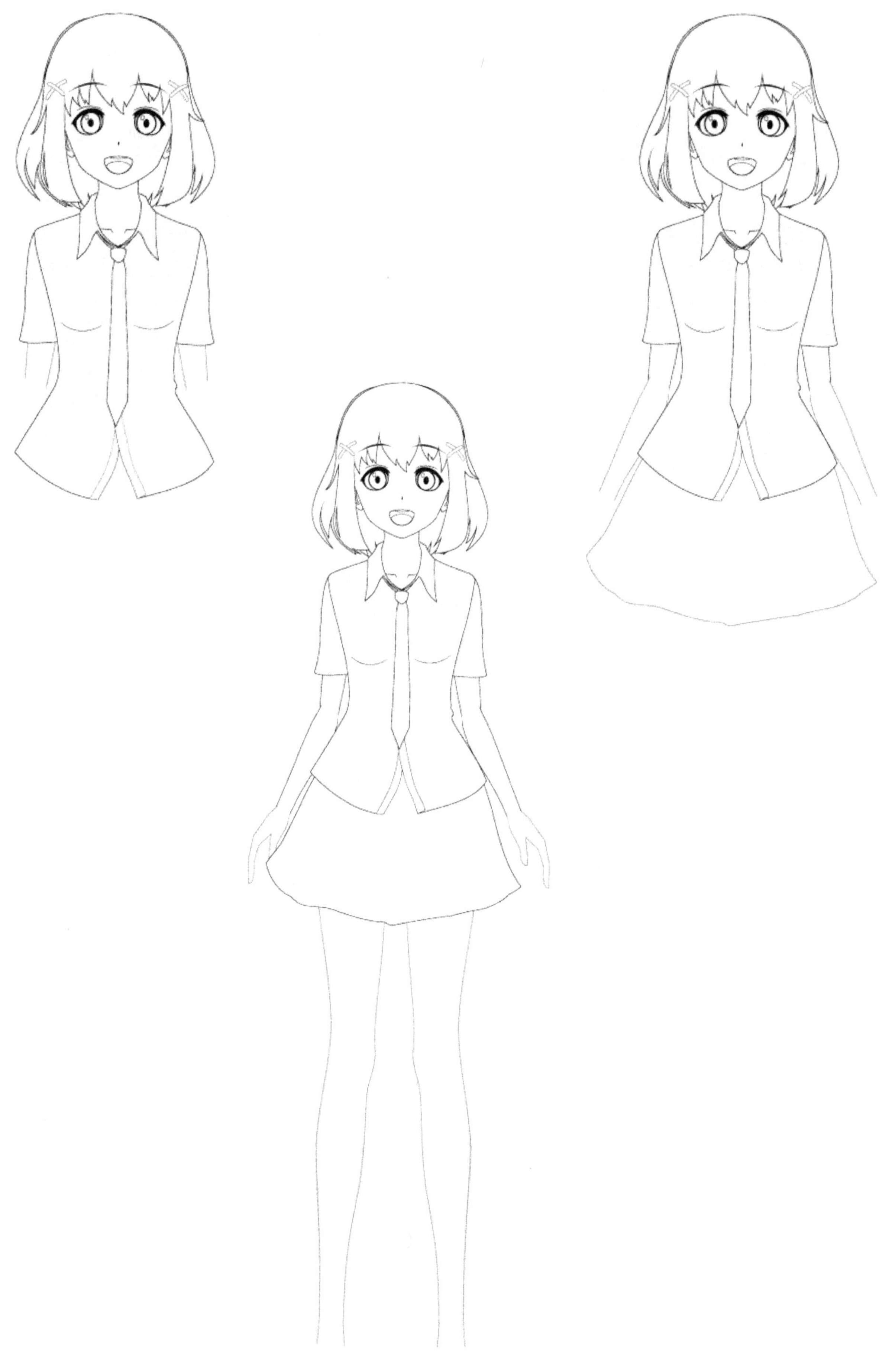

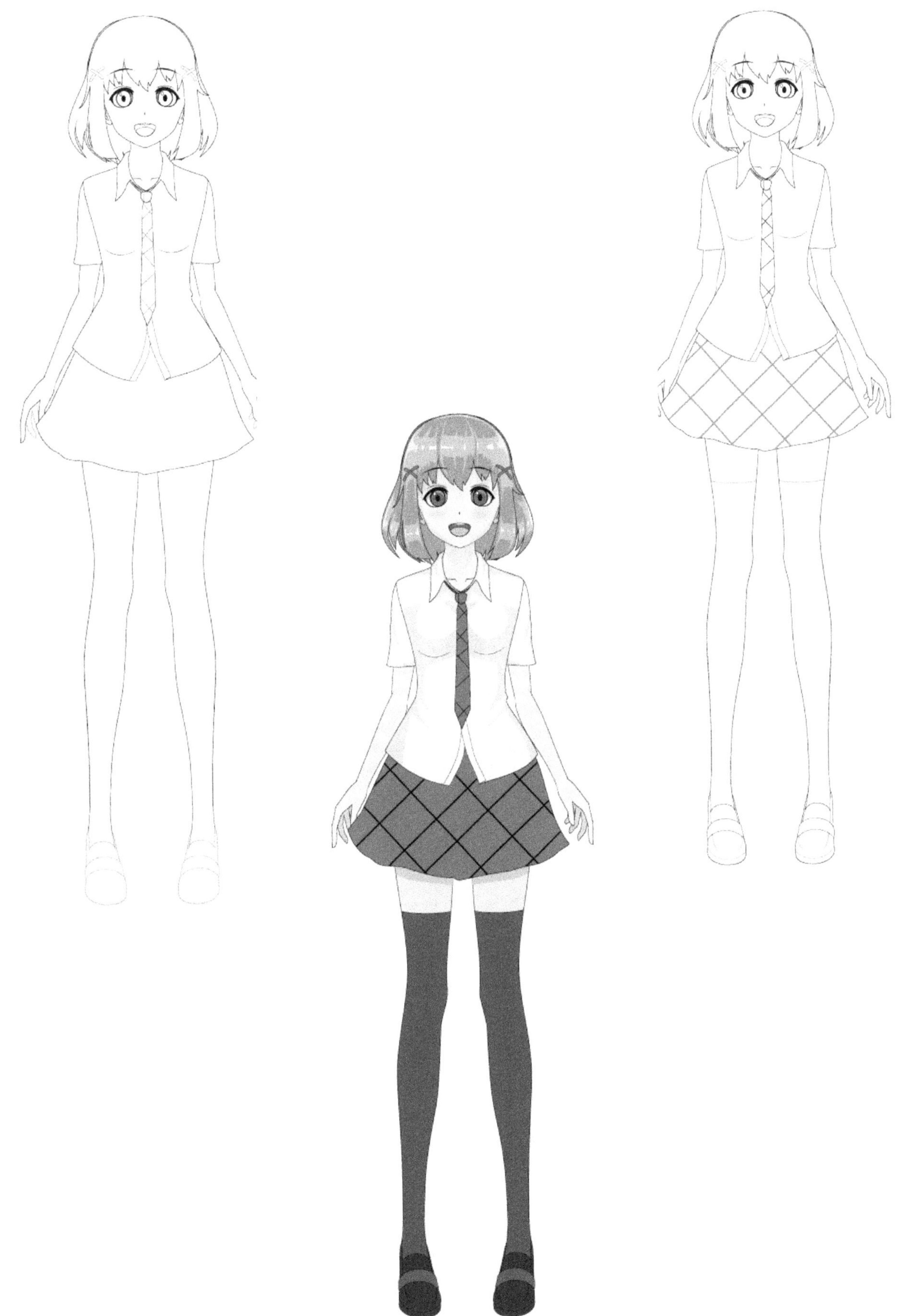

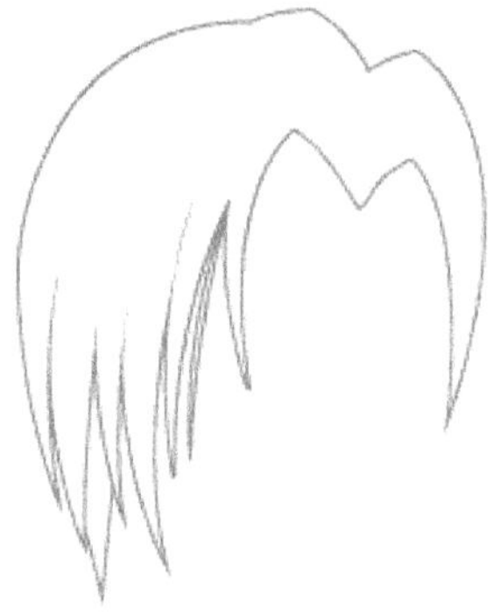

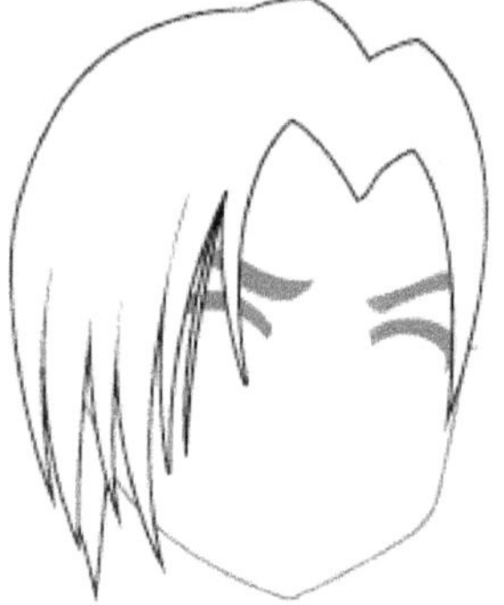

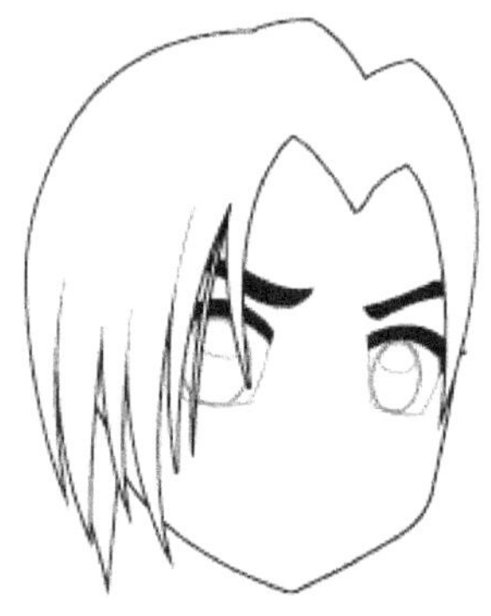

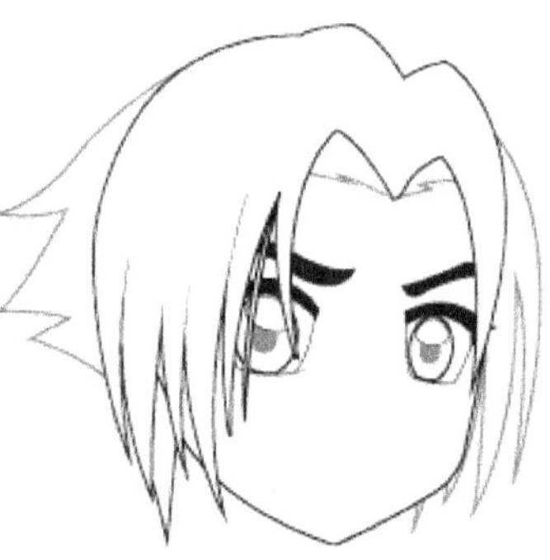

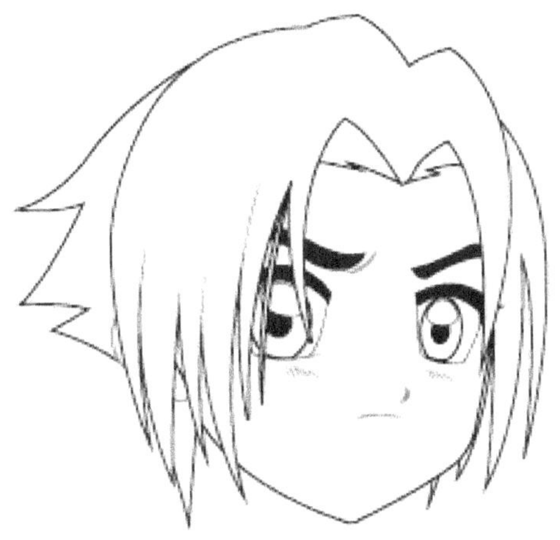

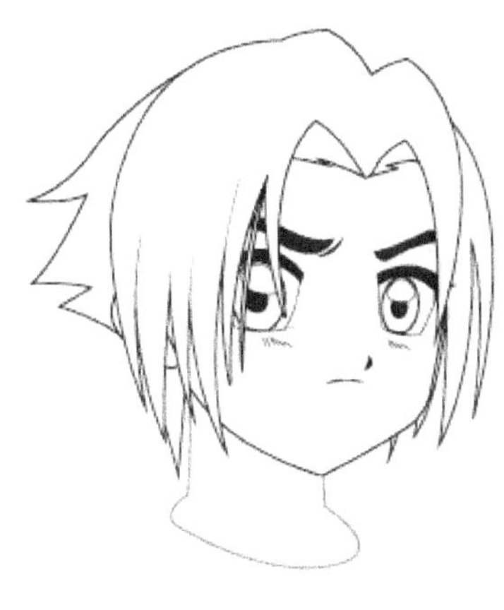

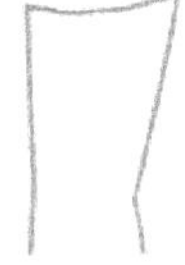

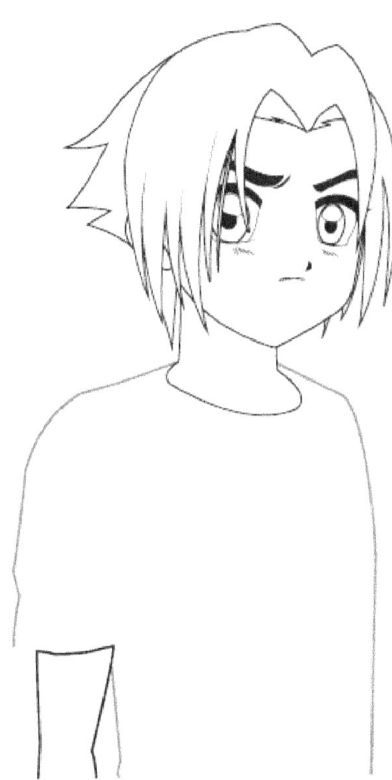

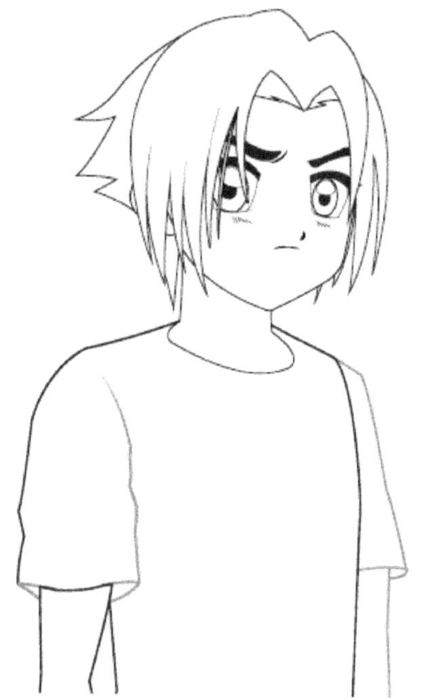
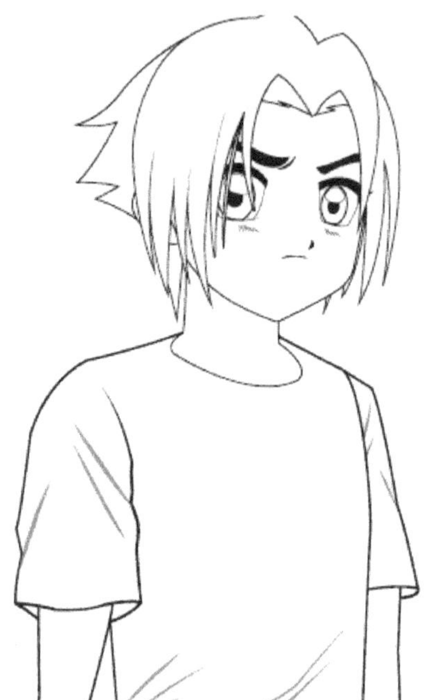
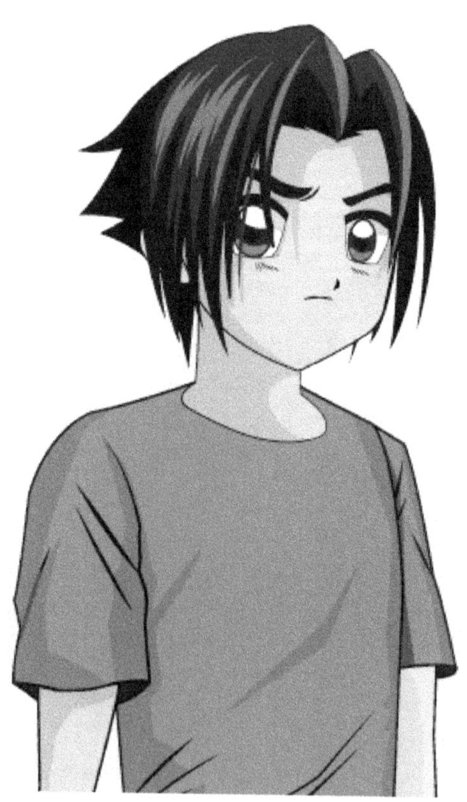

1

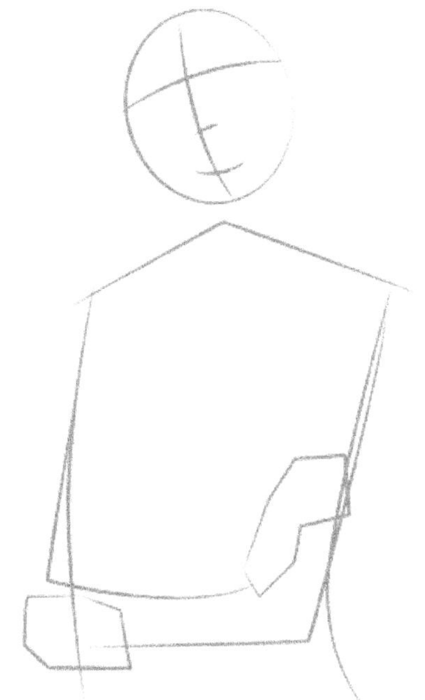

2

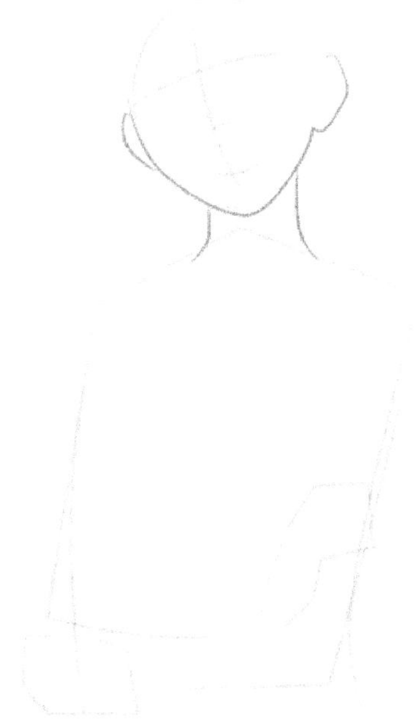

3

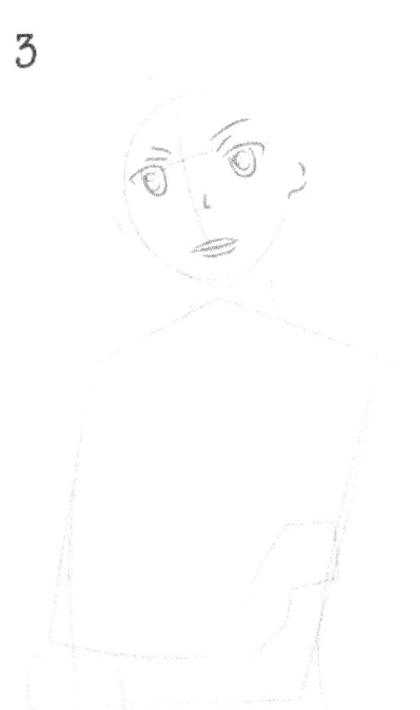

4

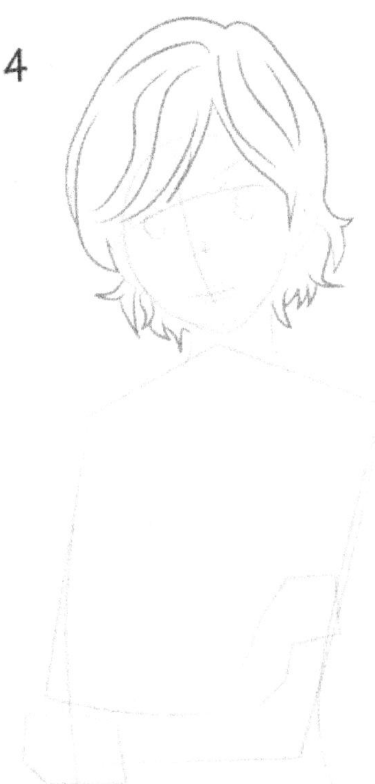

5

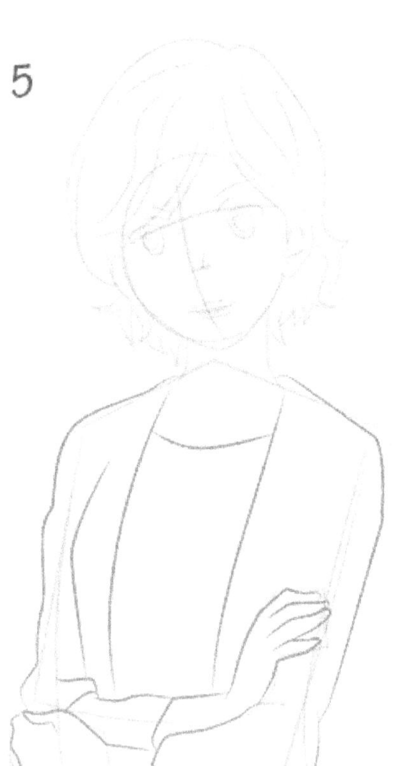

6

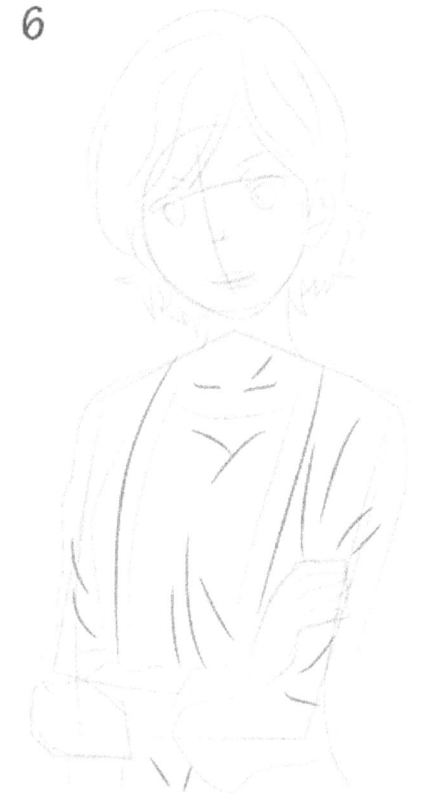

7

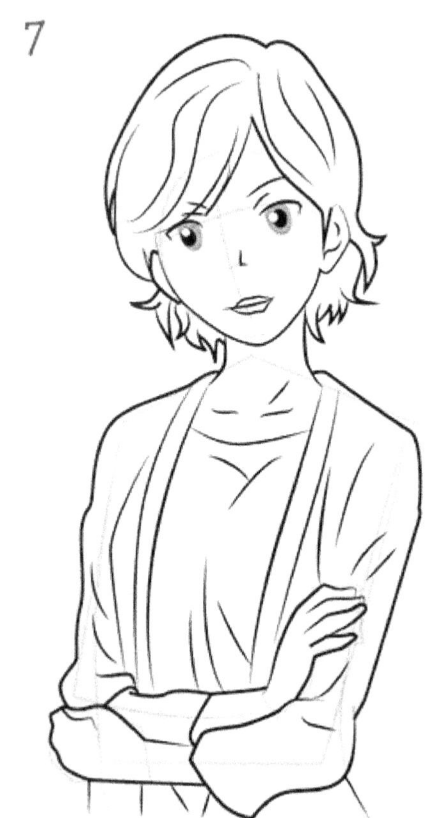

8

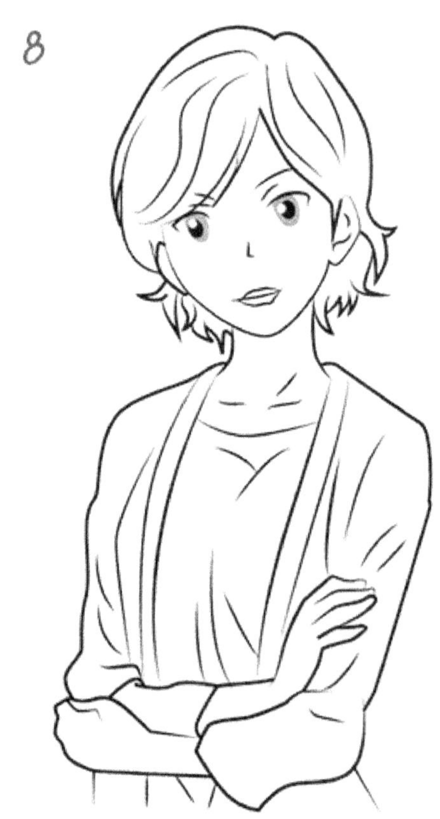

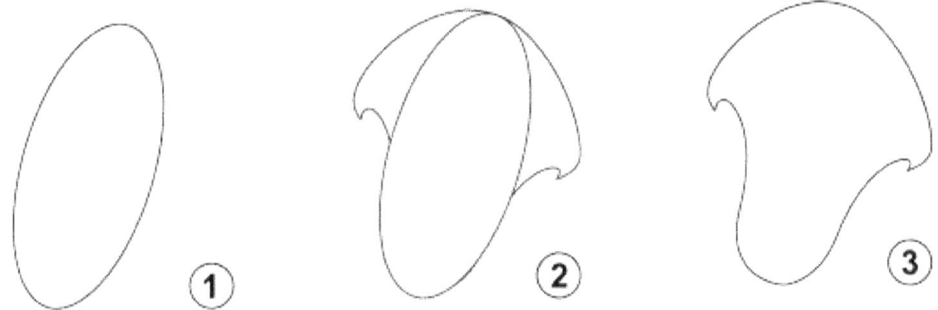

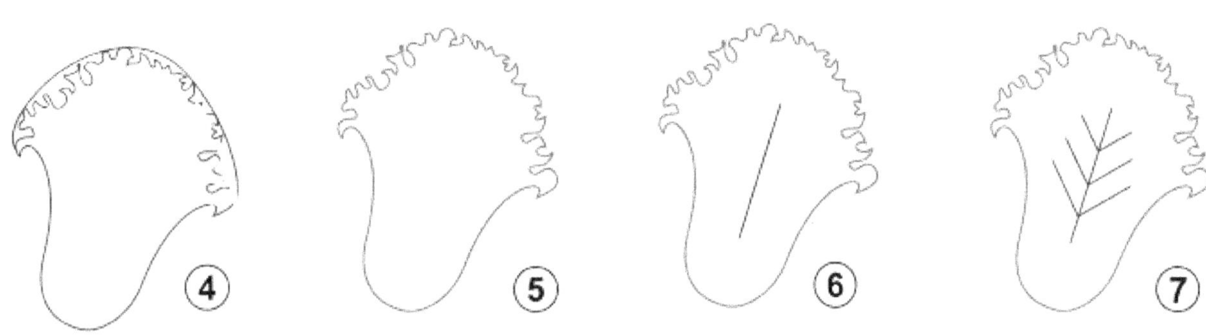

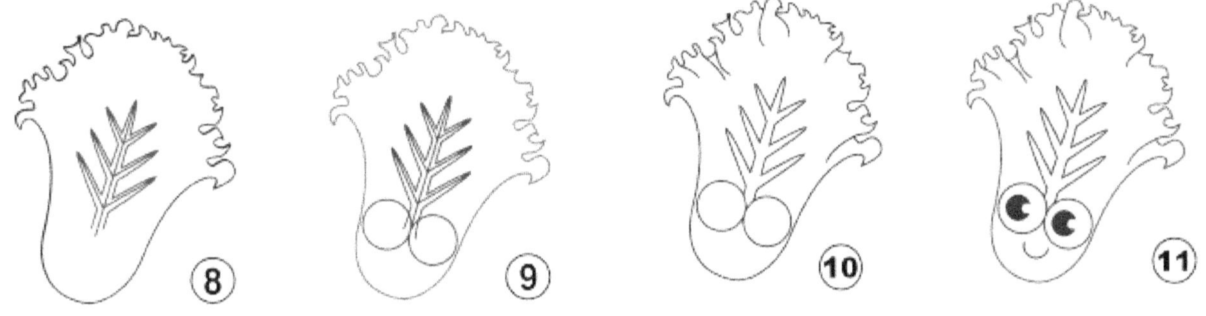

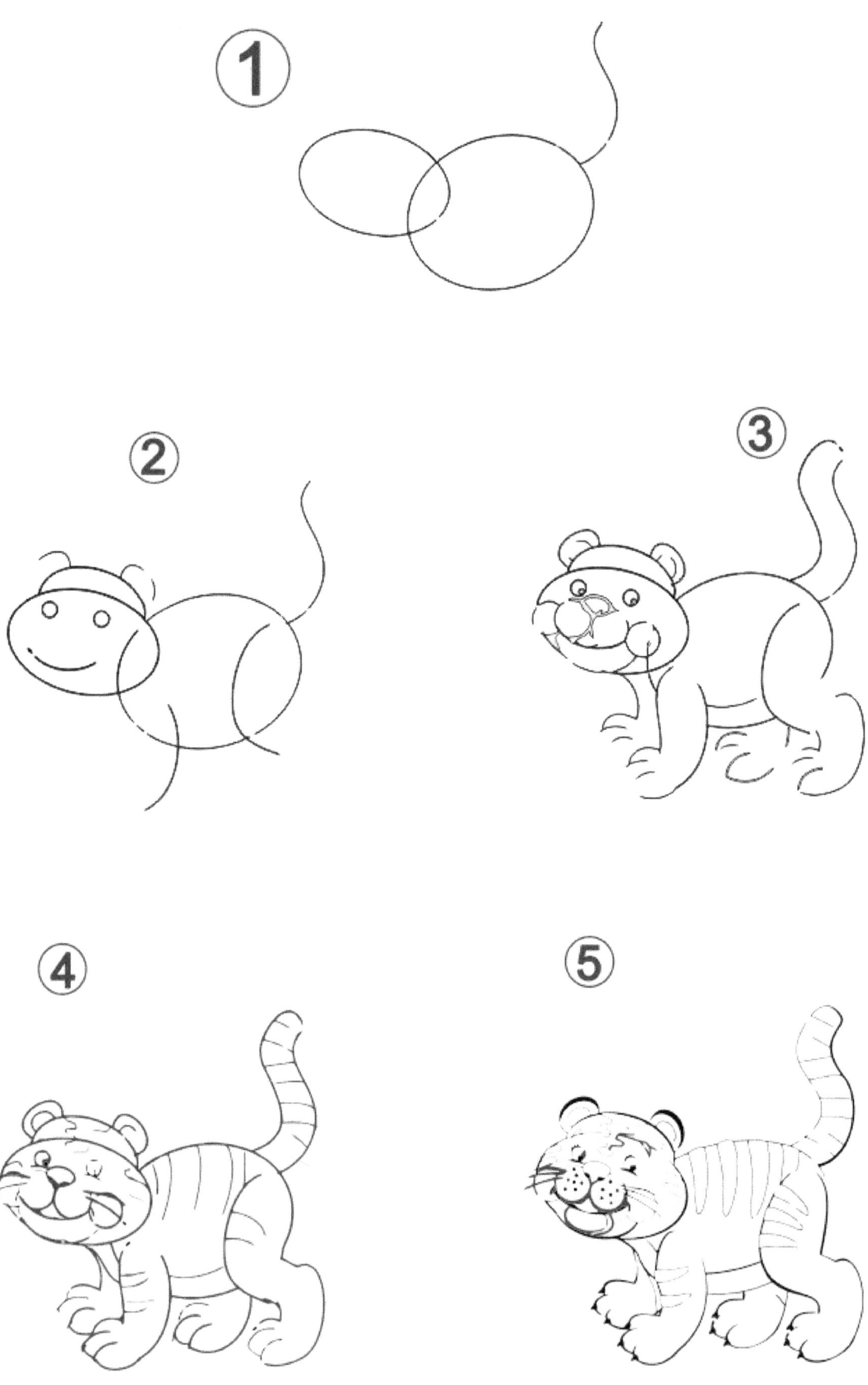

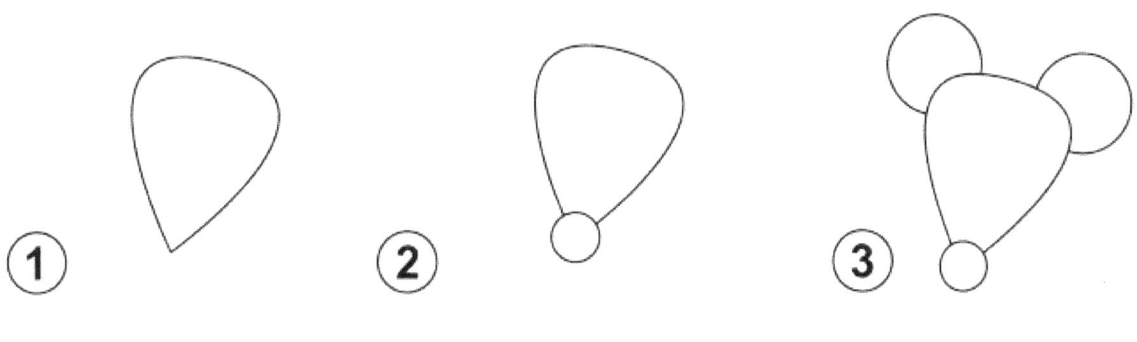

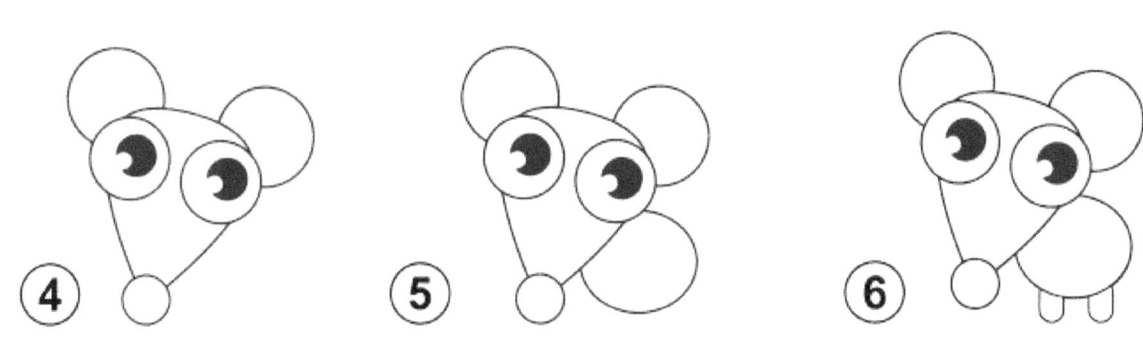

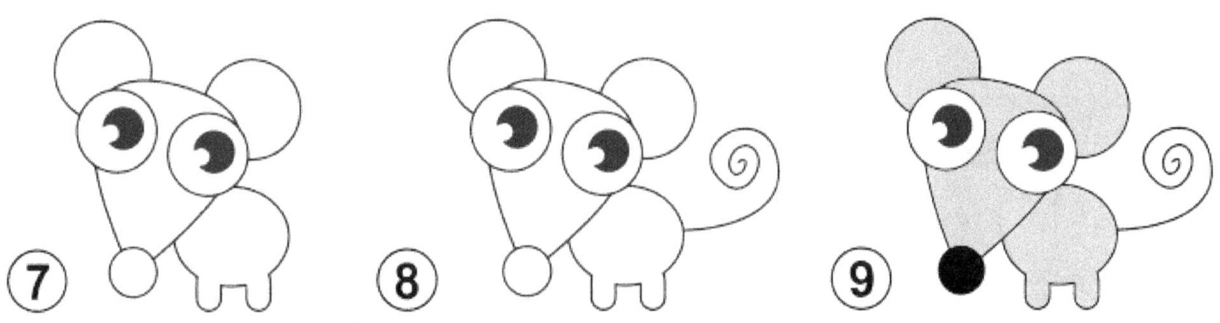

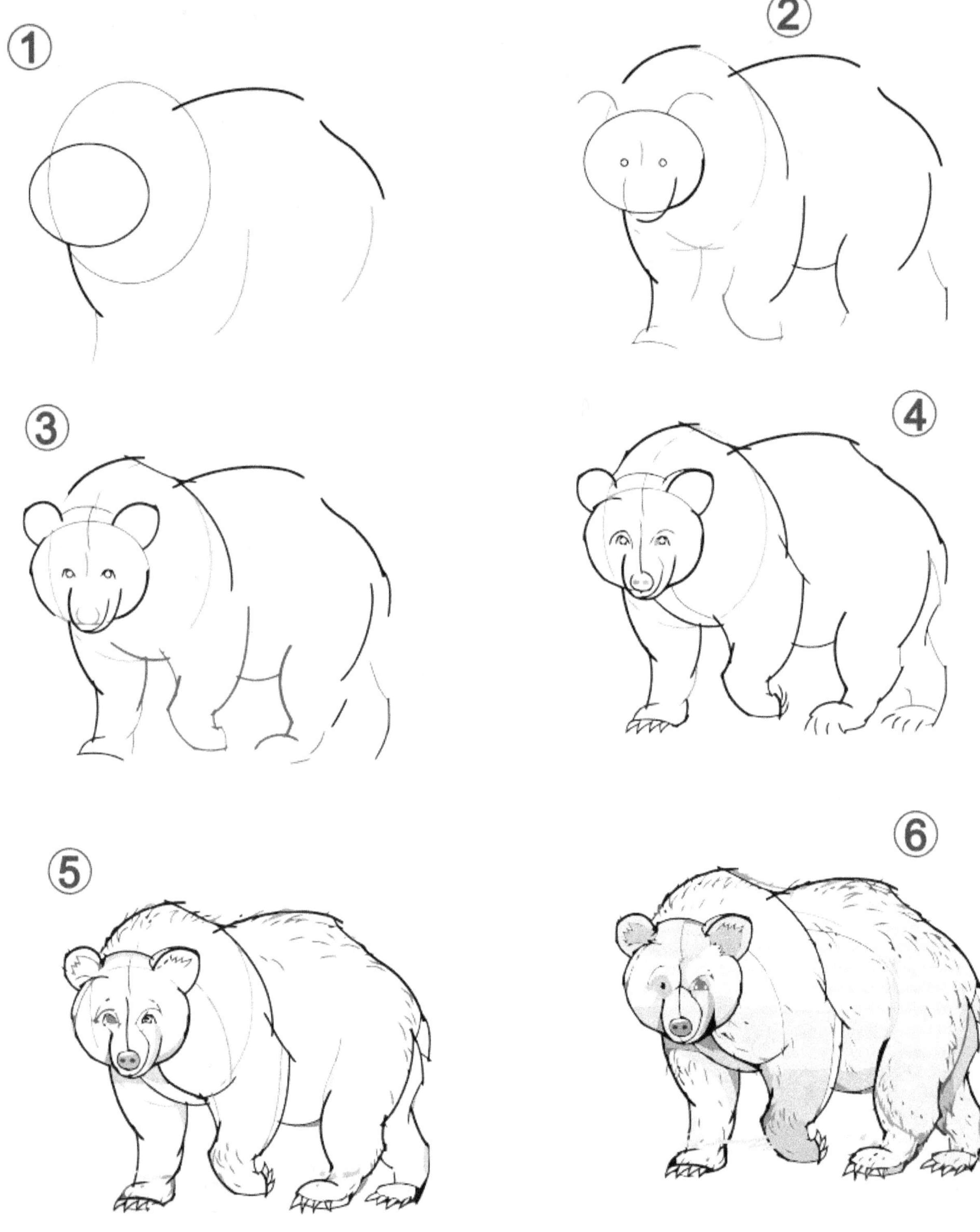

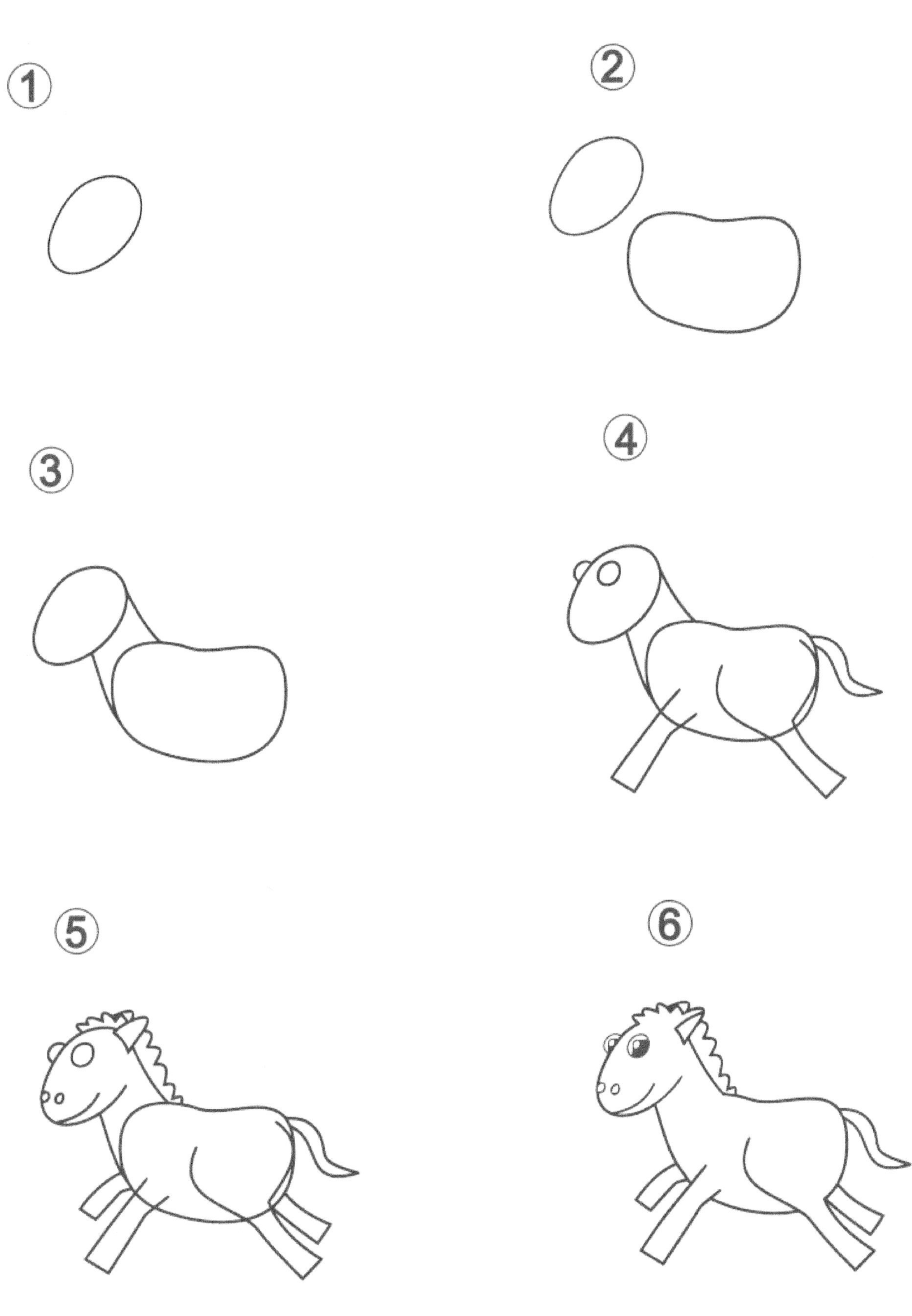

1
2
3
4
5
6

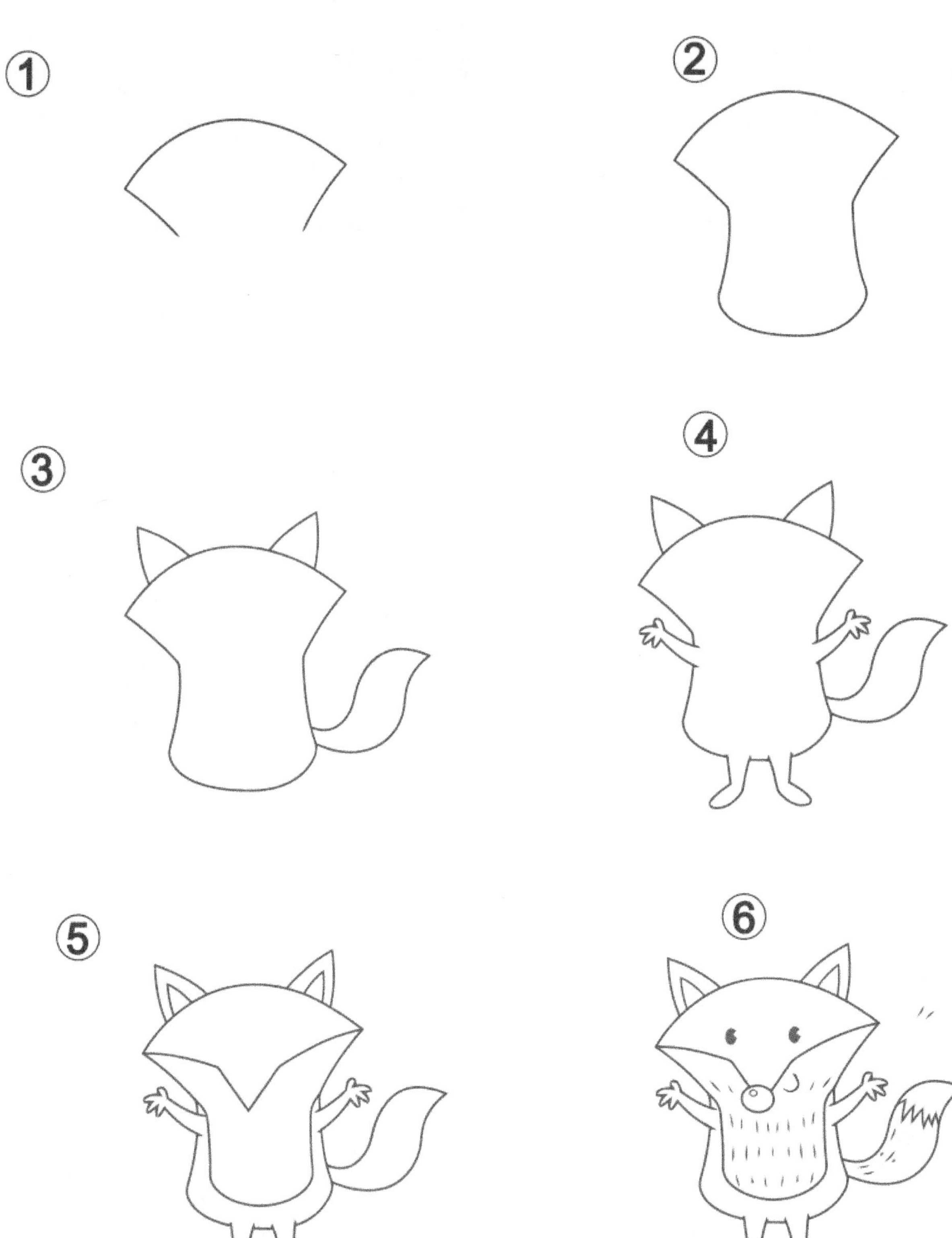

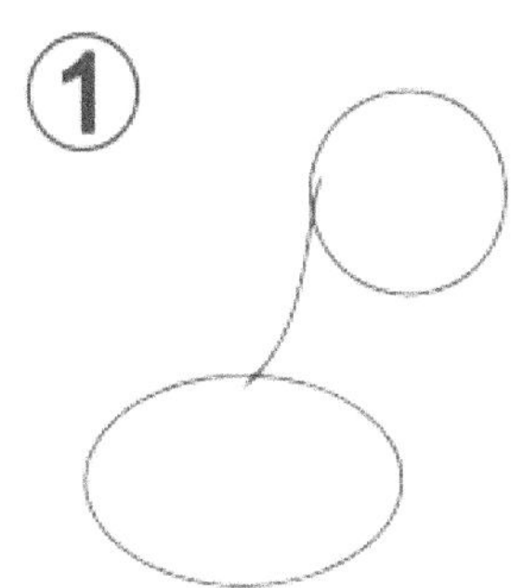

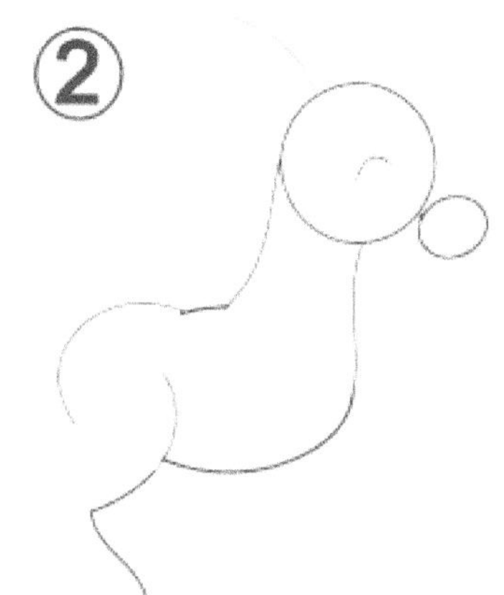

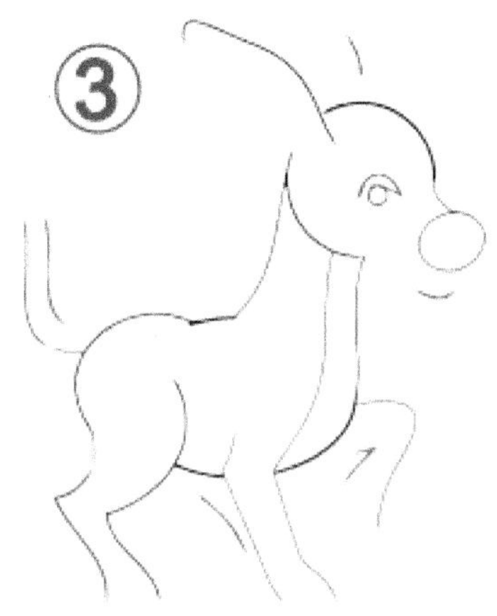

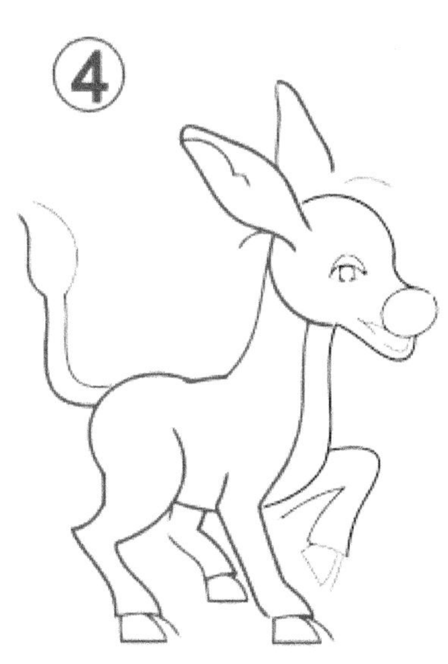

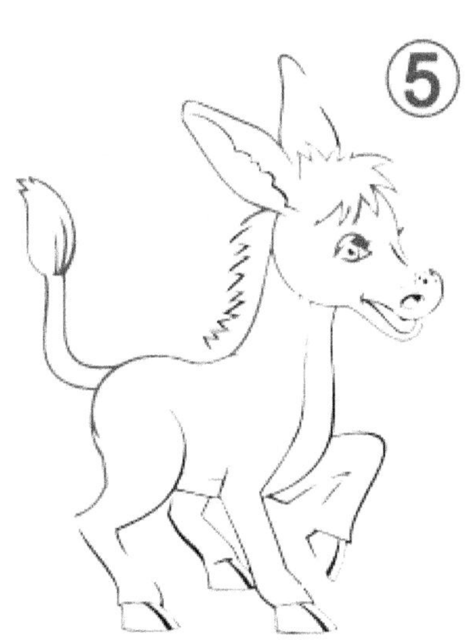

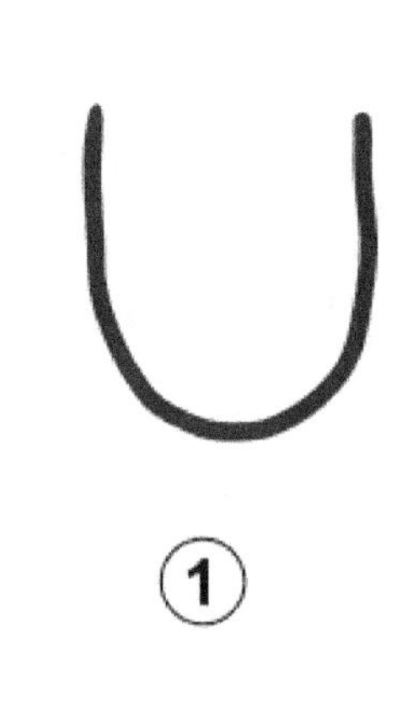

1

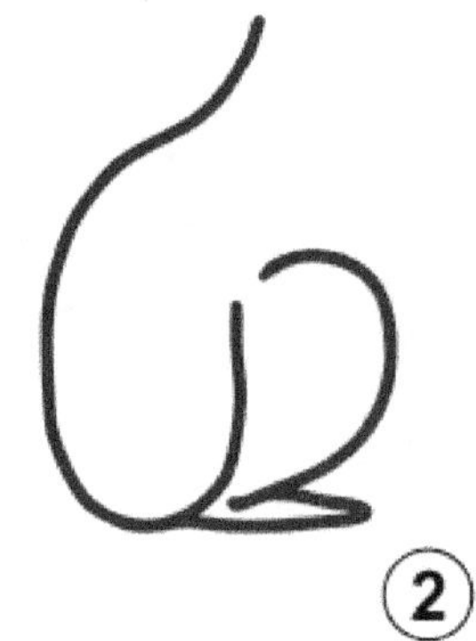

2

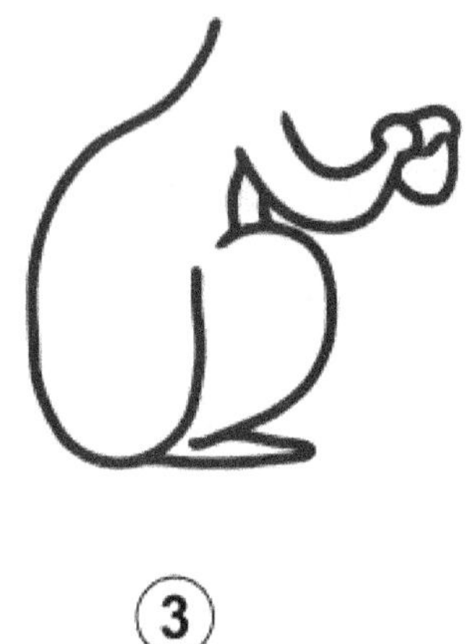

3

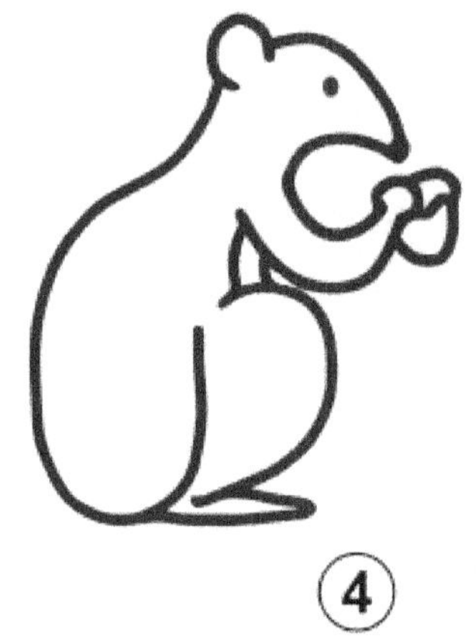

4

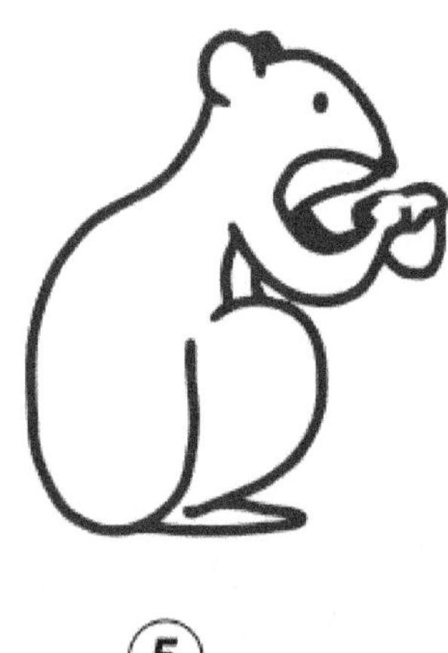

5

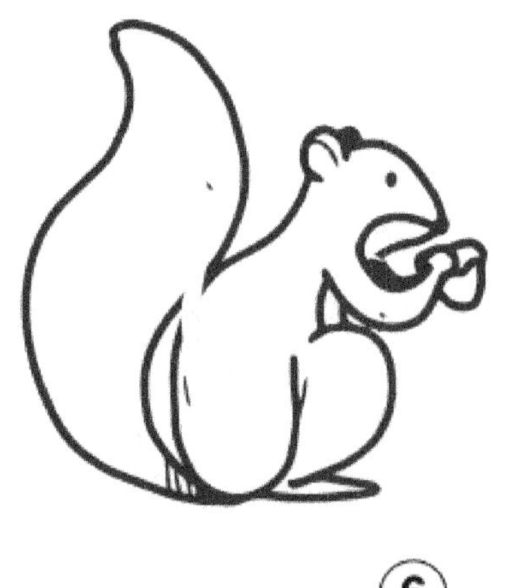

6

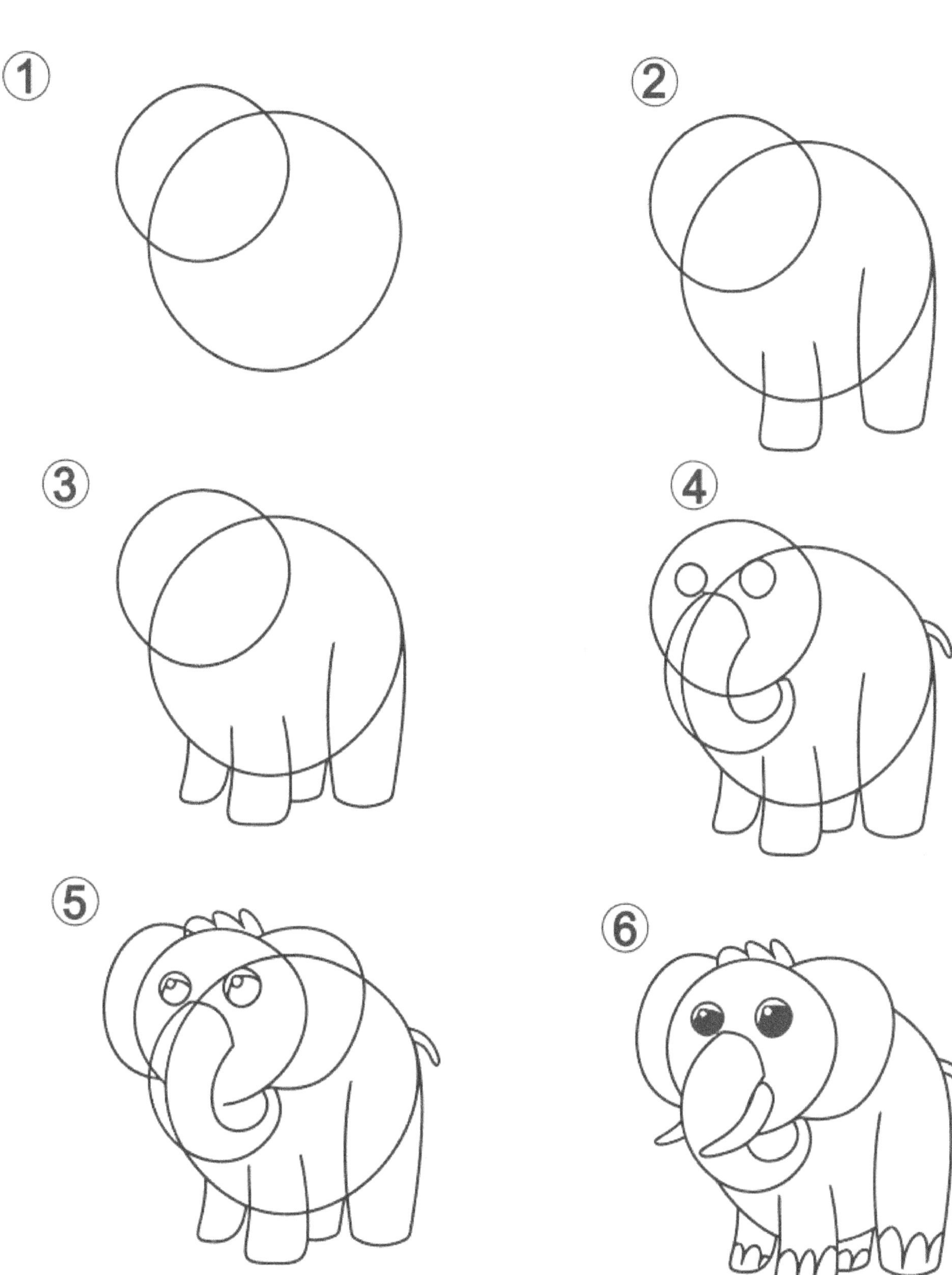

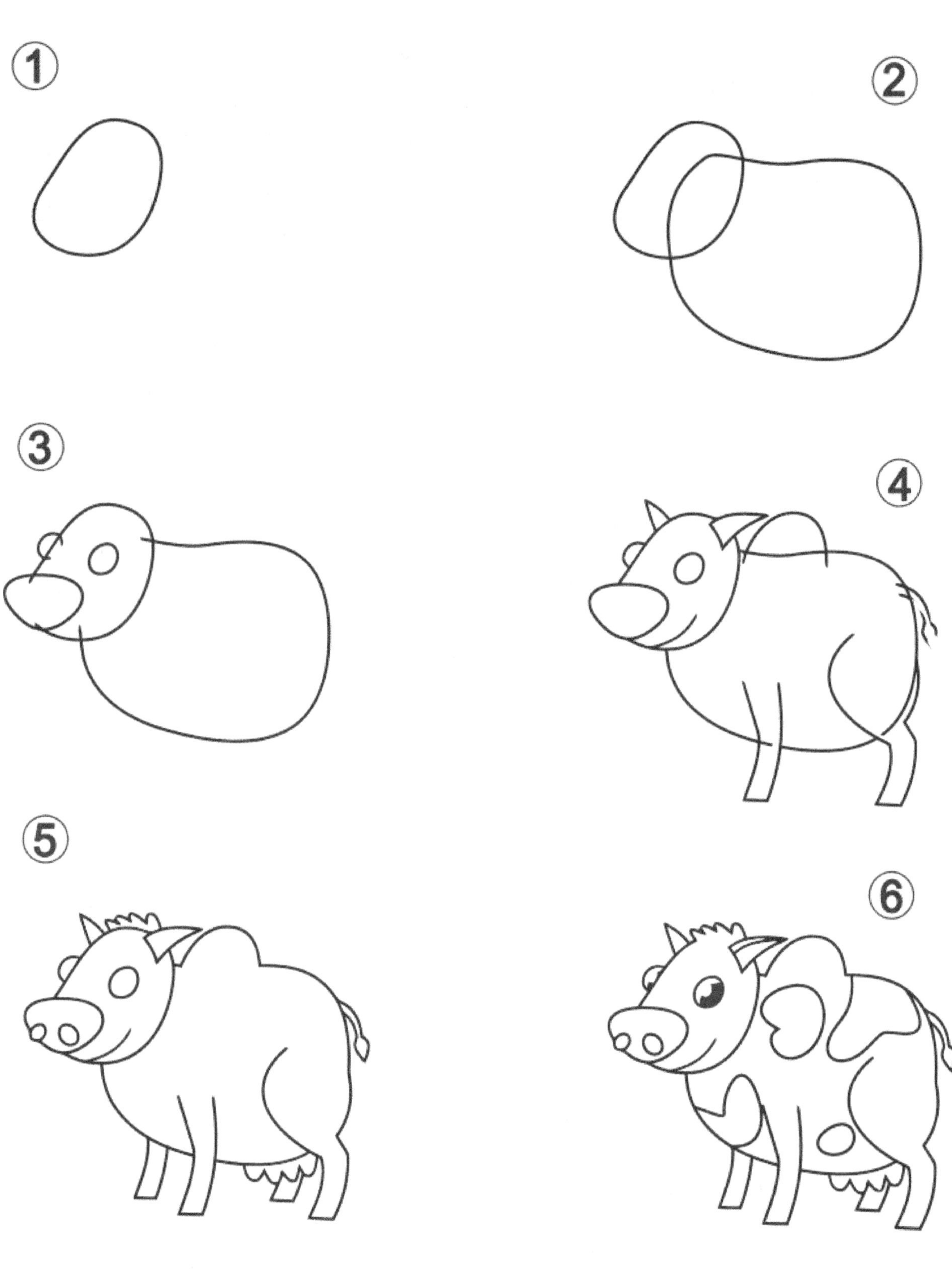

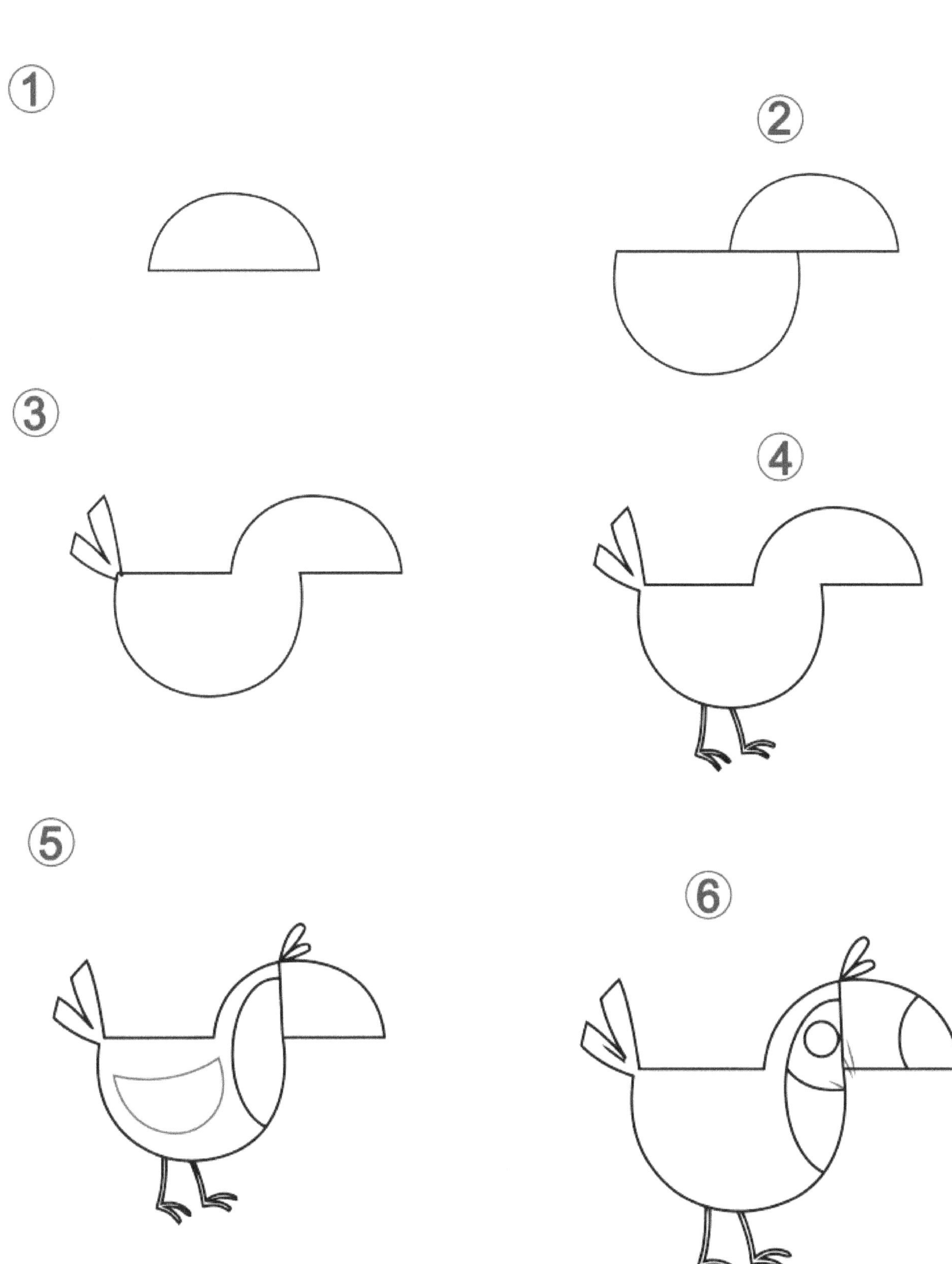

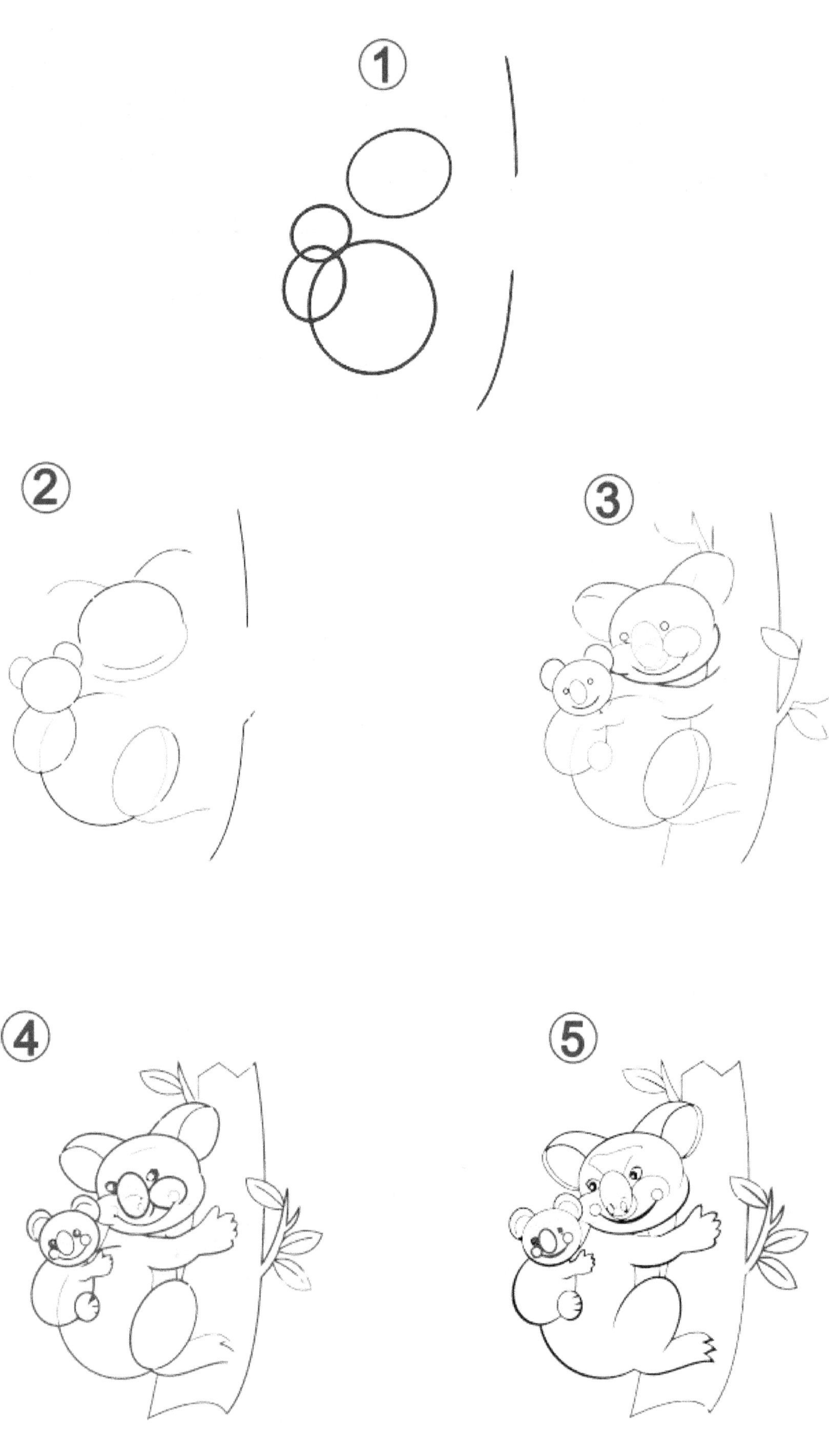

BONUS
20 cute stuff
included

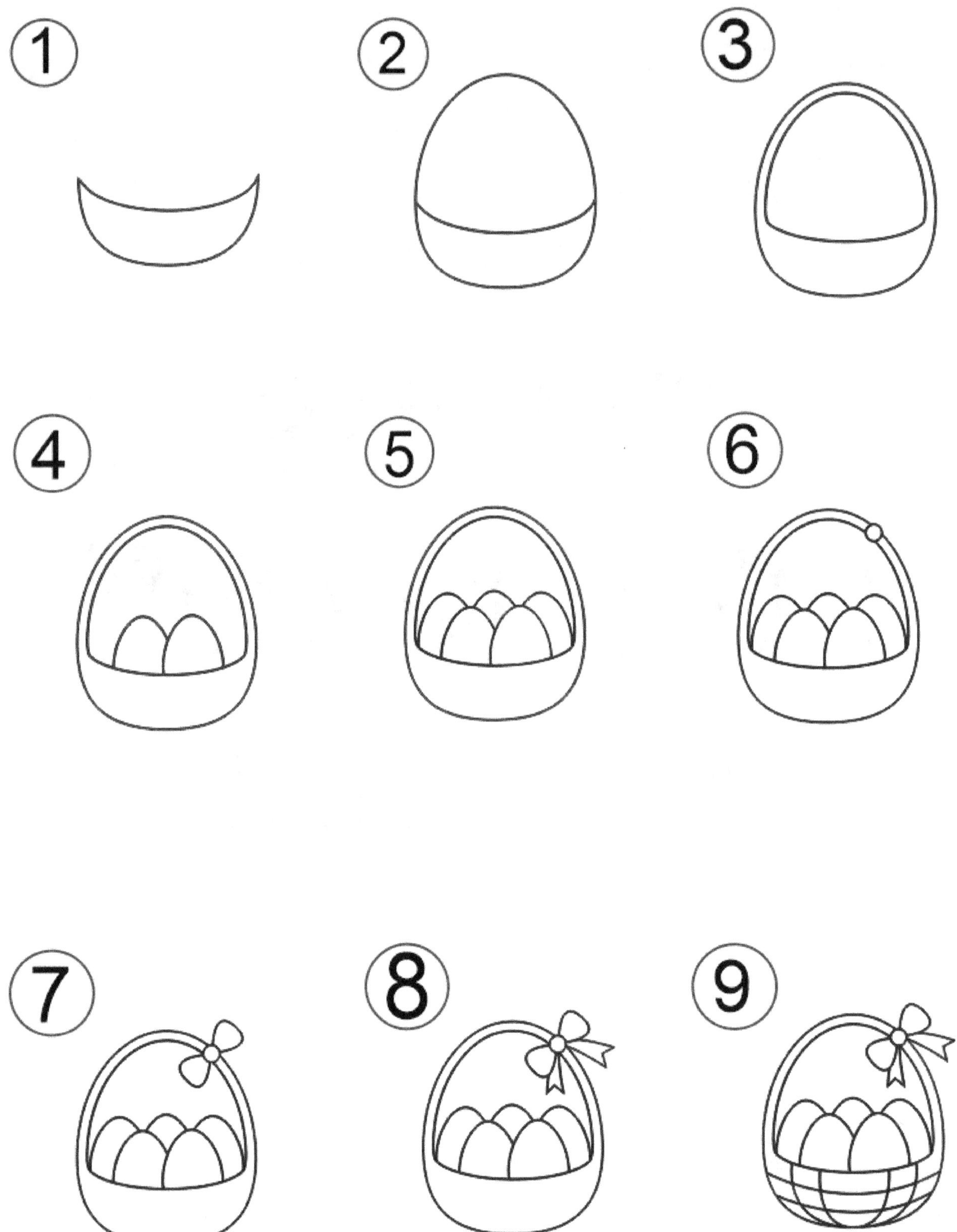

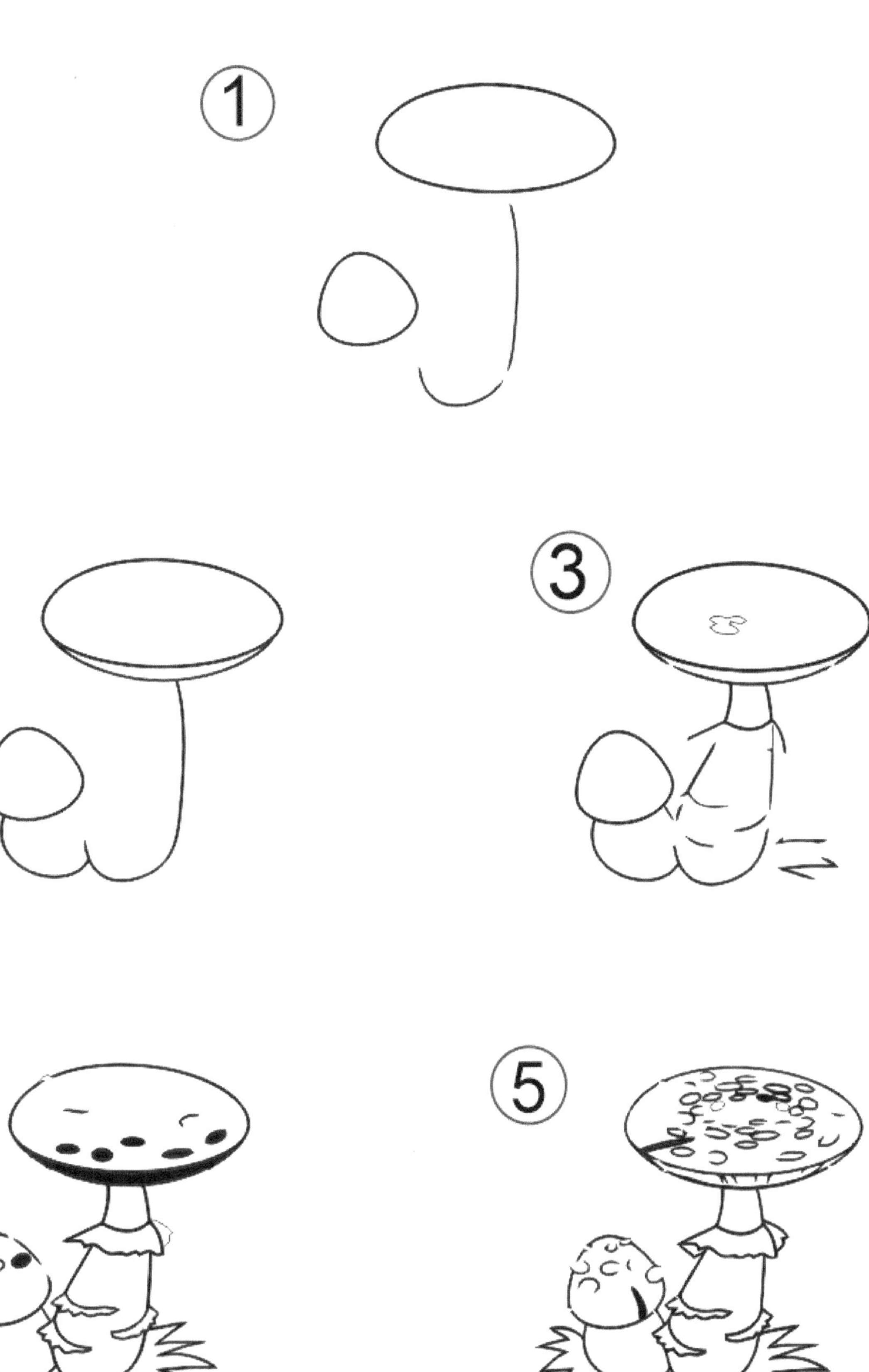

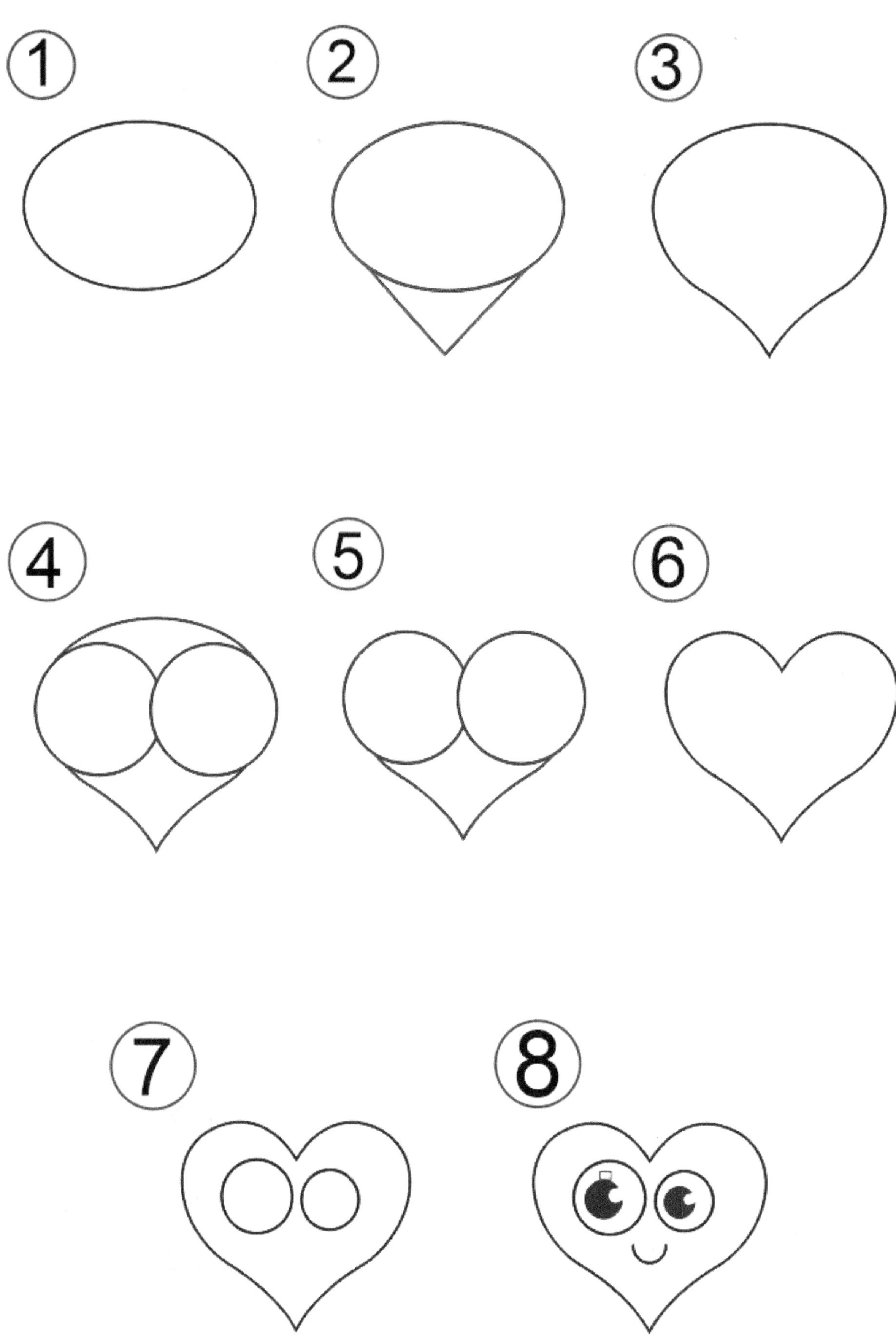

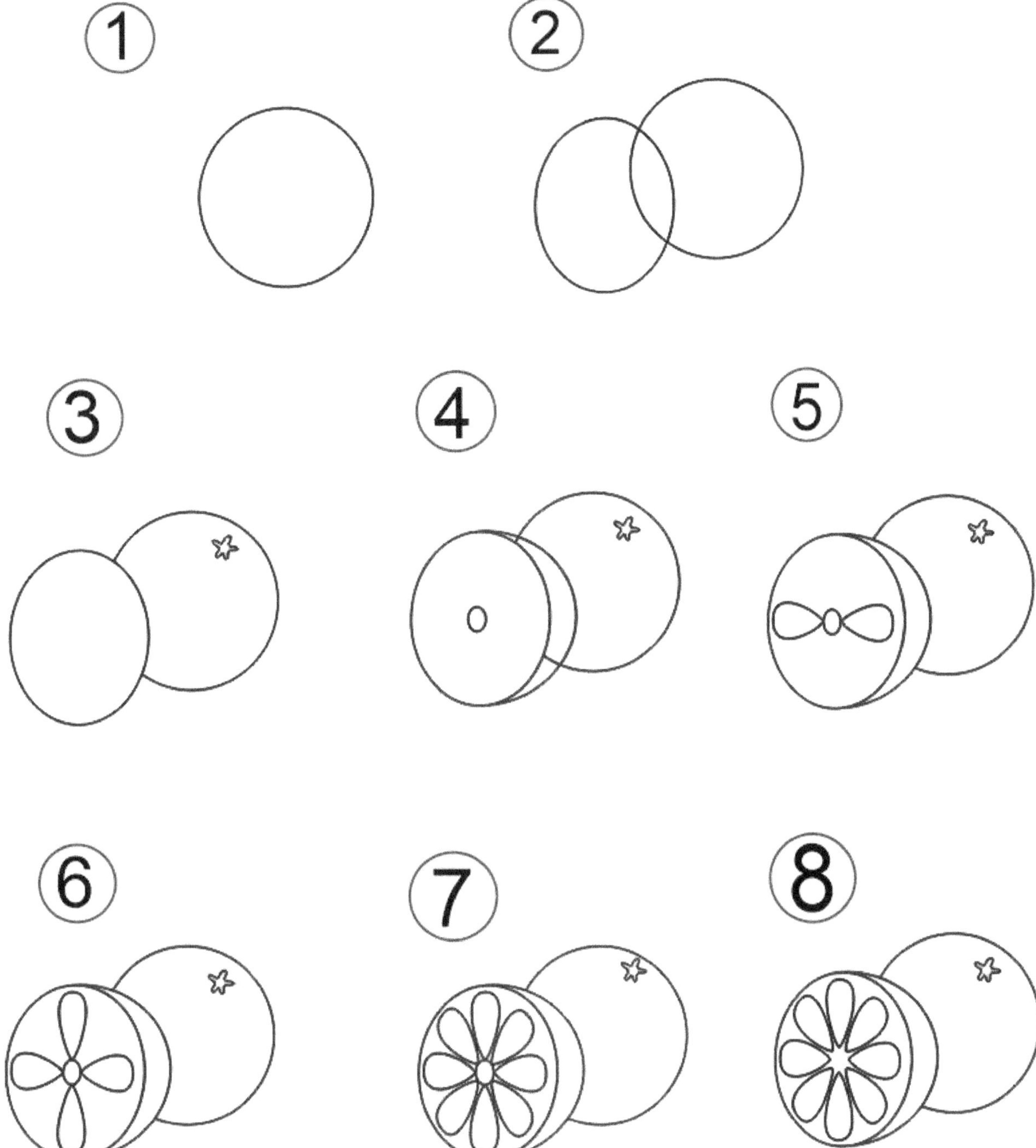

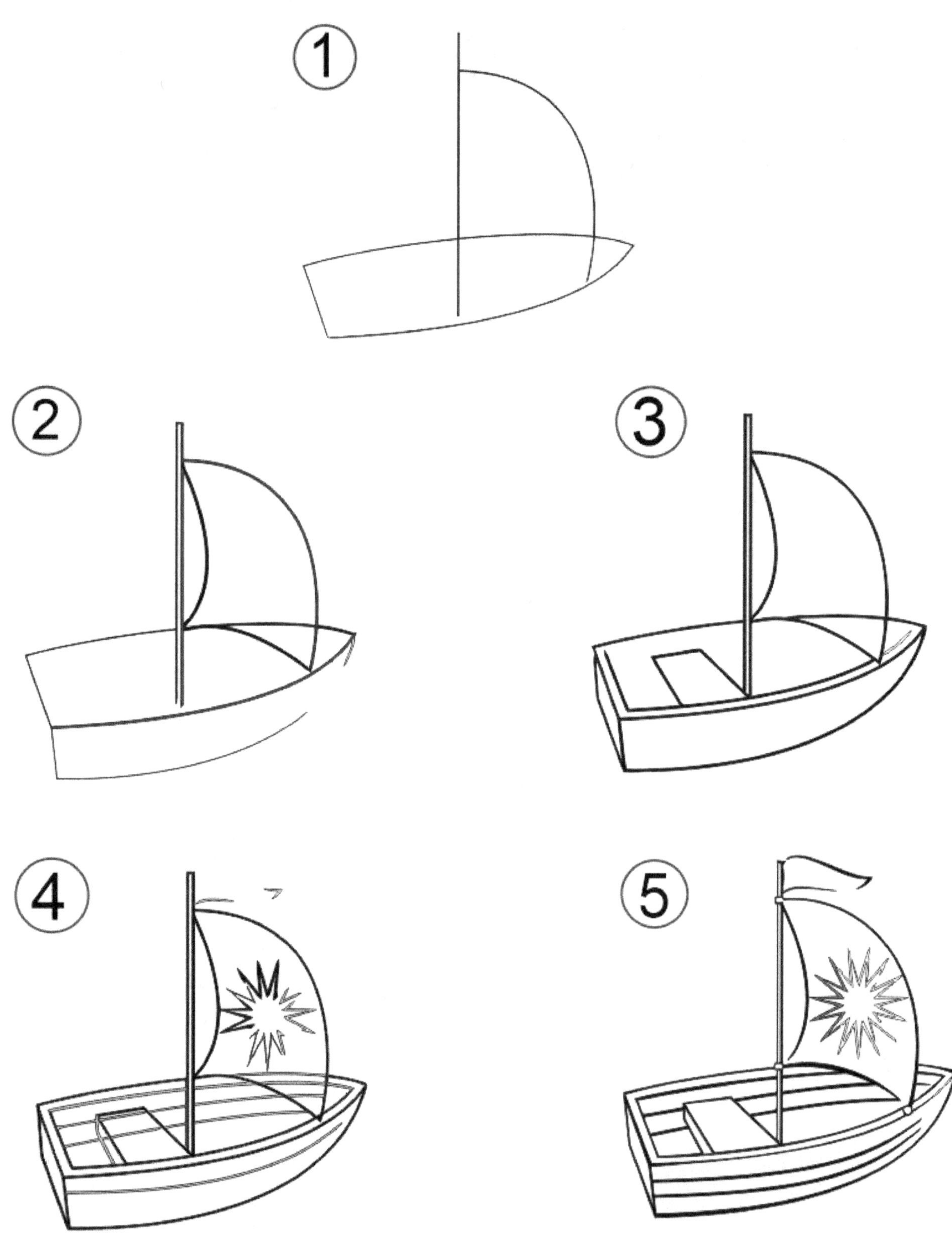

1
2
3
4
5

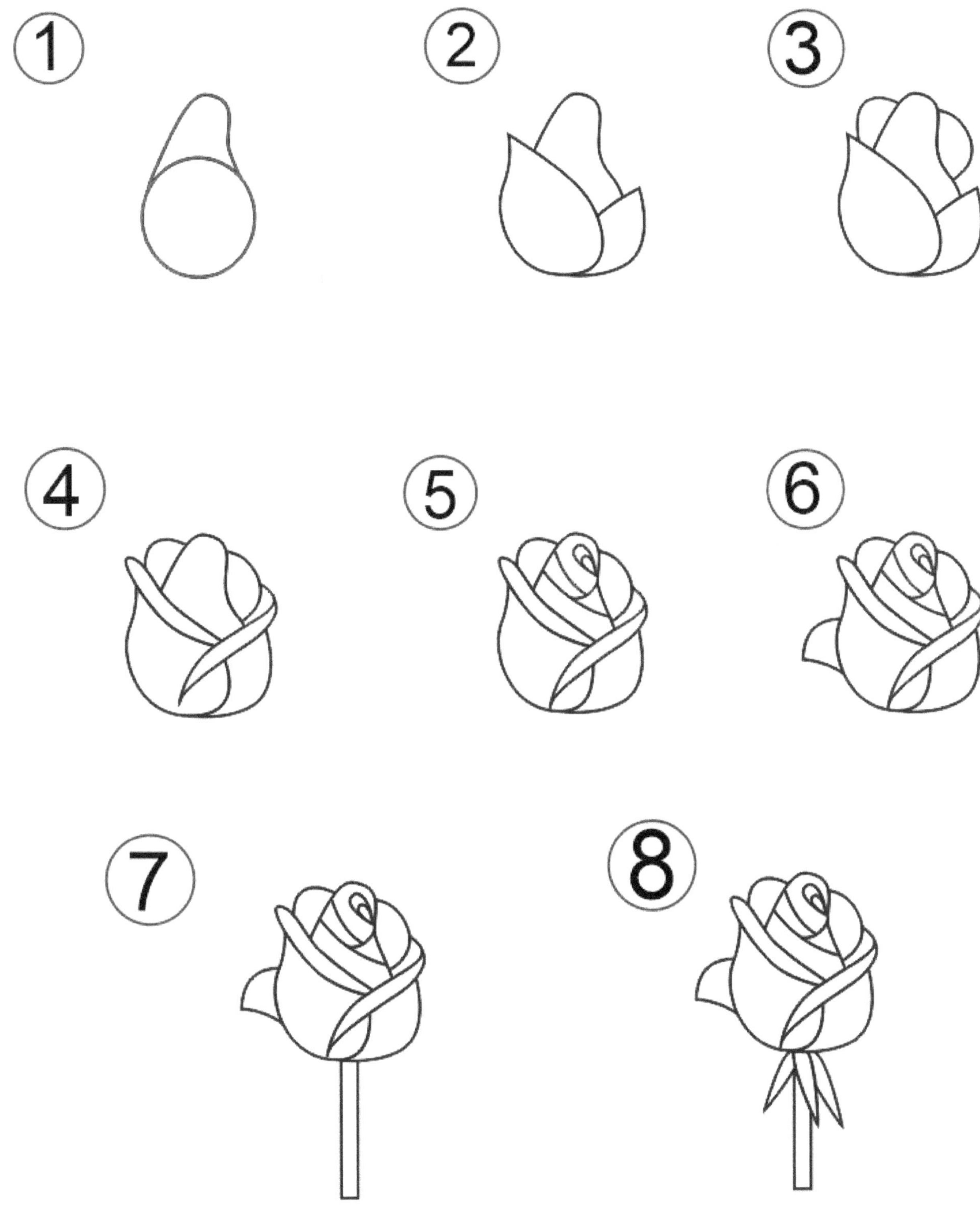

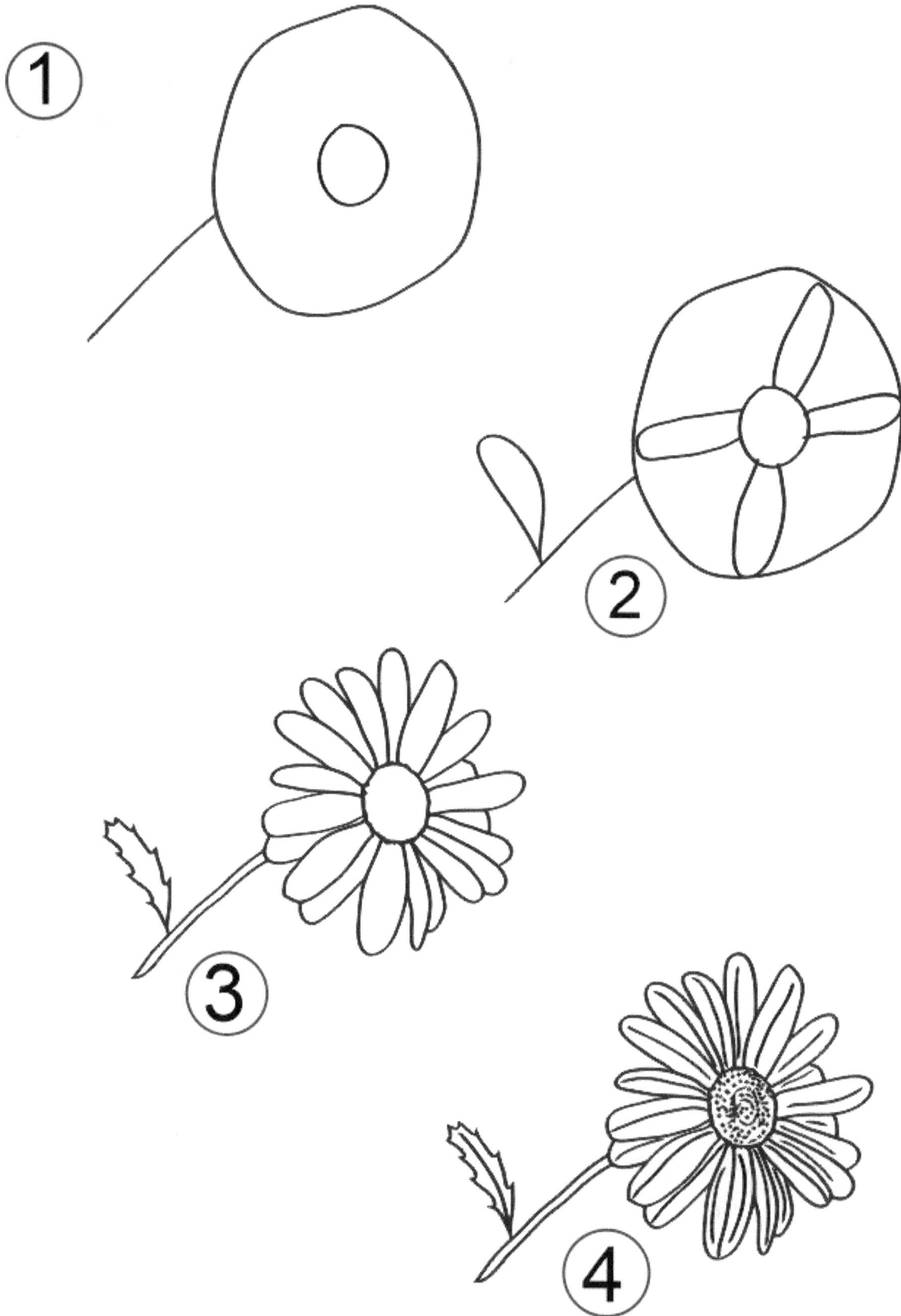

① ②

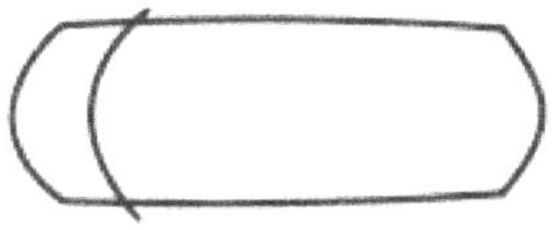

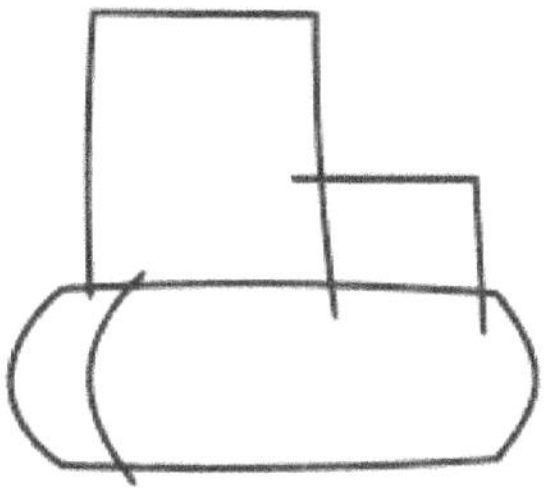

③ 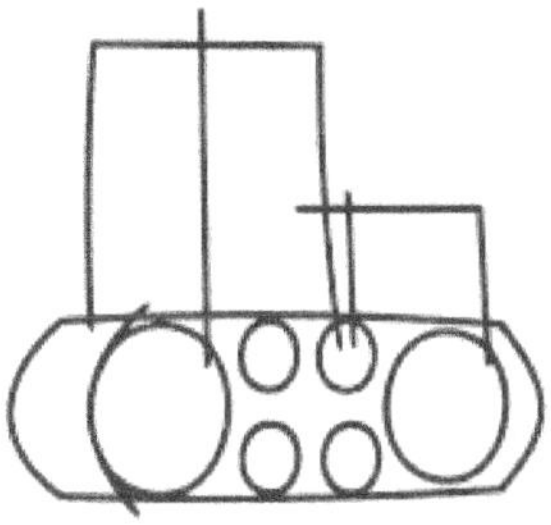 ④

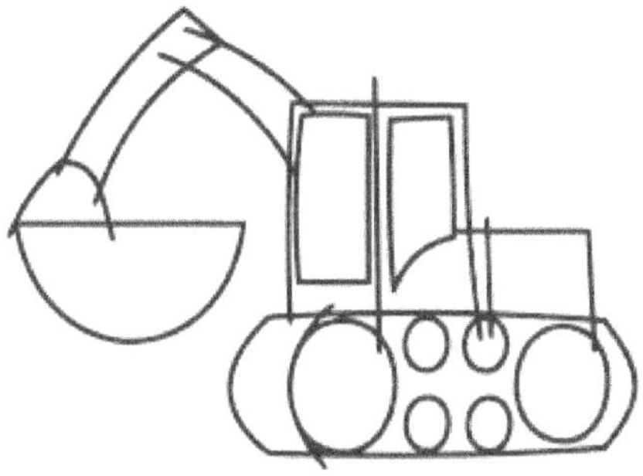

⑤ ⑥

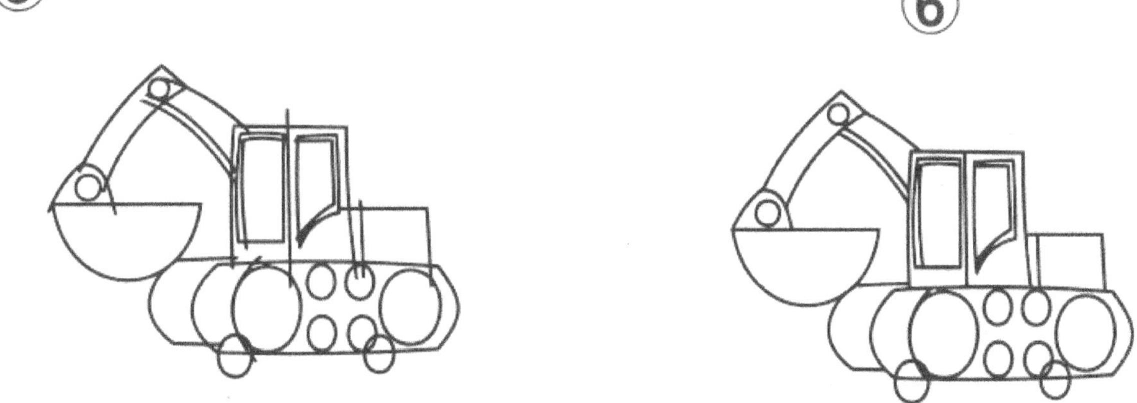

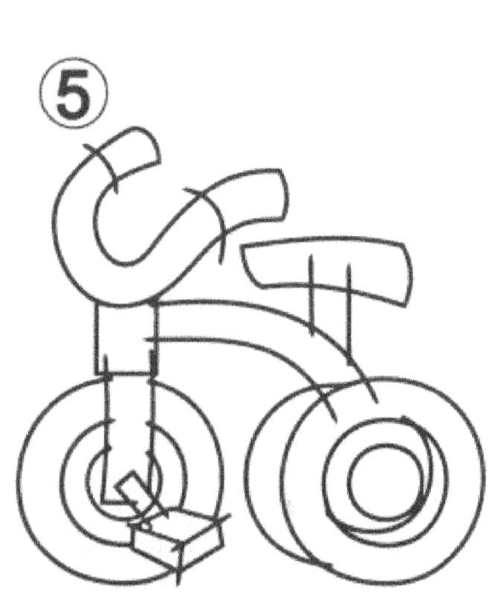

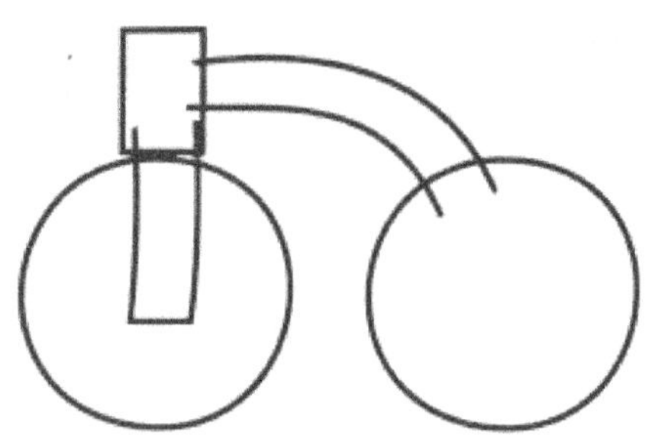
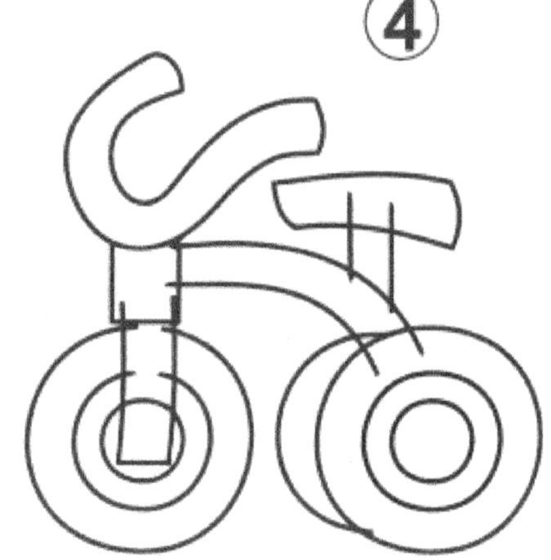
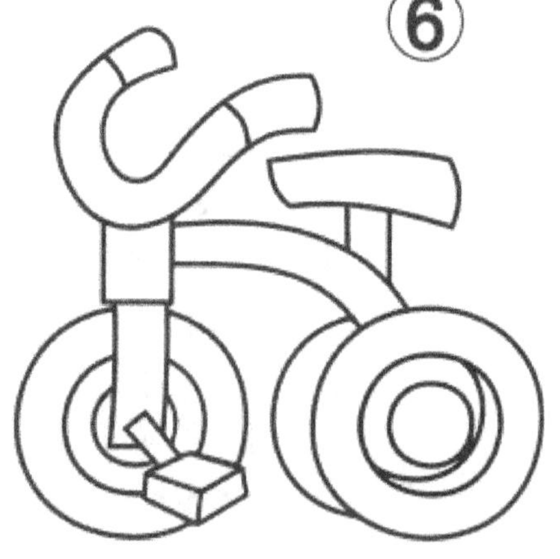

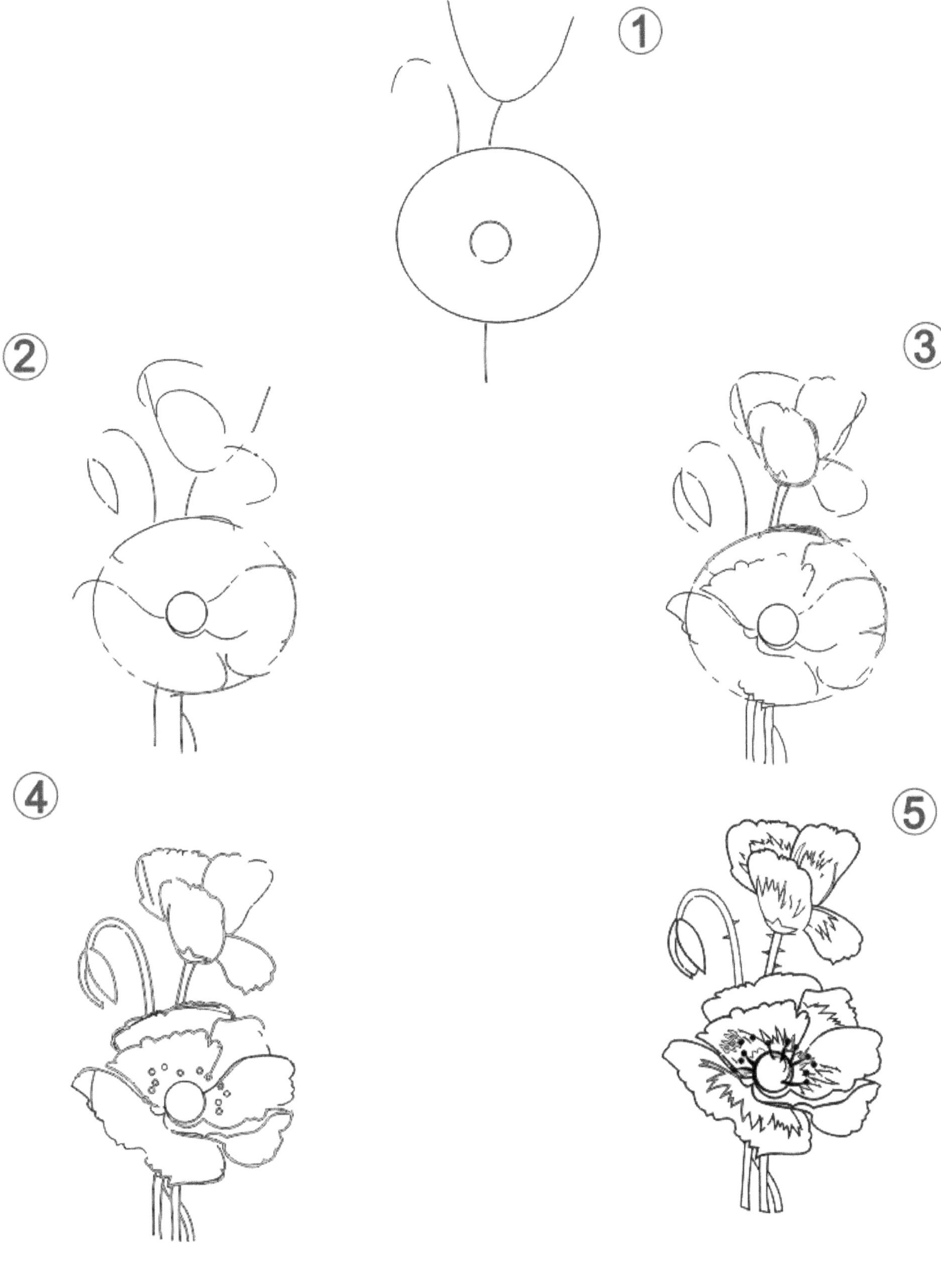

1
2
3
4
5

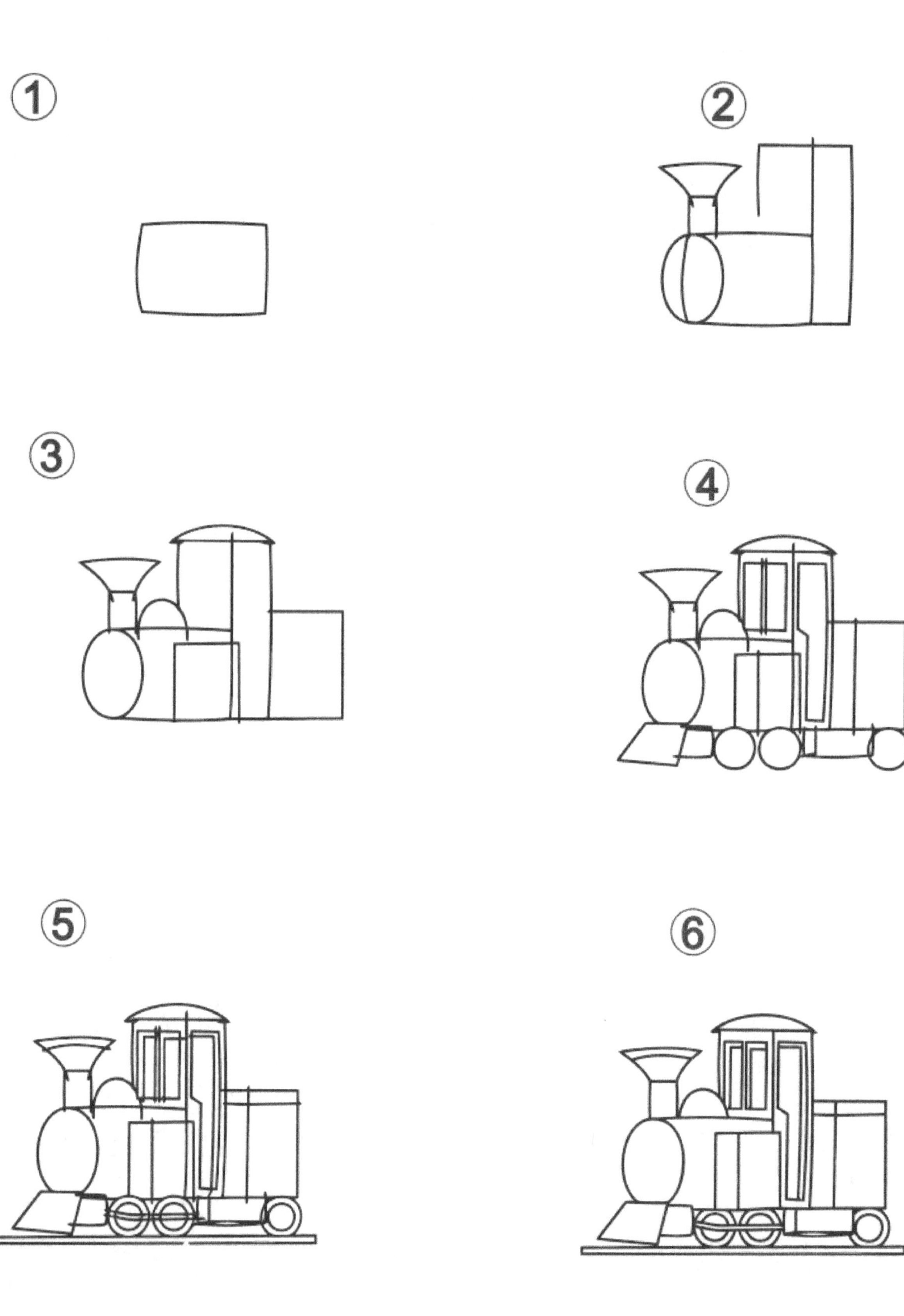

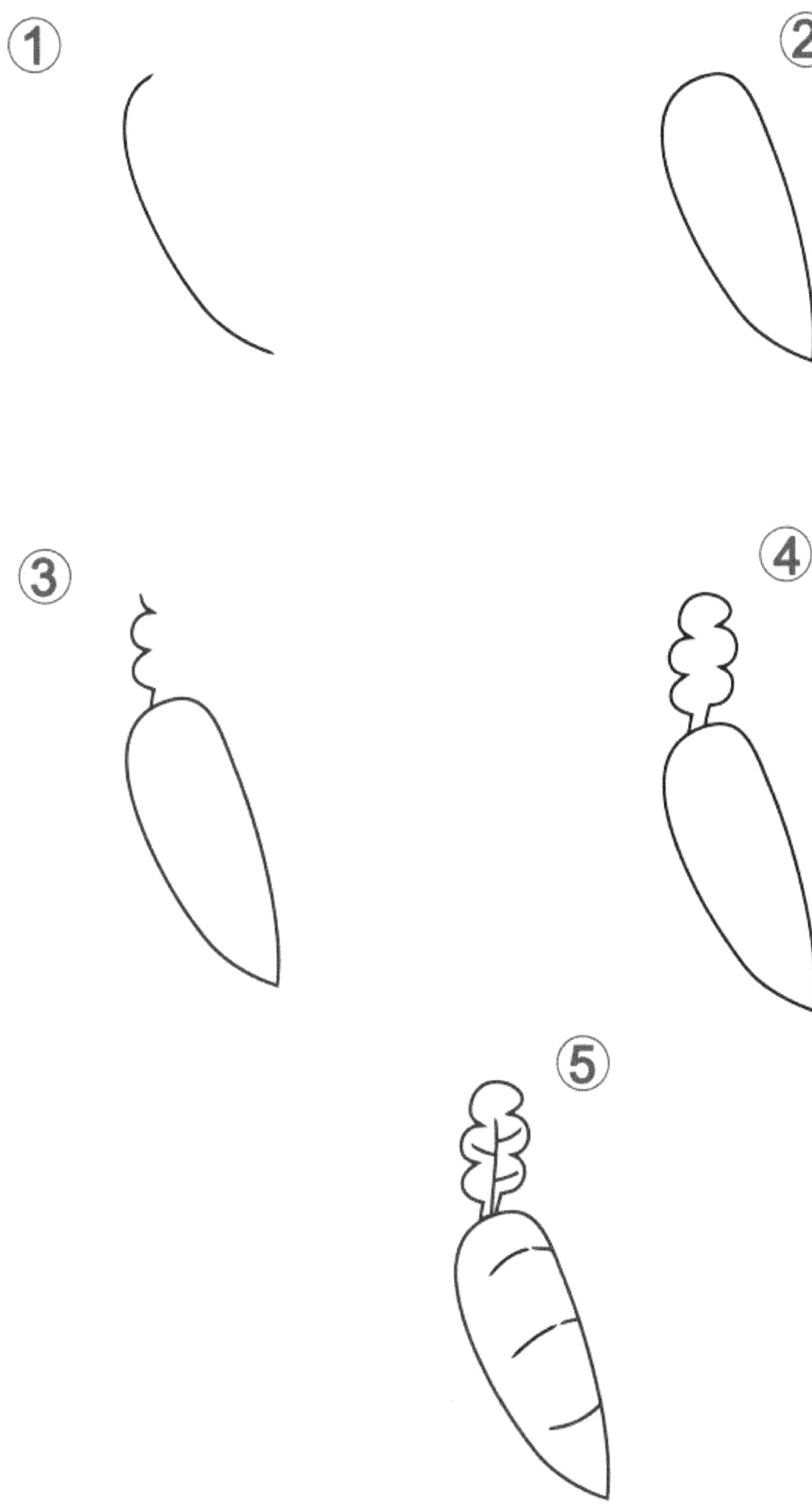

1
2
3
4
5

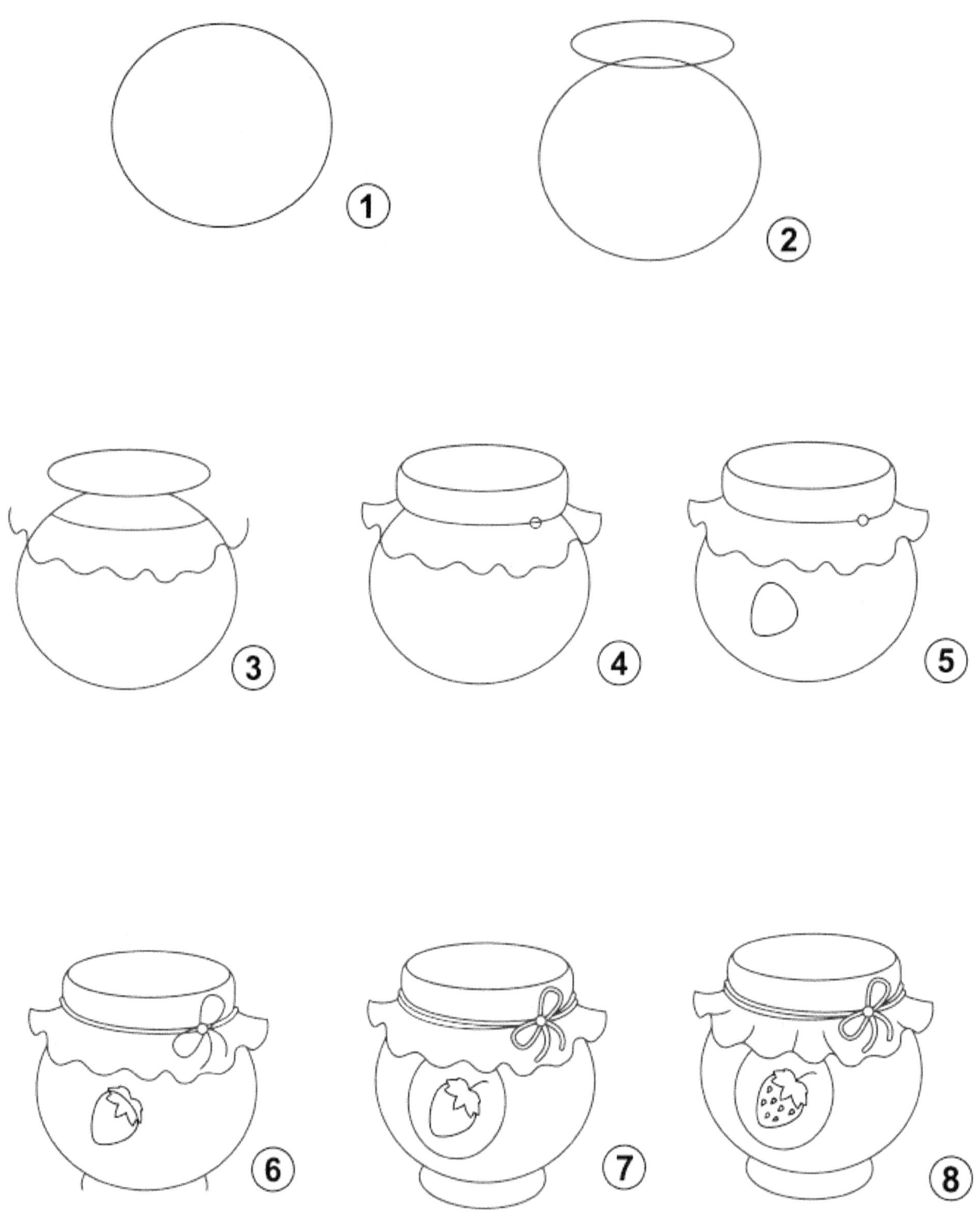

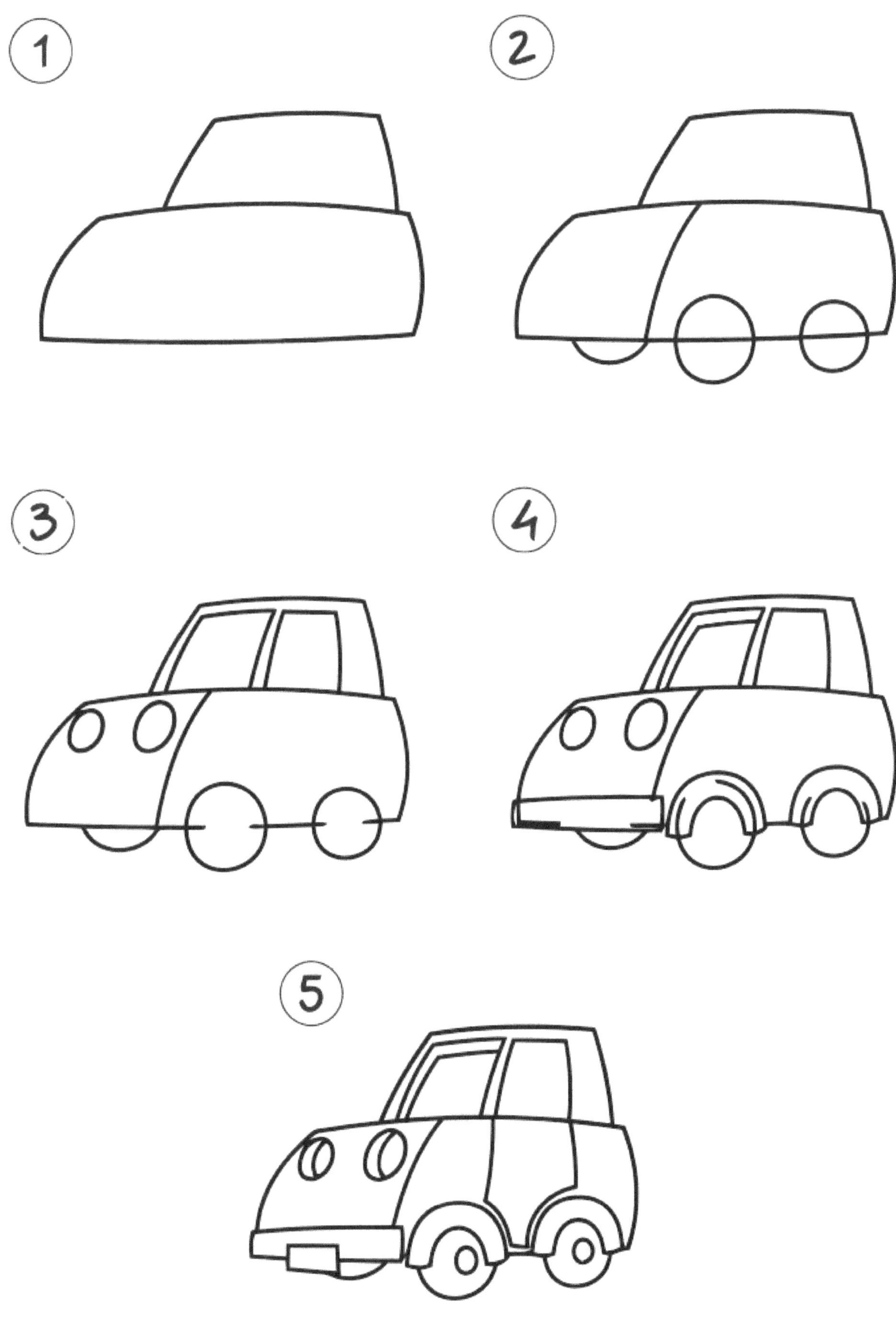

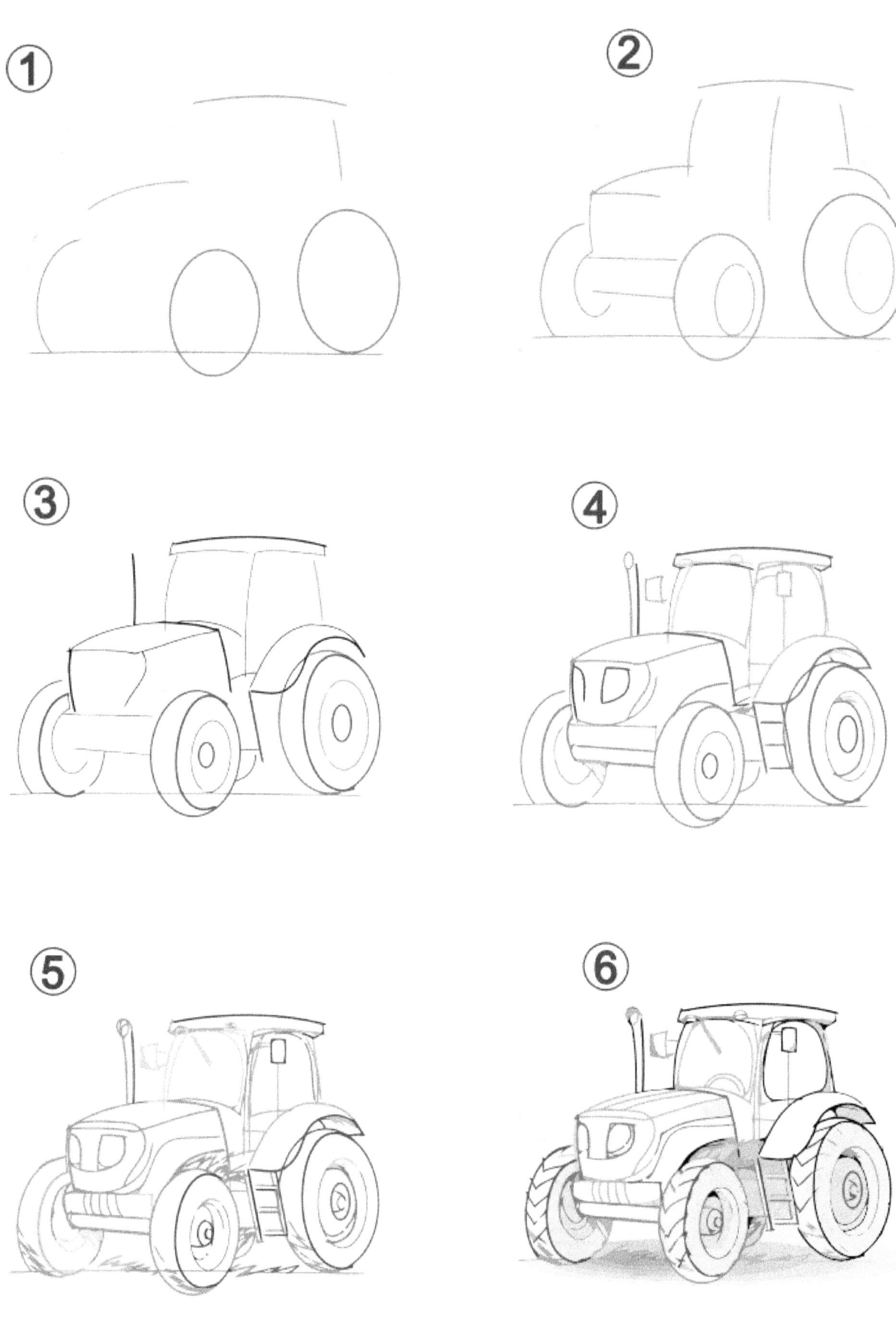

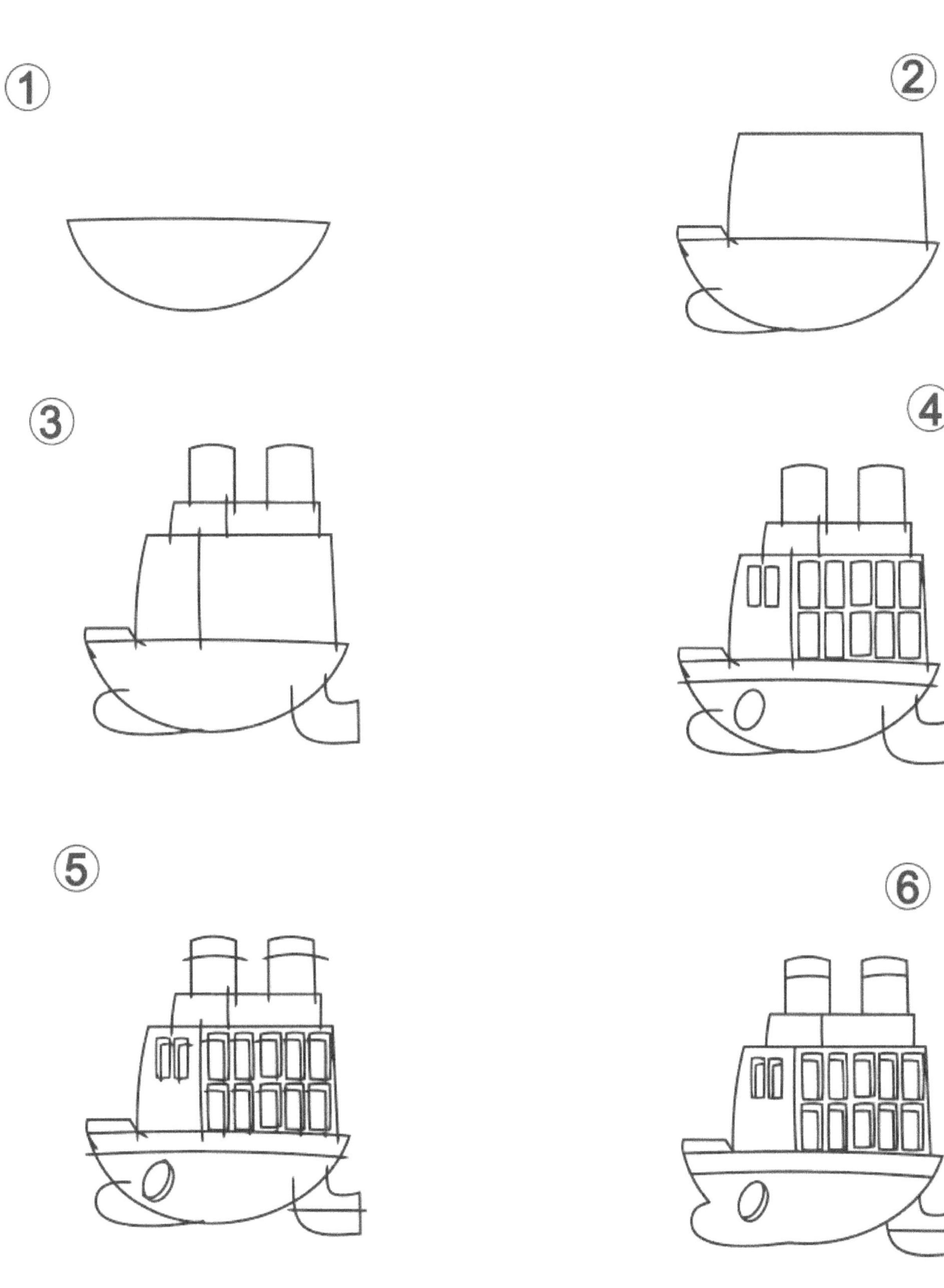

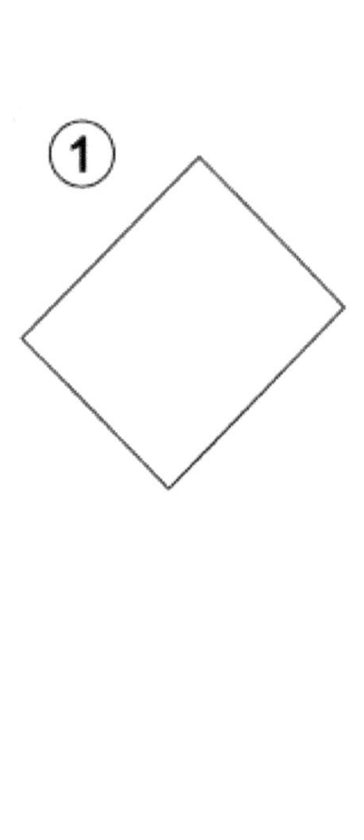

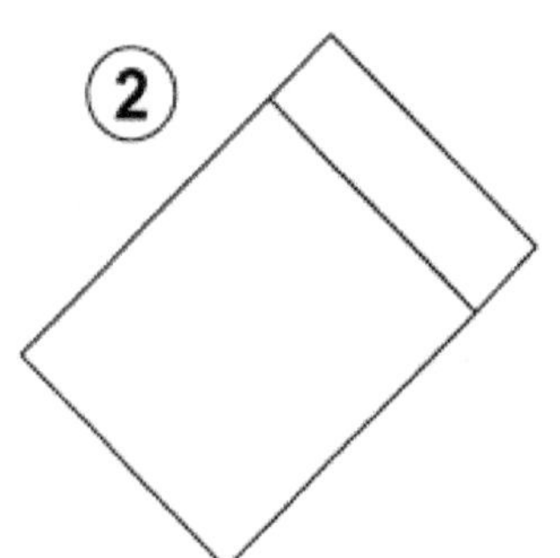

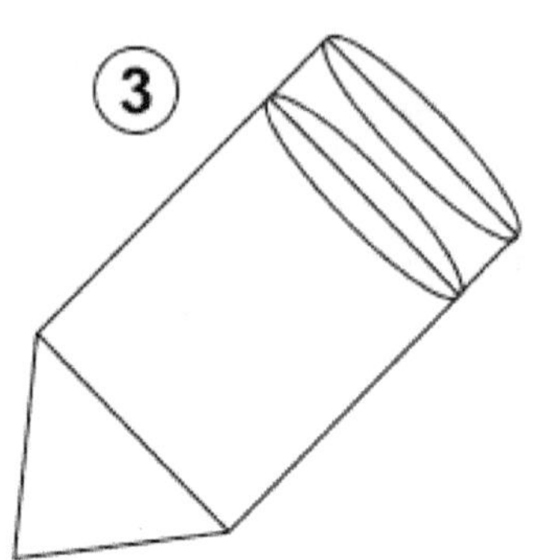

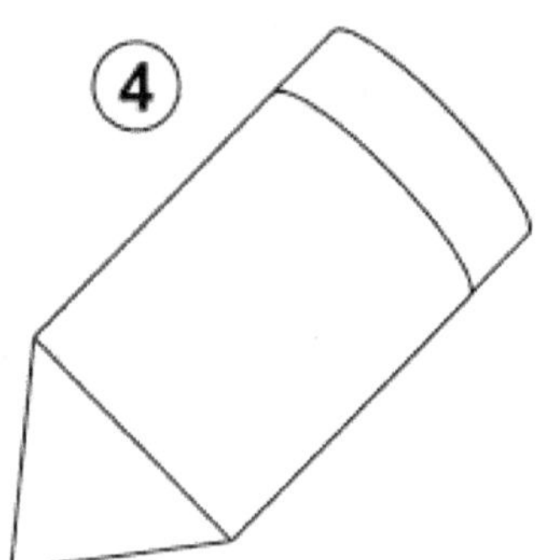

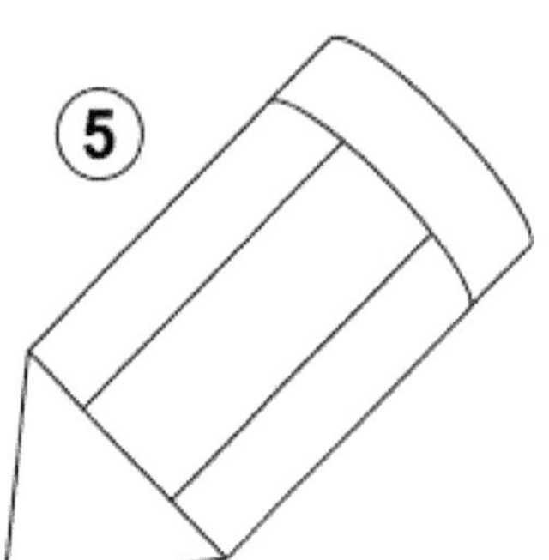

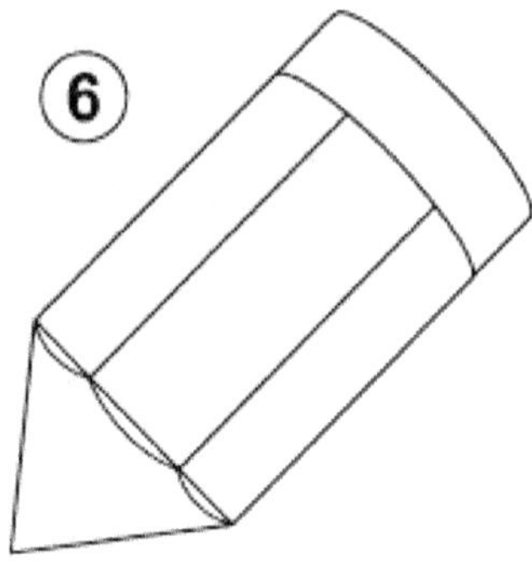

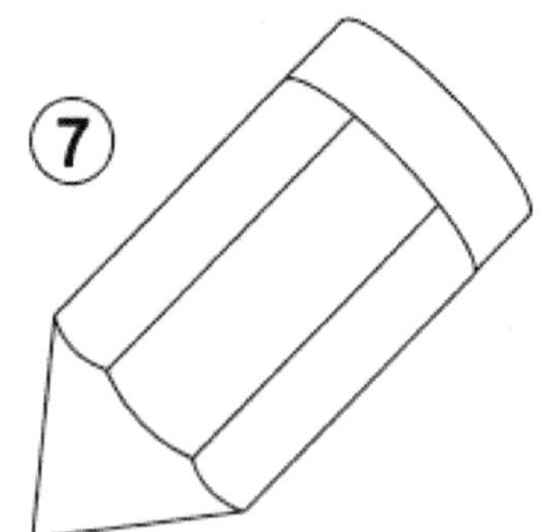

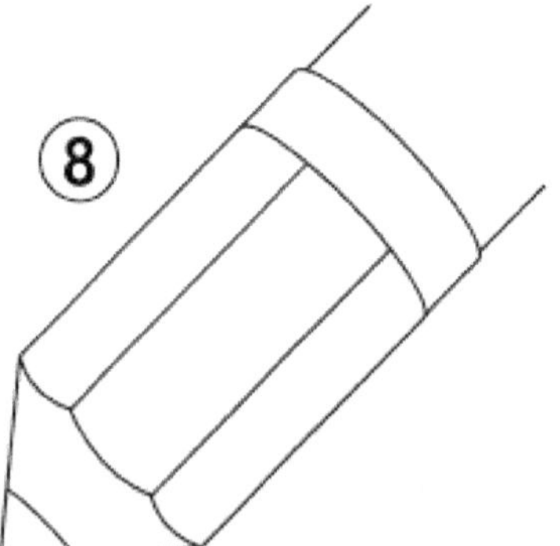

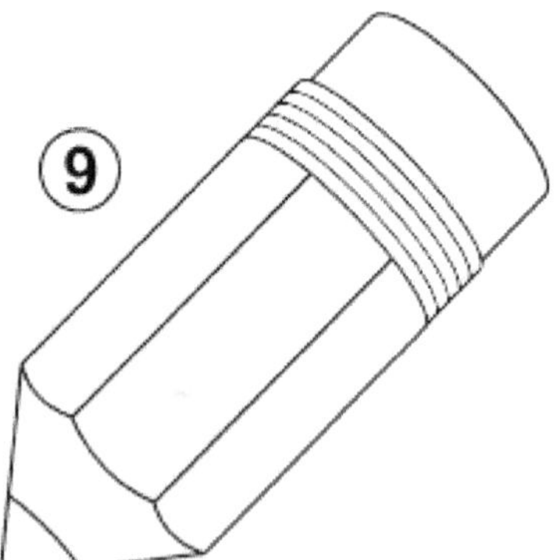

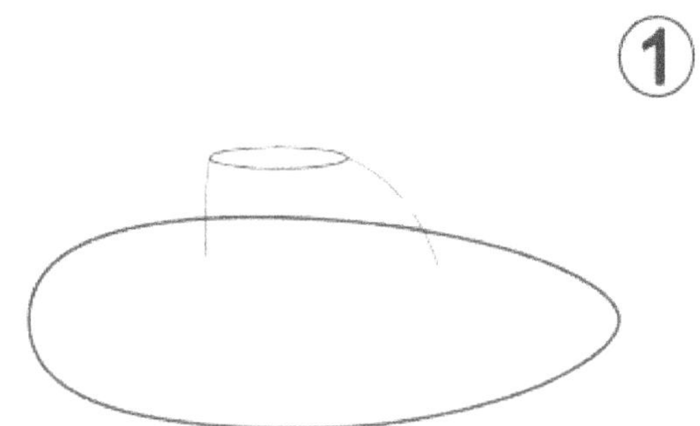

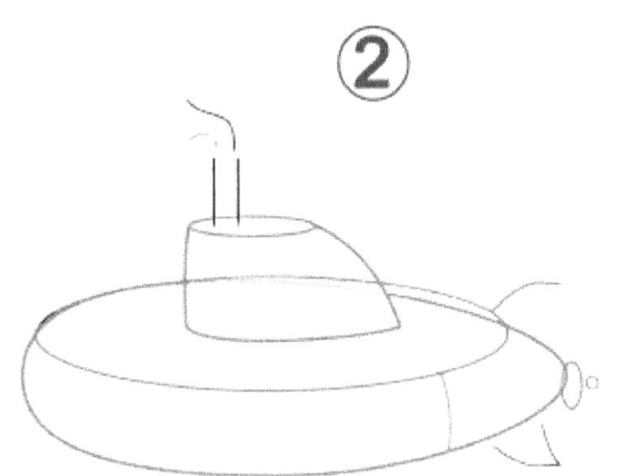

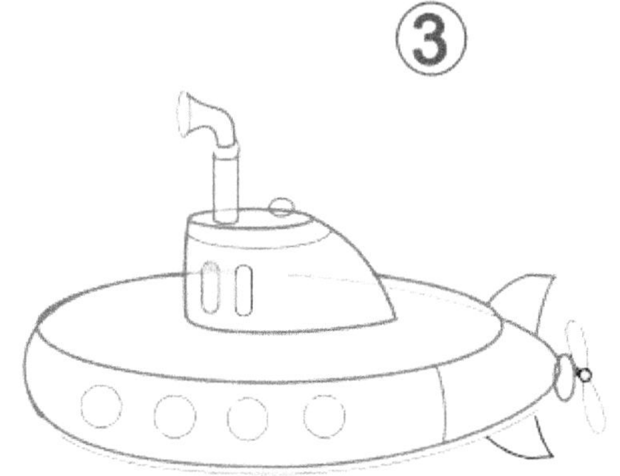

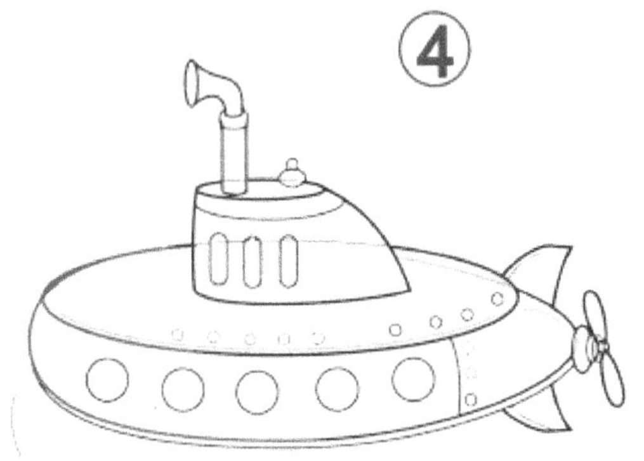

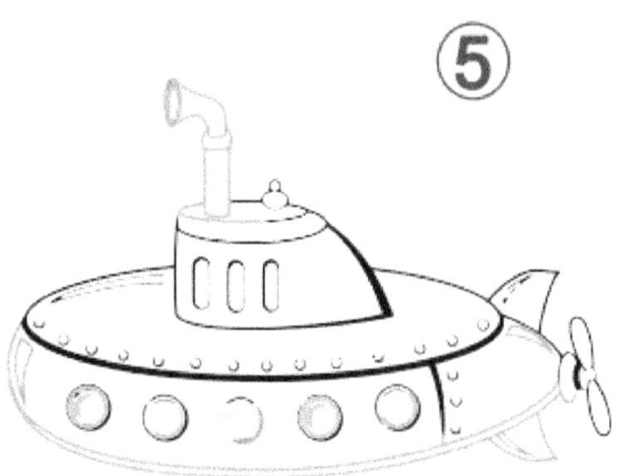

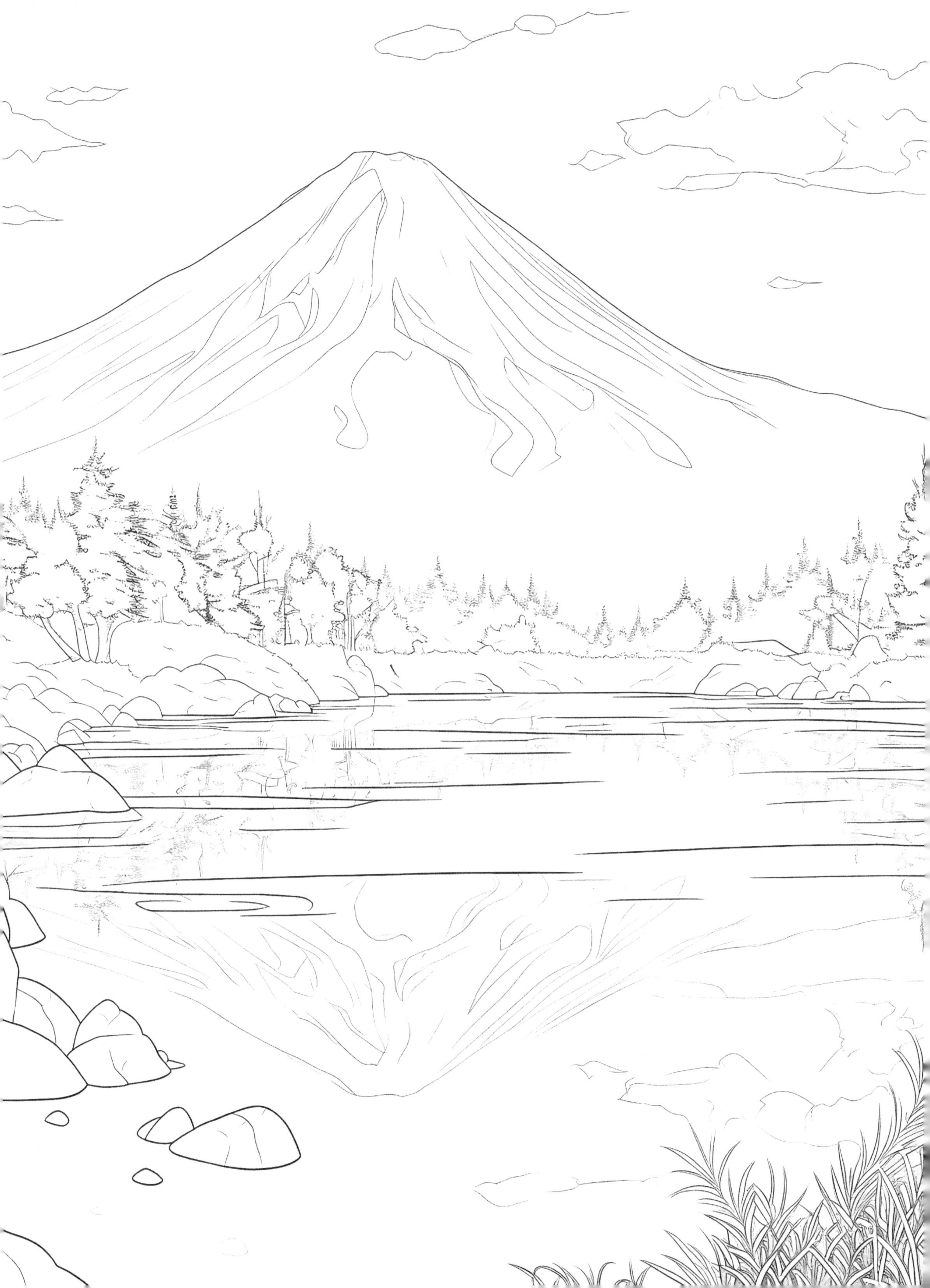

城を築く勇気は困難に立ち向かう力

The courage to build a castle is the power
to face adversity

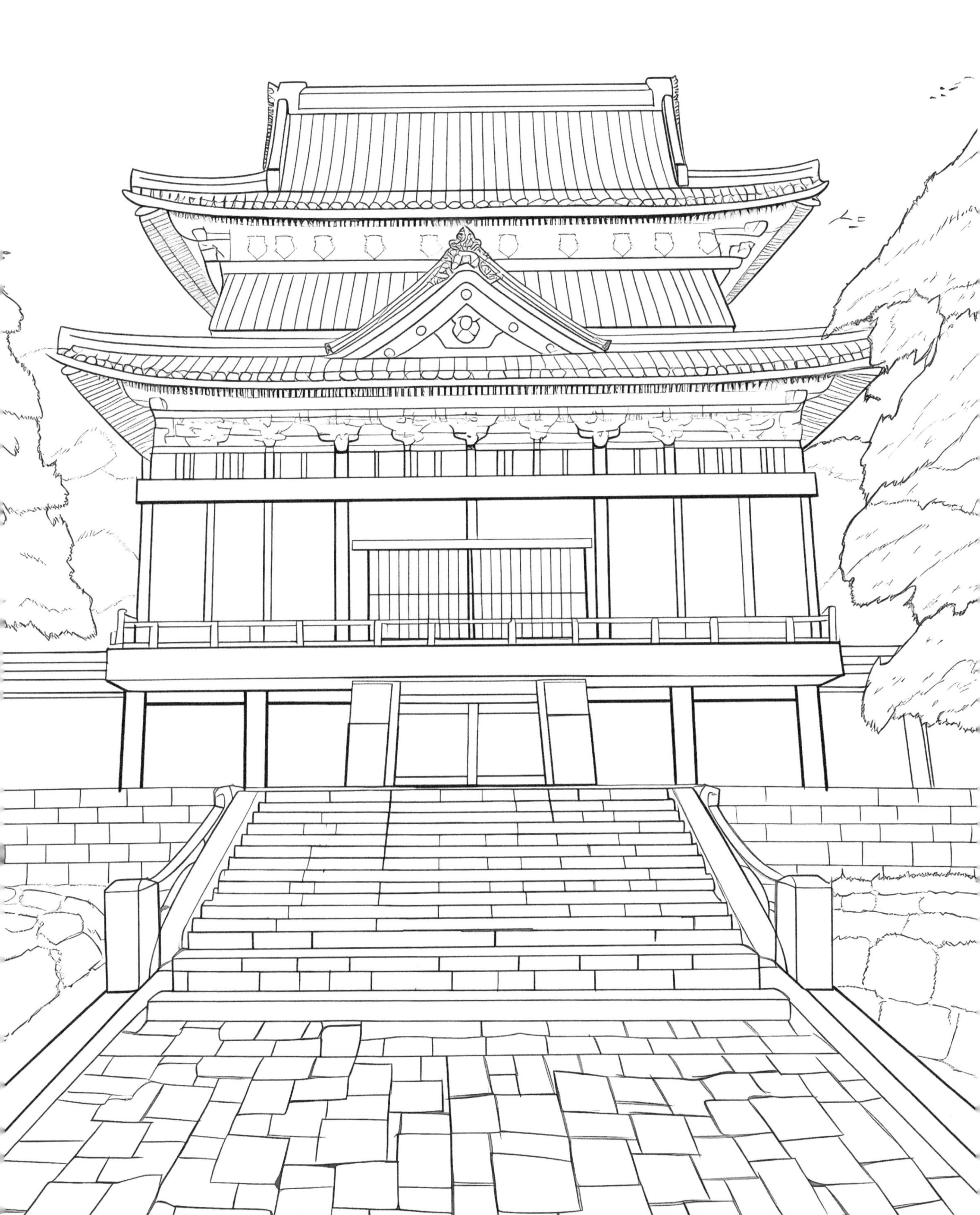

木々のさえずり、自然の歌

The chirping of trees, the song of nature.

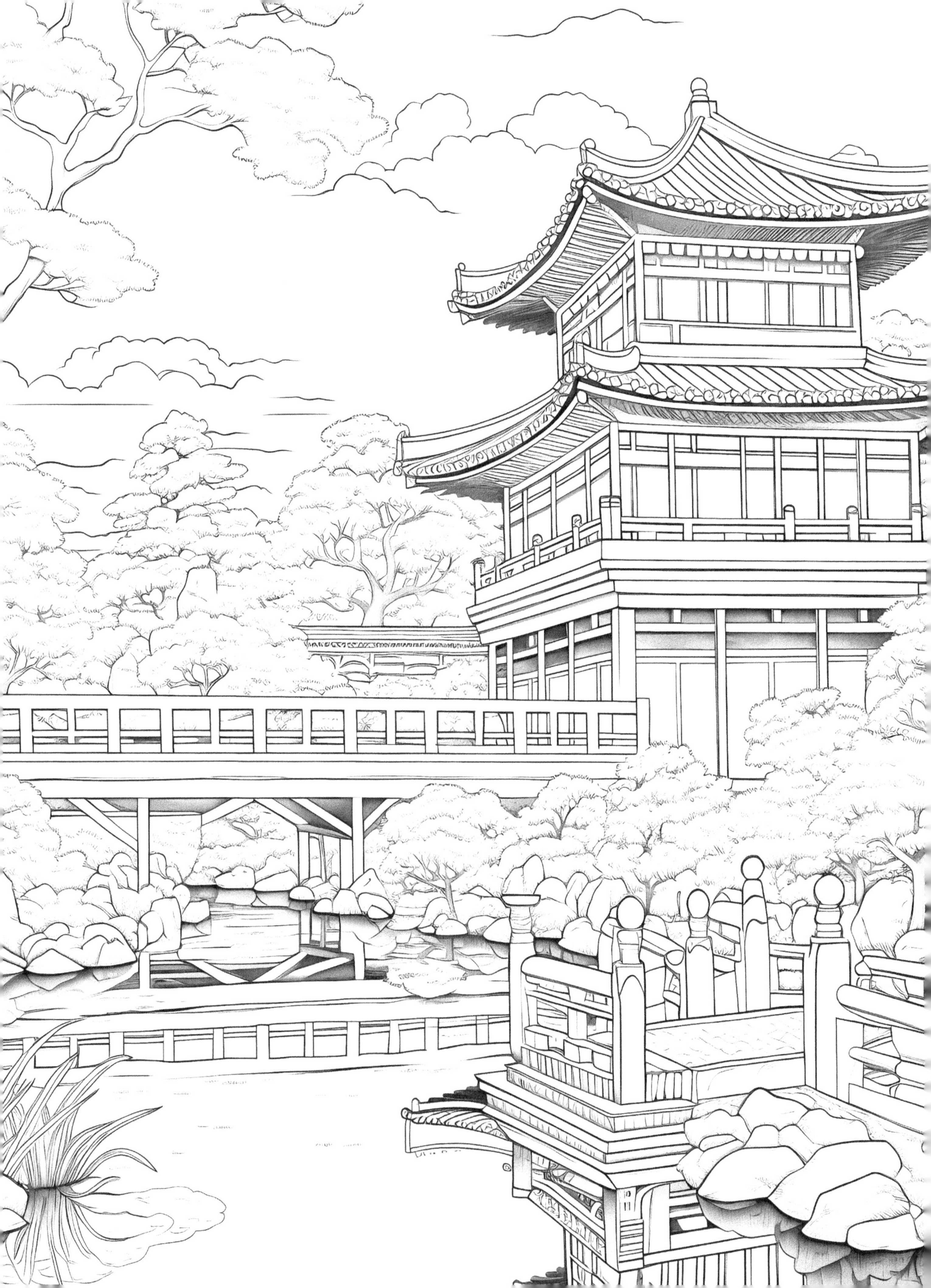

大仏の微笑み、悟りの境地

The smile of the Great Buddha, the state
of enlightenment

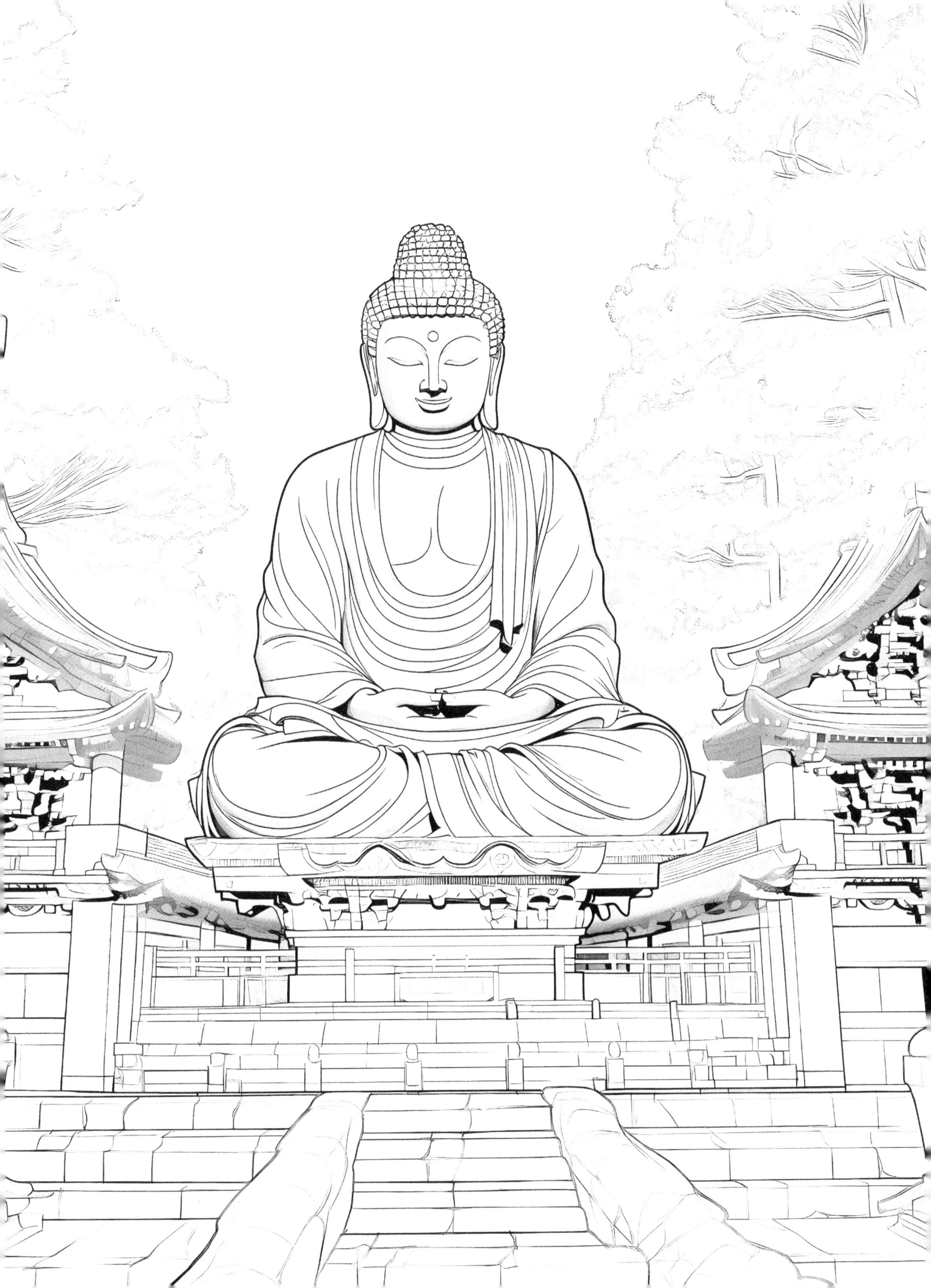

竹林のなか、心が静まる

Amidst the bamboo grove, the heart finds
tranquility.

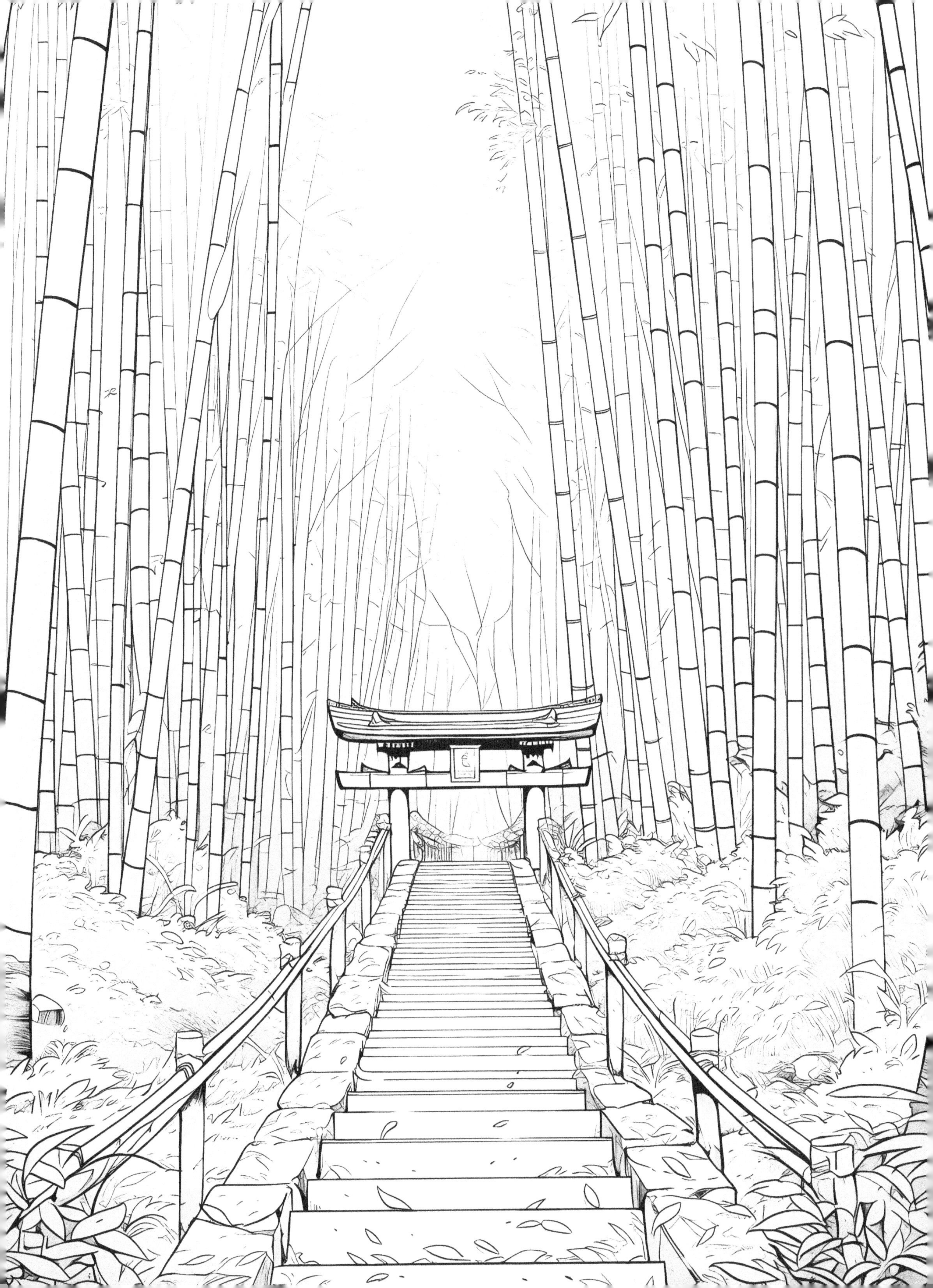

お月見の夜、心ときめく

Moon-viewing night, a heartwarming experience.

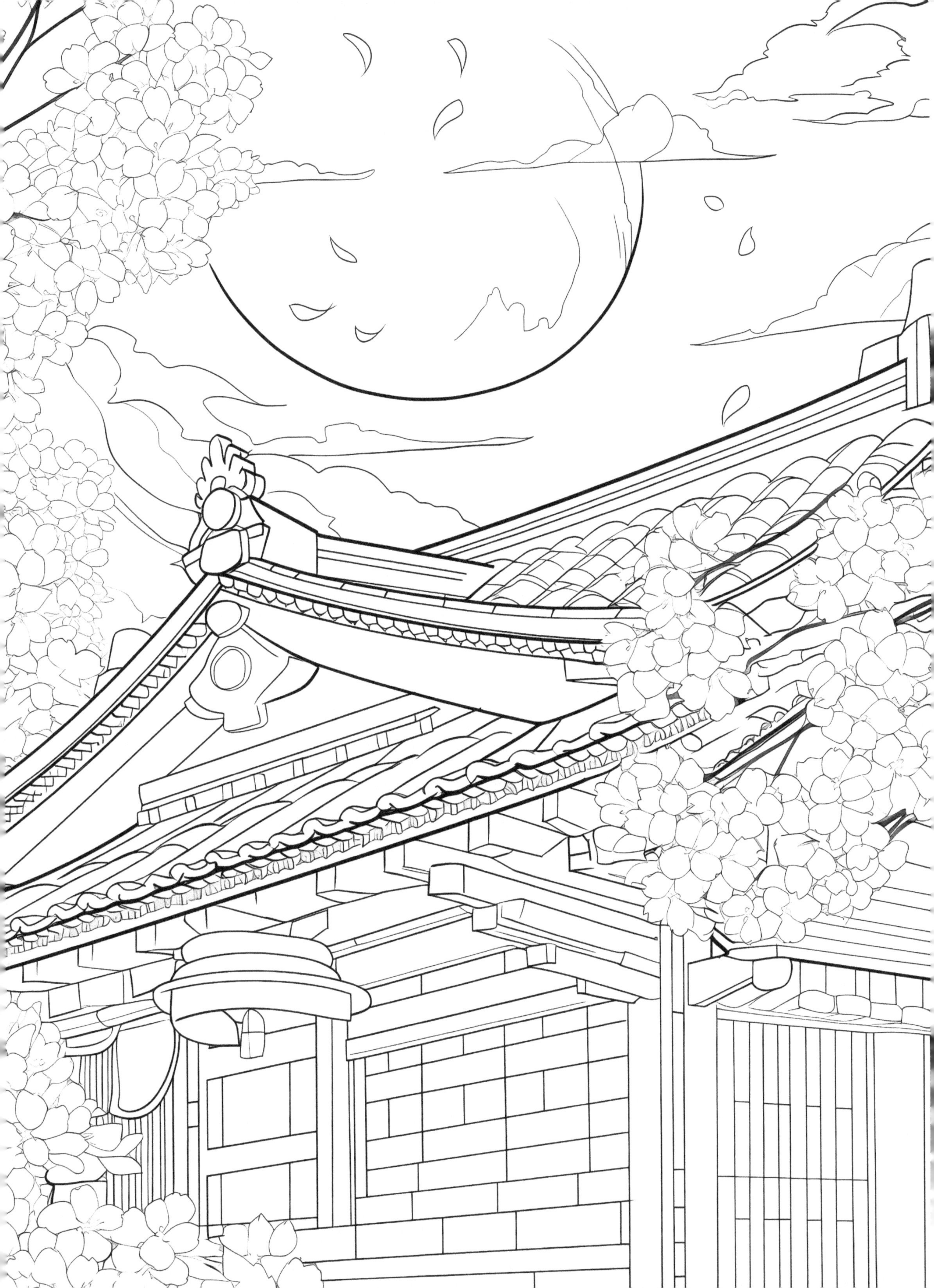

お寺の静けさ、心の平穏

The tranquility of temples, peace for the heart

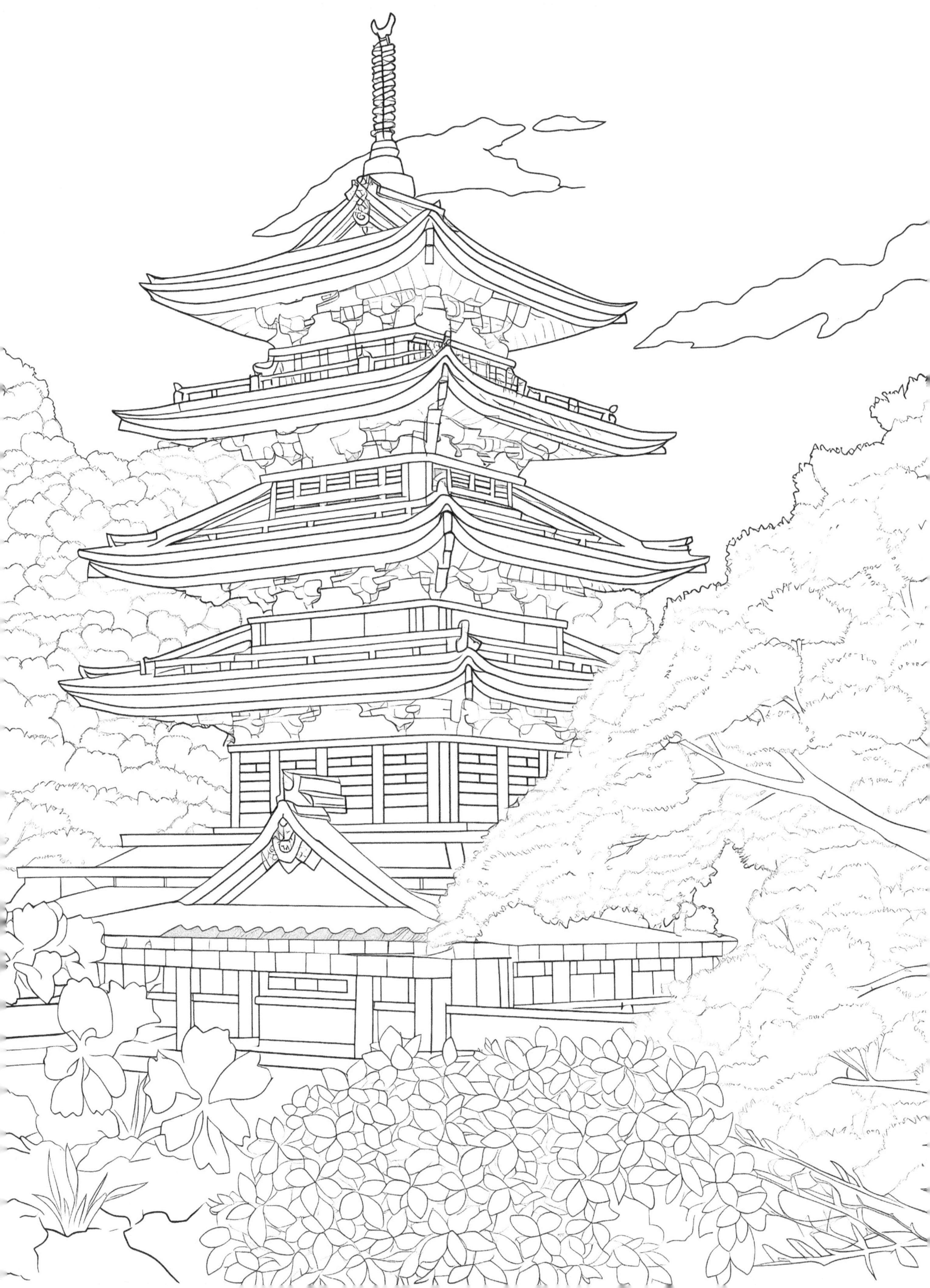

平和は心の花で育てるもの

Peace is something nurtured like a
flower in the heart.

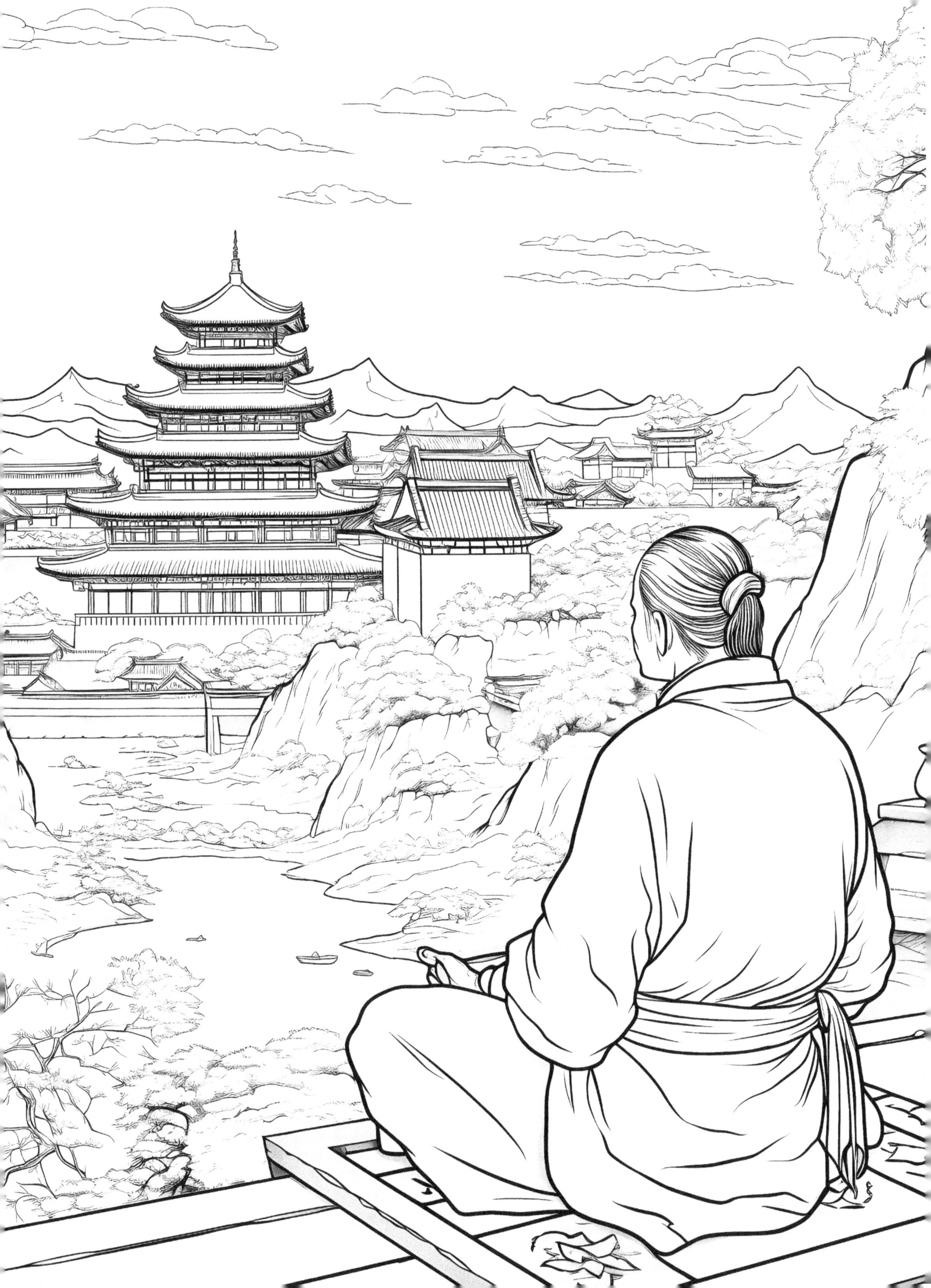

世界を見つめる瞳には無限の可能性が広がる

In the eyes that gaze at the world, infinite
possibilities unfold

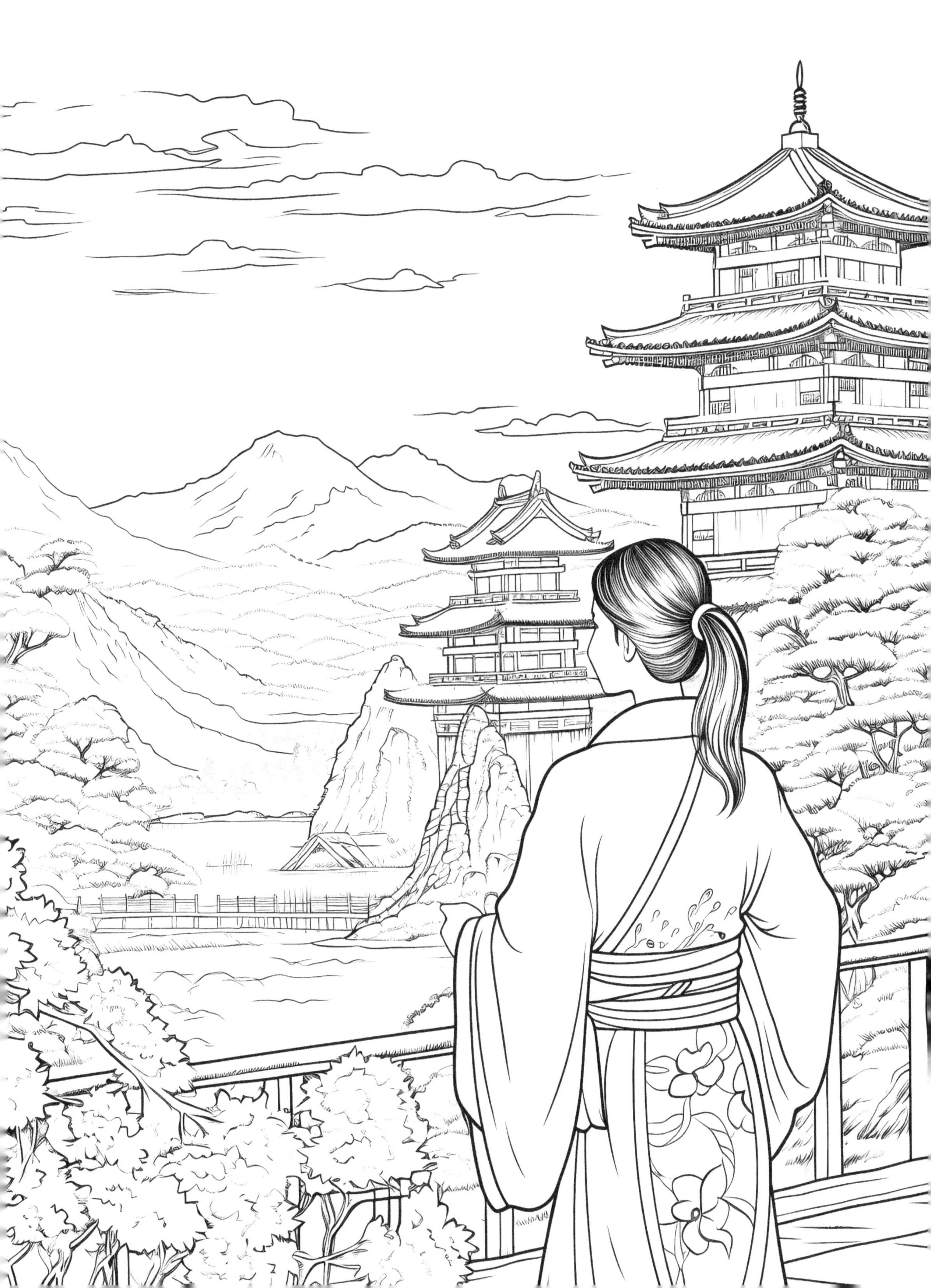

桜舞う春の夜、月の光が心を満たす

On a spring night when cherry blossoms dance, the moonlight fills the heart

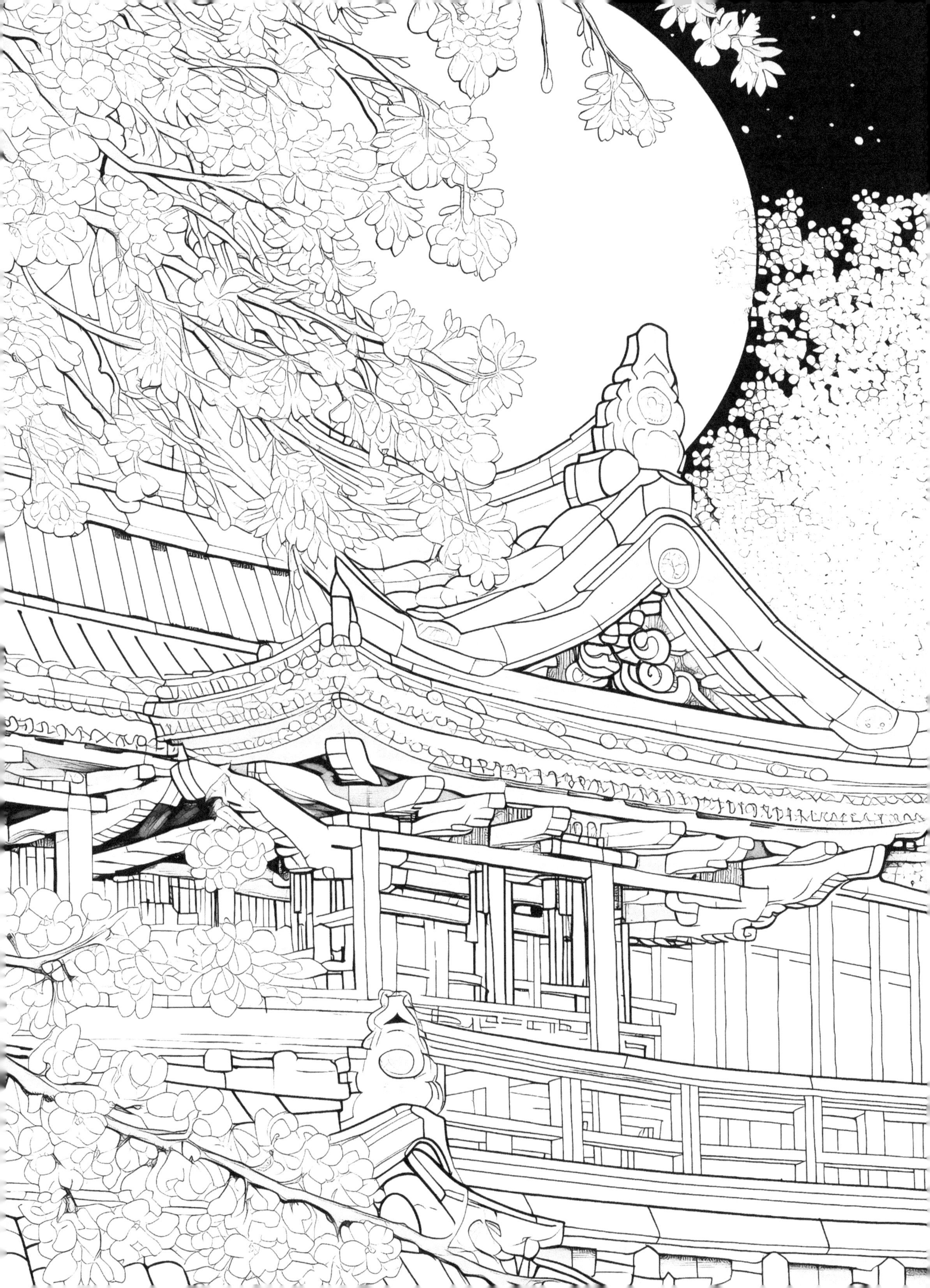